BY ROYAL APPOINTMENT

BY ROYAL APPOINTMENT

TALES FROM THE PRIVY COUNCIL –
THE UNKNOWN ARM OF GOVERNMENT

DAVID ROGERS

Biteback Publishing

First published in Great Britain in 2015 by
Biteback Publishing Ltd
Westminster Tower
3 Albert Embankment
London SE1 7SP
Copyright © David Rogers 2015

ISBN 978-1-84954-856-4

10 9 8 7 6 5 4 3 2 1

A CIP catalogue record for this book is available from the British Library.

Set in Bulmer

Printed and bound in Great Britain by
CPI Group (UK) Ltd, Croydon CR0 4YY

For

Erica

Andrew and Stephen

Hannah, Robert, Jacob and Lois

CONTENTS

CHAPTER ONE

INTRODUCTION

I T WAS 29 NOVEMBER. The sixty-first year of the queen's reign. At Windsor Castle, the oldest institution of government in the world, the Sovereign's Privy Council, was about to issue a proclamation for the proroguing of the British Parliament. The Clerk to the Council handed the monarch the document to be signed. The queen reached out for her pen. It wasn't there. Consternation. For once, the well-oiled royal machinery had broken down. The old guard sprang into action. The Clerk, Sir Almeric Fitzroy, Knight Commander of the Most Honourable Order of the Bath and Knight Commander of the Royal Victorian Order, having made a quick but fruitless inspection of the table, flung open the door and yelled for the duty Groom-in-Waiting. Old Etonian Lt Col. Lord Edward Pelham-Clinton, younger son of the Duke of Newcastle, was an elderly war veteran who moved slowly, but it was well within his capabilities to search the castle and find a pen to allow the Council to complete its business, and Parliament was duly closed.

That incident happened in 1898 and is recorded by Sir Almeric Fitzroy in his *Memoirs*. It is notable for two reasons. Queen Victoria, even if she didn't actually find it amusing, did say, 'It is very funny!' More importantly, it is rare for either counsellors or the Clerk to comment on the contents of meetings of the Privy. Rare, but not unknown. Especially in more recent times, when Cabinet ministers – all of whom are sworn to the Privy Council (along with, among others, leaders of the main opposition parties) – are keen to rush into print with diaries, autobiographies and memoirs. One breach of secrecy that occurred regularly was the telling of the Privy Council oath. Sir Neville Leigh, who was Clerk when Willie Whitelaw was Lord President of the Council in the 1980s (it was a job and title that often went with one of Viscount Whitelaw's other posts, Leader of the House of Lords), said, 'The problem was that politicians found the ancient ceremony of swearing in both so impressive and so bizarre that they just couldn't help telling their families and friends all about it.' This was in spite of the fact that failing to keep the secrecy of the oath was a statutory act of treason. By the end of the twentieth century it would have been unrealistic to attempt a prosecution on those grounds, so the protocol of secrecy was abolished in 1998.

The taking of the oath is the culmination of a centuries-old ceremony. Now in the public domain, it can be freely published:

> You do swear by Almighty God to be a true and faithful Servant unto the Queen's Majesty as one of Her Majesty's Privy Council. You will not know or understand of any manner or thing to be attempted, done or spoken against Her Majesty's Person, Honour, Crown or Dignity Royal, but you will lett and withstand the same to the uttermost of your power, and either cause it to be revealed to Her Majesty Herself, or to

such of Her Privy Council as shall advertise Her Majesty of the same. You will in all things to be moved, treated and debated in Council, faithfully and truly declare your Mind and Opinion, according to your Heart and Conscience; and will keep secret all Matters committed and revealed unto you, or that shall be treated of secretly in Council. And if any of the said Treaties or Councils shall touch any of the Counsellors, you will not reveal it unto him, but will keep the same until such time as, by the Consent of Her Majesty, or of the Council, Publication shall be made thereof. You will to your uttermost bear Faith and Allegiance unto the Queen's Majesty; and will assist and defend all Jurisdictions, Pre-eminences and Authorities granted to Her Majesty and annexed to the Crown by Acts of Parliament, or otherwise, against all Foreign Princes, Persons, Prelates, States or Potentates. And generally in all things you will do as a Faithful and true Servant ought to do to Her Majesty. So help you God.

Most new members of the Privy Council confess that they are perplexed by the wording of the oath and some admit to being so nervous before the ceremony that they hardly remember anything at all – though there has been no recent occasion (at any rate, not on record) to compare with the time in June 1904 when Sir Gainsford Bruce, a retiring High Court judge, steadied his nerves to such an extent that he was paralytic and had to be held up on one side by the Colonial Secretary and former England cricketer Alfred Lyttelton, with a knight of the realm propping up his other side. So alarmed was the king, Edward VII, that he cut the ritual short and had Sir Gainsford escorted to his carriage.

Nerves are understandable. A newly appointed Cabinet minister, especially in a change of government following a general election, has a hundred and one matters to worry about. If in charge of a new department of state, there are all the problems of buildings and staff. Civil servants will be pressing for policy decisions to be made. Lobbyists will be circling and the media wanting interviews. Places on Cabinet committees will be jostled for, and, if time, special advisers pacified. The amount of background reading to be done is enormous. On top of that comes a demand from the Clerk of the Privy Council to attend a rehearsal for the kissing of hands. It is vital that the Clerk gets this done. The Privy Council oath binds the Cabinet to a whole range of national secrets. Without access to that information, they could not function. So, for over an hour on what is one of the busiest days of their political careers, these now most powerful Members of Parliament practise kneeling on one knee on a stool, raising the Bible in the right hand, standing, slowly walking three paces forward, kissing the monarch's hand and walking backwards without treading on the stool or the corgis. The Queen then normally tells them that they have done very well and the new counsellors get into their official cars and go off to run the country. Most counsellors find this impressive. The one notable exception was the Labour Cabinet minister Richard Crossman MP, later to become Lord President of the Council. In *The Crossman Diaries*, he writes, 'I don't suppose anything more dull, pretentious, or plain silly has ever been invented. There we were, sixteen grown men. For over an hour we were taught how to stand up, how to kneel one knee on a cushion, how to raise the right hand with the Bible in it.' Where necessary, the ceremony also involves the handing over of the seals of office.

If they think that is the end of their dealings with the Privy Council, then the new ministers are very much mistaken. At perhaps the most mundane and perfunctory level, every time a Bill completes its passage through the Houses of Parliament – first formal reading, second reading debate, committee stage, report stage, final reading (both in the Commons and the Lords) – it cannot become law as an Act of Parliament until it is signed by the Queen in the presence of Privy Counsellors. This goes back to the time when Parliament did not trust the monarch and thought it at least a possibility that the Sovereign might ever so slightly change the wording. It is true that these meetings don't take long. This is partly because all the participants have to remain standing. This was an innovation introduced by Queen Victoria. There is no written record of why she did this. Some say it was to continue honouring the memory of Prince Albert. The less charitable say it was because she couldn't put up with Mr Gladstone going on and on.

Ministers should be grateful for this duty of the Privy Council. Once legislation is formulated in an Act, it is possible for it to be amended by an Order 'in' (sometimes, but only rarely, 'of') Council. And some Secretaries of State will find that the work of their department is closely tied in with the Privy Council, especially Justice, Education, and the Home Office.

But what exactly is the Privy Council? What is it for? How did it ever come into being? As we have no written constitution, there are no easy answers to these questions. Perhaps the most appropriate answer to why the Privy Council exists is the same as the official reply given to so many historical constitutional questions – ancient usage. Certainly, the Council is not as powerful as it once was. Indeed, many political writers ignore it entirely, the index in their books going from '*Private Eye*' to 'Profumo, John' without a pause. Some say it has no power at all, though I don't think you would agree if you had been sentenced to death in a former British overseas territory that still used the Judicial Committee of the Privy Council as its court of appeal; or if you were a lecturer having a row with your college where the University Chancellor, or the Official Visitor, was a member of the royal family; or if you were a priest who had been defrocked by the Church of England's Court of Arches. Or indeed if you were a Prime Minister trying to establish a Royal Charter to control the press.

But throughout recent history the question has been asked, and

occasionally answers have been attempted. In 1832, Lord Meath argued
in Parliament that the role of the Privy Council was to set up governmen-
tal committees and that the Cabinet only had any power because it was a
committee of the Privy Council. Almost a hundred years later there was
an interesting answer given to a question from Captain Wedgwood Benn
MP, who was asking what statutory authority the Privy Council had. The
pretext was an enquiry about export licences during the First World War.
It was obvious that the minister's civil servants had researched long and
hard for an acceptable reply but with little luck. The best the minister
could come up with was: 'I am advised that there is no statutory authority but that the power to grant licences has been exercised by the Privy
Council in time of war at least as far back as the eighteenth century as
one of the powers inherent in the Privy Council.' Two phrases there of
which Sir Humphrey from the BBC's *Yes Minister*, would be proud: 'at
least as far back' and 'powers inherent in the Privy Council'. In 1957, Captain Wedgwood Benn's son Tony wrote a Fabian Tract suggesting the
best role for the Privy Council would be to replace the House of Lords
as the second chamber at Westminster.

   The Privy Council cannot simply be dismissed as having only a ceremonial role today. Indeed, in some way there is less ceremony than
there used to be, though that could be changing. The practice of wearing Privy Council uniforms on state occasions, which was abandoned
in the second half of the twentieth century, was suddenly revived by one
counsellor in 2013. To the surprise of many, the Rt Hon. Alan Duncan,
Conservative Member of Parliament for Rutland & Melton, turned up
in 'full levee' Privy Council uniform (borrowed from the Privy Council Office), with the fore-and-aft cocked hat tucked under his arm, at St
Paul's Cathedral for the ceremonial funeral of Margaret Thatcher. 'What
on earth is he wearing?' one television commentator asked on air, and it
took some time before researchers got the right answer into his earpiece.

The tentacles of the Council spread to every area of parliamentary and public life. Royal brides, battleships and burial plots: all these are affected by the current workings of the Privy Council, as is the governance of the Channel Islands and the Isle of Man, where the Crown, acting through the Privy Council, is the ultimate authority. The Council also has responsibility for looking after the thousand or so organisations, charities, companies and institutions that are incorporated by Royal Charter. Most of its work is devolved onto committees, with the entire Council only being summoned on two very specific occasions: on the death or abdication of the Sovereign, or when the monarch announces her, or his, engagement. Last happened in 1839!

The relationship between the Queen and her counsellors can best be expressed as the actual working practice of the rights of a constitutional monarch as now accepted by all governments of whatever political flavour. This agreement was defined in 1867 by our greatest constitutional expert, Walter Bagehot, as 'the right to be consulted; the right to warn; and the right to encourage'. Throughout history, the most important expression of this has been a declaration of war, which is exercised through the royal prerogative. There have been attempts to change that, to say that it should be Parliament that makes and announces a decision of that significance. But in the early years of the twenty-first century, the pragmatic view has been maintained that in uncertain times it would only help an enemy to learn how many MPs – and which ones – had voted against going to war, and give little comfort to our troops. Although in recent years governments have held parliamentary debates on going to war, as in the cases of Iraq and Syria, these debates and any subsequent votes are not constitutionally binding on the government.

It is in times of war that the Privy Council is at its busiest in getting the correct legal wording for protocols and proclamations. The classic example is the commonly retailed story, perhaps apocryphal, that there was confusion at the end of the Crimean War when the Privy Council forgot to put the name of the town of Berwick-upon-Tweed on the peace treaty with Russia. Since 1502, in order to confirm that Berwick was English and not Scottish, the Privy Council had insisted that the town's name be on all foreign treaties. So, up until the 1960s, when this slip was corrected, some people argued that Berwick was still officially at war with the Soviet Union. For the Boer War, the clerks had to refer back to Charles I and a document of 1625 for the right terminology to 'man the navy'. At the time of the First World War, King George V made a Declaration in Council renouncing 'the Foreign Titles and Arms of the Duke of Saxony and Prince of Saxe Coburg and Gotha' and changed the name of the royal family to Windsor. In the Second World War, George VI very reluctantly agreed to the request of the Prime Minister Winston Churchill to appoint the proprietor of Express Newspapers, Lord Beaverbrook, to the Privy Council.

What of the Privy Counsellors themselves? For many people, membership of the Council is regarded as a great social cachet. Some claim that membership gives personal access to the monarch, but access should not be taken to mean a private audience. There was a convention that counsellors sitting in the House of Commons were called to speak before other members, but *Erskine May* is keen to stress that is in entirely in the gift of the Speaker. One perk to be enjoyed on special occasions is the right to sit on the steps of the throne in the House of Lords to listen to debates. Membership is awarded to some politicians as a sop for not getting into the Cabinet, where it is mandatory that all members become Privy Counsellors. One of Margaret Thatcher's Chancellors of the Exchequer, Nigel Lawson, writes in his autobiography, *The View From No. 11*, that when, as a junior Treasury minister in 1981, he was passed over for promotion to the Cabinet, his elevation to the Privy Council, and therefore the distinction to style himself as 'The Right Honourable', was 'a consolation prize'.

Indeed, some who in their parliamentary career miss out on the Cabinet altogether actually try to claim membership as a kind of retirement gift. One such was Bob Boothby, the flamboyant, larger than life Member of Parliament for East Aberdeenshire in the post-war years. As a regular on the BBC's *Any Questions?* radio programme, he was one of the first media-star politicians. Stories about him abounded. How, when meeting Hitler, he responded to the Führer's salute by clicking his heels together, thrusting his arm upwards and yelling 'Boothby!' The press dwelled on his association with the gangster twins the Krays, and, slowly, as press interest in the personal lives of politicians became more intrusive, his love affair with Lady Dorothy Macmillan, the wife of the Prime Minister Harold Macmillan. In spite, or perhaps because, of Boothby's complex relationship with the Macmillans, the PM did offer Boothby a peerage – which he accepted. Macmillan even gave him a choice of becoming one of the last hereditary lords or taking one of the first life peerages. He took a life peerage, but it was not enough. On 27 December 1983 – against all protocol – he wrote to the Queen asking to become a member of the Privy Council. Robert Rhodes James in his book *Bob Boothby: A Portrait* describes how this was dealt with. 'He received a flattering and smooth reply from one of her private secretaries: "As regards a Privy Councillorship this is of course something which is given by the Queen on the advice of her Prime Minister." No such advice was given.' So that glittering prize eluded Boothby.

Membership of the Council used to be dependent on the wishes of the monarch. A change of Sovereign led to a change in the Council. Today, membership is normally for life, though an expectation has grown up since the middle of the twentieth century that any member whose behaviour in their personal life could bring the Council into disrepute shall resign. Inevitably, this brings the actual existence of the Privy Council to the attention of the media, academics and the general public. So those counsellors who resigned in disgrace or embarrassment because of their criminal, sexual or financial activities during the period from the 1960s to the 2010s ensured that the publicity over their antics reminded students of politics that the institution was still in being. Being able to resign was a new development and it is still questionable whether this is constitutionally correct. In October 1918, Sir Edgar Speyer tried to resign his counsellorship after much public debate as to whether or not he was a German spy. After much furore, the establishment of the day decided that was treating the honour with disrespect and that only the monarch could remove a member from the Council.

Since then, however, John Profumo (lying to the House of Commons), Jonathan Aitken (perjury), Chris Huhne (attempting to pervert the course of justice) and others have been spared that indignity and allowed to remove themselves – though the Privy Council can expel members if it is felt that they are a bit slow in doing the honourable thing. This happened in 2011 when the Labour MP Elliot Morley was convicted and imprisoned for fraud in relation to his parliamentary expenses. It is an interesting political footnote that one of the longest-serving members of the Privy Council, the Rt Hon. John Jeremy Thorpe – he was appointed in 1967 – was acquitted in a sensational conspiracy to murder case but never recovered a seat in the House of Commons or went to the House of Lords, and has virtually been written out of history as a leader of the Liberal Party, but remained a Privy Counsellor until his death in 2014. He also had been one of the first political media stars.

The Privy Council has always included, among the mostly staid, upright, and respectable men and women of the establishment, members with extreme personalities, ambitions and aspirations; heroes and rogues; saints and sinners. (Indeed, at the start of the twenty-first century, over 50 per cent of the Saints and Sinners Club meeting for their festive whitebait meal at Greenwich to usher in the new millennium were

Privy Counsellors.) It is from among the stories of the lives of these people that the historical significance and constitutional role of the Privy Council emerges.

As most people now have longer life spans, it is unsurprising that (with life membership) the size of the Council is gradually increasing. At the start of 2015, there were around 600 members, the most senior being HRH the Duke of Edinburgh, who was sworn in 1951. The oldest Privy Counsellor is the Rt Hon. Lord (Denis) Healey, who was born in 1917 and served as Chancellor of the Exchequer under Wilson and Callaghan. At the time of the first Queen Elizabeth there were forty counsellors. The number of members has fluctuated throughout the centuries, the Council being abolished entirely from 1649 to 1660 during the time of Oliver Cromwell's Commonwealth.

To arrive at an accurate definition of what the Privy Council actually does in the context of the constitutional and political life of the United Kingdom is difficult. There has been little academic study or research in this area, except on the Council's judicial role. Only one major general study has been published, *The History of The Privy Council*, written by the former Clerk we met earlier, Sir Almeric Fitzroy. That was in 1928. In his history, Fitzroy pays tribute to the most quoted reference on the subject, *The Privy Council* by Albert Dicey, the outstanding lawyer and Fellow of All Souls College, Oxford. This was published in 1887 and is an extended tract of an essay of Professor Dicey's that won the Arnold Award at Oxford in 1860. Fitzroy agrees with Dicey that 'its history stretches back to remote antiquity'.

It therefore should share a place in the understanding of our heritage alongside the other three main institutions of state: the monarchy, Parliament and the judiciary. But while all of those three have been extensively studied and written about, the Privy Council has not enjoyed similar attention. This is because both Parliament – especially Cabinet government

– and the structure of our law courts have grown out of the Privy Council (and its offshoot the Star Chamber) itself. So the activities of the Council have faded into the constitutional background. This is understandable. The relationship between the monarchy and the Council had its origins in secrecy. This characteristic has continued over the centuries. The very words, the Privy Council, give the clue. This was the king's Privy Council, made up of those people closest to the monarch. They gave him counsel. They were privy to his thoughts. From these courtiers, all the great offices and officers of state developed – the chancellors, chamberlains, earl marshals and stewards.

Therefore, the starting point of any attempt to understand the Privy Council is impossible to pinpoint. It is, as Dicey and Fitzroy had it, in 'remote antiquity', long before the days of thorough written accounts and records. Throughout history, leaders have emerged in many different ways. But whether by birth, election, appointment or force – either of arms or personality – in their leadership of tribes, communities or nations, they have needed supporters and advisers. Often, this body of people harboured opportunists and traitors and, in different times and in various circumstances, there was the potential for both the good and the bad, those faithful and those unfaithful to their leader, to prosper. This was the background to the formation of the Privy Council. Its essence developed from the relationship between monarch and advisers. The role of the Council in its early years depended very much on the character of the king. But, as the power of the monarch decreased and the role of parliamentary government increased, so the function of the Council and the part played by its members changed.

Sometimes a strong monarch meant a weak Council and vice versa. It acted very differently under King John than it did under Richard II. Sometimes a far-sighted king would develop and nurture the work of his stewards. Often there were specific circumstances to be dealt with.

William I had to use his advisers to help enforce an idea of kingship and national rule on a Saxon population that had developed firm systems of local government. The Tudor monarchs used the Council to oversee what we would now consider to be regional matters, from dealing with the disputes between town and gown at Oxford to deciding how to respond to a plea from the organisers of bear-baiting competitions in the Vauxhall district of London to shut the theatres on at least one day a week because they were losing them audiences. The Council played a major role in the exploration, trade, conflict and agreements that lead to the creation of the British Empire, and the colonies dealt with the Privy Council rather than the developing democratic parliament at Westminster. In the early part of the twentieth century, until 1921, it was the duty of the Privy Council to see that Lords-Lieutenant raised their quotas of local militia. Later in that century, it could be argued that their most important role was in taking authority for Charters and Royal Commissions. Prime Minister Harold Macmillan ordered the Privy Council Radcliffe Report into the identification of communists after the spy George Blake escaped from prison to go and live in Russia. The Franks Commission, set up to study the lessons of the 1982 Falklands War, consisted of five Privy Counsellors.

In order to attempt an understanding of how all this came about, we have to go back to beyond 1009, when the Witenagemot elected (yes, elected!) the Danish King Sweyn's son Canute to become an Anglo-Saxon king. Back, indeed, to 'remote antiquity'.

CHAPTER TWO

REMOTE ANTIQUITY: MYTHS ANCIENT AND MODERN

'OH HOW MUCH I want you at my birthday party. You'll make the day so much more fun.' This is a translation from a cheerful letter written on wood (now in the British Museum) by Claudia Severa, the wife of a Roman soldier stationed at the auxiliary fort of Vindolanda, south of Hadrian's Wall near what is now Bardon Mill in Northumberland. She was writing at the turn of the first century AD to her sister Sulpicia Lepidina, the wife of the high-ranking Flavious Cerialis, the Prefect of the Ninth Cohort of the Batavians. Her invitation, together with other documents discovered at the same place and now known as the Vindolanda Tablets are, at this date, the oldest surviving written British historical records. As such they are a benchmark in historic research. Before that time, the British narrative of history depended on storytelling, which, if it was recorded in writing at a later date, was often embellished by false memory and the motivation of personal aspiration. To the delight of scholars, the desire to embellish history did not diminish but grew as written records proliferated over the next 2,000 years. How true is the warning given to their readers by W. C. Sellar and R. J. Yeatman in their classic book *1066 and All That*: 'History is not what you thought. It is what you can remember.' Because we have no written constitution, embellishment, not to say invention, is an ever-present danger in research into constitutional issues. Stray outside of Magna Carta in 1215 or the 1689 Bill of Rights and you do so at your peril. There used to be an old doorkeeper at the House of Lords who, when asked by tourists why the bishops sat in the House of Lords, would look in turn thoughtful and then puzzled before replying, 'Well, you know it's such a long time ago. I can't rightly remember.' The parliamentary handbook *Vacher's*, published quarterly since 1832, is just as honest, admitting that they don't know the reason other than it is 'by ancient usage' that the two Anglican archbishops and the bishops of London, Durham and Winchester automatically have seats in the House of Lords.

Throughout its long and mostly unwritten history, the Privy Council contains many examples of monarchs, politicians and civil servants being involved in matters where they are unsure of the correct constitutional position – or even if there is one. For instance, in the nineteenth century the Princess Royal was included in the list of counsellors because the Lord President at the time made the assumption that all members of the royal family were born Privy Counsellors in the same way that they were born princes and princesses. 'Oh, never make assumptions,' wrote Professor Albert Dicey of All Souls in 1887. This was with special reference to constitutional history. Things changed, Dicey warned scholars.

The concept of the Privy Council giving advice to a monarch was different in the nineteenth century than it was in the eleventh century. In his Arnold essay of 1860, he writes that 'according to the ideas prevailing at that time of William I, it was rather the king's privilege than his duty to receive counsel from the great men of his kingdom. Their recommendations were not, like the advice of modern parliaments or ministers, commands, veiled under a polite name.'

This was also a warning that Dicey felt necessary to give to all those who might follow his advice and try to find the roots of the Privy Council in remote antiquity. There is so little written evidence available that all assumptions must be made with great caution. The origins, development and present activity of the Privy Council straddle the whole range of possibilities that have been available for historical research. From too little hard evidence of its beginnings to now, in the twenty-first century, perhaps too much information and analysis. We are approaching, if not at, what Richard Hoggart, author of the seminal book *Uses of Literacy*, described as the Ambridge situation. He once had an MA student in Media Studies doing research on the BBC radio soap opera based around the fictional village of Ambridge. At that time, in the 1960s, it was possible for that researcher to actually listen to all the recordings of the programme that the BBC had kept and use that as basic source material. Hoggart made the point that there would come a time when, even if his student devoted all his waking hours on the course to listening to *The Archers*, he would not have time to hear the whole canon of broadcasts. So how then would he organise his research material? On most subjects there has now been so much written and recorded that it is difficult to establish criteria by which to decide whose previous work to trust, especially when it comes to identifying a valid starting point.

The problem is compounded by the way in which history is currently presented. History used to be taught in terms of great events and

prominent people, beginning with old stories, where facts were mixed
with myths and legends. This approach, enthusiastically championed
in the early 2010s by the Conservative Secretary of State for Education
Michael Gove, was well summarised by H. E. Marshall in her brilliantly
readable book *Our Island Story*, first published in 1905 and reissued 100
years later. She wrote:

> This is not a history lesson, but a story book ... You will find some
> stories that are not to be found in your school books – stories which
> wise people say are only fairy tales and not history. But it seems to me
> that they are part of Our Island Story and ought not to be forgotten.

So the chronicle of our nation from the Roman occupation and the coming of Christianity leads on through Boadicea, Hengist and Horsa, King
Arthur and the Knights of the Round Table, and Alfred burning the
cakes, to the more certain facts of the Battle of Hastings, the murder of
Becket, Agincourt, the Wars of the Roses, the wives of Henry VIII, the
Armada, the Fire of London, the Industrial Revolution, Nelson, Wellington, the Great War and so on. This was the stuff of history lessons, some
of which became confused in the minds of young scholars by periods of
English literature, where Shakespeare added his own spin to make the
distinction between fact and fiction more difficult but very interesting.

The difference between fact and fiction – what is truth and how to teach
it – occupied the minds of educationalists concerned with the subject
of 'curriculum development' until the middle of the twentieth century.
Some Christian Biblical scholars devised for themselves a really satisfactory answer. All the Bible was true but some was literal truth while the
rest was poetic, or spiritual, truth. The problem, of course, was – and still
is – that one person's poetic truth is another's literal truth.

Then, in the 1960s, history teaching changed. Much of it stopped being about teaching pupils how some men and women achieved greatness and started concentrating on the idea of empathy. The emphasis changed to studying ordinary people and how they lived in past times. Questions would be set along the lines of 'Imagine how you would feel if your home was destroyed in the Fire of London?' It was felt that there was a balance to be corrected. And perhaps there was. Certainly many people, not just children, developed an enthusiasm for finding out about their own family histories, and fascinating stories emerged throwing different lights on national events such as the First World War and the struggle for women's emancipation.

In the second decade of the twenty-first century, there was a new development. Totally unforeseen. The new technology that brought about social media, blogging, Facebook, YouTube, Twitter etc. also created, or perhaps fuelled, a desire, especially among the young, for people to record their own lives. Far from photographs, home movies and videos being for just special occasions such as weddings and holidays, digital images became a constant companion. Some people developed the mindset that if an event wasn't recorded, it didn't happen.

The impact on future historical research will be enormous. The Privy Council offers a good example of this. For instance, in the period from the mid-1950s until today, anyone studying the lives of members of the Privy Council in the nineteenth century at the time when Professor Dicey was at All Souls would base their work on the primary material of letters, memoirs, biographies, newspapers, magazines, wills, contracts, parliamentary reports, court cases and other documents. And, a big bonus, they could also use living memory. In the 1950s, I talked to an old lady who could recall conversations with Gladstone, and many members of the House of Lords have family recollections going further back than that. One baroness I knew was Lady Elliot of Harwood, who was born in 1903, the daughter of Sir Charles Tennant, who had been born in 1862.

Her paternal grandfather remembered the British slave trade being abolished. One of the consequences of the botched reform of the Lords by the Labour government in the early years of the twenty-first century was lamented by an American researcher I showed round Westminster. She said, 'You have destroyed a living, breathing, walking, talking library of history, anecdote and legend.' When I murmured something about the Lords not being a democratic institution of government, she took great delight in coming back at me with this comment from hereditary peer Viscount Cranbourne, directed at life peer Baroness Jay: 'We both sit unelected in this House because of patronage. The only difference is that my patron has been dead for over 500 years while yours is still alive. So who is likely to be more independent?' Exchanges about the future of the Lords have often produced perceptive comments. Enoch Powell once stumped Harold Wilson by asking, 'I don't understand. Are you trying to reform the House of Lords to make it more effective or less effective?'

Now consider the problems in 100 years' time of doing research on today's Privy Counsellors. Not only are there more Privy Counsellors than in the nineteenth century – over 600, many of them active in the House of Lords – but an increasing number, especially if they are younger, active politicians, are blogging and tweeting like mad, and film and television footage of them is growing at a geometric rate. Another example of the Ambridge problem.

This has produced a problem with myths. When Dicey and Fitzroy were writing in the nineteenth and early twentieth centuries, they assumed that any study of the Privy Council would start with the old myths and legends of centuries past and move on to deal with facts and certainties based on written material. They could not foresee that the development of mass communication would result in the growth – and often the manufactured growth – of modern myths. This can be observed especially in politics and among MPs and in particular among senior politicians, the Privy Counsellors.

It is not possible to know exactly what Cnut (known to generations of schoolchildren brought up in schools before the 1960s as King Canute) said to his advisers or was told by them as he sat on the beach with the waves lapping at his feet. Or to decide whether Robin Hood was a great archer and a popular rascal in the reign of Richard I or was really the Earl of Huntingdon in disguise who resigned his privy counsellorship under Edward II to lead the outlaws in Sherwood Forest. And how did a story about a cat, written in 1605, link the animal to Sir Richard Whittington, who was sworn to the Privy Council over 200 years earlier in 1397, becoming an established feature of our modern pantomime productions?

Modern myths are just as difficult to decipher and indeed they can flourish because of clever spin doctors and devious or sloppy journalism. This was recognised by Enoch Powell, who incidentally often saw comparisons with contemporary politics and historic events involving the Privy Council. Simon Heffer's biography notes that when Powell joined Harold Macmillan's Cabinet and was sworn to the Privy Council after the Prime Minister's panic reshuffle of the 'night of the long knives' in 1962 (a description taken from June 1934, when, on Hitler's instructions, the Gestapo and SS murdered over 100 Germans opposed to Hitler's regime), he said that it was 'like Henry VIII's Privy Council reassembling after several of their number had been beheaded'. Powell went on to say that he seemed to see an axe leaning against the PM's chair.

There were at least two myths concerning Powell's membership of the Privy Council. A story circulated that during Margaret Thatcher's premiership he was one of her key secret advisers, even though he was not then a member of the Conservative Party. This myth gained currency when, during the Falklands War, television cameras showed him striding into 10 Downing Street. What commentators didn't bother to find out was that he was attending a Privy Council briefing for opposition parties and that he was there because he was the only Privy Counsellor in the Official Unionist Party – the party he then represented in Parliament. Another myth about Powell was that after the furore following his 'rivers of blood' speech, he took his name out of public telephone books and went ex-directory. As Powell said, if only those perpetuating that story had checked, they would have discovered that his first name was John and he had been listed in the London telephone directory long before he became sworn to the Privy Council and entitled to put the prefix Rt Hon. in front of his name. The man known to many people as Enoch was simply listed as Powell, J. E.

Some modern political myths have grown out of supposed quotations where words are twisted just ever so slightly to make a headline – or sometimes completely invented. There is one example of each concerning comments made by Privy Counsellors when they were prime ministers. In a speech at Bedford on 20 July 1957, Harold Macmillan did not say, 'You've never had it so good.' Indeed, he was at pains not to use those exact words as they had been the slogan of the Democratic Party in their election campaign in the United States in 1952 and he did not want to align the British Conservative Party with an American political party two years before a general election. What he actually said was: 'Let's be frank about it; most of our people have never had it so good.' Subtly, but importantly, different. When, during the 'winter of discontent' in 1978/79, Jim Callaghan returned from an international summit in sunny Guadeloupe, he was asked about the situation in the UK and replied, 'I don't think other people in the world will share the view that there is mounting chaos.' This was translated by the *Sun* newspaper as, 'Crisis? What crisis?' A phrase much more likely to stick in the mind and go down in history, to be used time and time again by commentators not prepared to go back to the original film footage. And did Prime Minister David Cameron really say, 'Hug a hoodie', or was it a husky? This is all part of what is known in the international speech-writing trade as the Bogart syndrome. Thousands of people who have watched the film *Casablanca* will swear that they heard Humphrey Bogart say, 'Play it again, Sam.' But he didn't. He stuck to the actual words of the script-writers, Julius Epstein, Philip Epstein and Howard Koch, and said, 'If she can stand it, I can. Play it.'

So from King Cnut, Robin Hood and Dick Whittington to Macmillan, Callaghan and Powell, the existence of myths is a continuing part of the historical process. One area of fertile ground where political myths can flourish is in the relationship between leaders and their advisers. When things go well, there is goodwill, secrecy and respect. When things go wrong, all hell can break loose. This is as true today as it has been throughout history, and can result in significantly shattering events such as Henry II, Thomas a Becket and the unruly knights, or become just another entirely inconsequential bit of soon-to-be-forgotten gossip in the Westminster Village, such as the dismay in the Labour Party when Charlie Whelan, an unelected special adviser to the Chancellor of the Exchequer Gordon Brown in Tony Blair's government, claimed in a television programme that people like him (Whelan) – his words – had far more effect on government policy than elected MPs who had been appointed to middle-ranking ministerial jobs. This was no surprise to many commentators who had become used to the assumption that, at a stage higher up the pay grade, advisers such as Alastair Campbell, the Prime Minister's press officer, though with a much grander title, was far more influential than the vast majority of the Cabinet. But while Campbell and Whelan were key advisers, neither of them was a Privy Counsellor. So was that a sign that in the twenty-first century the advisory role of the Privy Council had changed? And that counsellors were less influential than the new and growing breed of 'special advisers' with which ministers surrounded themselves? What was the Privy Council's status as an assembly? How did it reflect the changes in the leadership of the nation in the last 300 years, as governing power passed increasingly from the monarch to the office of the Prime Minister?

CHAPTER THREE

REMOTE ANTIQUITY: LEADERS, ADVISERS AND ASSEMBLIES

'HOW DO YOU ACTUALLY go about catching a bus?' According to popular legend, this was the question put to Prime Minister Harold Macmillan by his adviser and confidant John Wyndham during a lunch at the Savoy in the 1950s. Macmillan had first met Wyndham when he had entered Churchill's wartime government as a junior minister in the Department of Supply. Wyndham was his teenage private secretary, excused military service because of poor eyesight. 'Two short-sighted snobs,' said one Labour MP about the pair. Certainly, Macmillan, Eton- and Oxford-educated and related to the Duke of Devonshire, and Wyndham, Eton- and Cambridge-educated and related to Lord Leconfield, hit it off from the start. It was one of those relationships that sometimes develop in politics and Wyndham stayed with Macmillan under various titles in different posts for the rest of his working life. The story told by party workers at Conservative Central Office in 32 Smith Square in Westminster was that Wyndham adopted the pose with Macmillan that he had never travelled on a London bus. Macmillan, who revelled in occasionally being spotted standing in a queue at a bus stop, persuaded him that he should do so. When lunch was finished, Wyndham got on a bus in the Strand. The conductor asked him where he wanted to go and got the reply, '32 Smith Square'. After the conductor patiently explained that the bus didn't go that way, Wyndham had a word with the driver. Apparently money changed hands and, according to many party professionals who just happened to be looking out of the windows at that time, a London double-decker turned into the square and stopped outside the main entrance of No. 32 to let the Prime Minister's adviser get off and go back to work.

Thus the urbane life of an aristocratic political adviser in the mid-twentieth century. Fifty years later, one of Prime Minister Tony Blair's aides, his Director of Communication and Strategy, Alastair Campbell, grammar school- and Cambridge-educated, had the power, even if not perhaps the authority, to instruct a Cabinet minister to choose between staying with his wife or settling with his mistress and doing it now – making a public decision that day. Four hundred years earlier, Thomas Cromwell, the son of a blacksmith and cloth shearer, who had become a lawyer, a Privy Counsellor and adviser to the king, Henry VIII, was – after what many would say was a successful career (Professor David Starkey described him as Alastair Campbell with an axe) – tried, sentenced and beheaded under a law of treason that he had actually written himself.

These three examples – out of the many hundreds that could be picked – show that, over the centuries, political advisers have come in varying shapes and sizes with different powers, responsibilities and lifestyles. And with titles that changed and became grander as the years went by. This is a disease of politics. In Anthony Eden's Cabinet in 1955, out of eighteen members, only four were grand enough to be entitled Secretary of State. Most of those who looked after departments were called ministers, e.g. Minister of Education. Now they are almost all called Secretaries of State, e.g. Secretary of State for Education. And note the subtle change that has crept in. They are no longer 'of' a department but 'for' a department. This even spreads to local government, where some councillors boast of having Cabinet responsibilities and looking after their constituents, forgetting the fact that they are not actually elected in constituencies but in much smaller wards. Most sadly of all, the ancient and honourable office of Town Clerk has been replaced by the historically meaningless term chief executive officer. So it is with advisers. Nowadays there is a top grade for some of them and they are considered 'special'.

However, one thing is constant. In politics there always have been and always will be leaders. When you have leaders, around them, no matter what you call them, you will have advisers. Sometimes they are jealous of each other. One Privy Counsellor and member of Margaret Thatcher's government, Norman Fowler, was sufficiently concerned about the relationship between leaders and advisers that he even wrote a book, prompted by Margaret Thatcher, along the theme that ministers decide while advisers only advise. Some advisers' power may well outstrip their title. Some aides may become leaders. Some may lose their heads. Over the centuries, in this relationship has been found – and no doubt not found, but successfully covered up – both honour and treason. There has much been written on the subject, notably Machiavelli's fifteenth-century work *The Prince*, which has been the foundation for some fascinating comment on the relationship between a prince and his servant, not least in Lord McAlpine's book *The Servant* (1992). McAlpine was deputy chairman of the Conservative Party and a close adviser

to Margaret Thatcher. He writes of the relationship between Mr Pick-
wick and Sam Weller, and between Bertie Wooster and Jeeves, adding
that 'Dickens and Wodehouse are not authors aspiring politicians normally go to for advice; but they could do worse'.

It is certainly in that concept of the relationship between leader and
advisers that we shall find the seeds from which the Privy Council grew,
if both the foremost authorities on the Privy Council, Professor Albert
Dicey and Sir Almeric Fitzroy, are to be believed. 'Remote antiquity' certainly tells us of some of the earliest leaders in these islands, if not of their
aides and advisers. Indeed, the name of one of our first leaders, Cassivellaunus, is recorded on a monument to him at Devil's Dyke in Sussex.
Cassivellaunus was a British tribal chieftain who led an alliance of tribes
against Julius Caesar's second Roman invasion in 54 AD. Extreme caution must be taken in assessing the achievements of these early leaders for
two very obvious reasons. Firstly, hard evidence is slight. Secondly, most
of their exploits seem to concern their involvement with heroic deeds
and the temptation to embroider these narratives into exciting stories
with mass appeal has been impossible to resist. Invention has been rife.
Leaders on both sides of the second Roman occupation have captured
public imagination. 'Sex-mad tyrant' was the most concise summary of
Tinto Brass's epic 1979 film *Caligula*. This bizarre general, who gained
notoriety for telling his troops to collect sea shells on the French sands
instead of crossing the Channel to invade Britain, is a familiar historical
figure. However, you will Google in vain for his opponent, King Guilderious, who mustered the tribes and waited for him on the Kent beaches.
Well, that is one story. The question is: did King Guilderious ever actually reign outside of the pages of Geoffrey of Monmouth's twelfth-century
volume, *The Kings of Briton*? Caractacus certainly deserved his fame as
a great warrior and noble orator. When he was captured by the Emperor
Claudius in 51 AD and taken back to Rome to be publicly executed,

apparently his dignity of bearing and the impact of his speech resulted in him and his family being granted liberty. But Robert Graves wrote a book not about him but about Claudius, which was made into a highly successful television series and catapulted Claudius, not Caractacus, into the position of one of the best-known figures of that period in our history. Boudicca (or Boadicea, as friends of King Canute would say) was also obviously a great leader and some historians maintain that she consulted her daughters wisely. Like Cassivellaunus and Caractacus, we can assume that she discussed matters with the various tribes involved in the preparation for their battles. But it does not seem as though there was any kind of formal structure for consultation. That had to wait for the Anglo-Saxons.

At this time, there was no concept of England developing as a nation. During the 400 years after the Romans had left there were tribes and various kings in different parts of the country. This was a period when, for the first time, there were contemporary and near contemporary written accounts of life and events. The problem is that historians – now with great certainty – regard much of these writings as either error or invention. For instance, Gildas, a monk who lived on the island of Flatholm in the Bristol Channel in the sixth century, wrote an account in *The Ruin of Britain* of the dreadful condition that Britain fell into after the Romans departed. He describes how one king, Constantine, was overthrown by his chief adviser, Vortigern. If true, this may be the first recorded instance of an adviser usurping a ruler. Vortigern had obtained control of the king's money to hire mercenaries to help defeat Constantine. He then, in 499, invited the Saxon leader Hengist to bring a party of soldiers to Kent to march north with him to help in his battle with the Picts and Scots. There is evidence to support Gildas's narrative. But the monk also writes that he, personally, helped King Arthur when he effectively intervened with his negotiating skills to help Arthur secure the release of Guinevere after she had been abducted. So it is not surprising that many dismiss him as a fantasist.

One of the other two great sources from this period is the Venerable Bede's *The Ecclesiastic of The English People*, written in 731. This book and the discussions at the Synod of Whitby in 664 are important in the search for the roots of the Privy Council. Not for what they say, but for early evidence that even though the country was not united politically, the Church – at local, national, and European level – was becoming one of the keystones of our unwritten constitution. There is constant and continual debate about the reliability of the *Anglo-Saxon Chronicles*, a narrative of English history from the birth of Christ until 1154. Many think that this work was inspired by Alfred the Great and that the recordings of the later years are much more accurate than those of the early centuries. One of the institutions mentioned in the *Chronicles* is the Witenagemot, an assembly or assemblies of the ruling class, and at various times in history there has been an attempt to look back to these assemblies and see a direct link from them to the King's Council (the Privy Council) and the parliamentary bodies of today. In terms of historical truth, this link may be dubious. In his masterful work of 1905, *Anglo-Saxon Institutions*, H. M. Chadwick wrote:

> I have not thought it necessary to discuss at length the nature of the powers possessed by the Council (i.e. the Witenagemot), for ... there can be little hope of arriving at any definite conclusions on this subject. Indeed it seems at least doubtful whether the functions of the Council were ever properly defined.

In his 1995 book *Alfred the Great*, David Sturdy goes further. Writing about the attempts of historians to look back a thousand years and see the beginnings of some of some of our institutions then, he says, 'Victorian notions of a national "witan" are crazy dreams, myths of a democratic parliament that never was.' If we are searching in remote antiquity for a predecessor to the Privy Council, a stronger link is probably to be found in what Biblical scholars would call poetic truth rather than actual truth. That is in the story of King Arthur and his Knights of the Round Table. It has everything: a king, his advisers, including Merlin the wizard – shades of Privy Counsellor Peter Mandelson (or is that being too unkind?) – and a place of assembly at the Round Table. Romance, sex, mystery, intrigue and treachery. No wonder the story has survived the centuries and grown its own subplots as it has captured the imagination of audiences in prose, poetry, theatre, music, dance, film and television. It may well be that the story has a basis in truth and that King Arthur really was the great Romano-British leader Ambrosius Aurelianus, who managed briefly to unite the old provinces of the Roman era for one final battle against the Anglo-Saxons before the country segregated into smaller, more compact communities. But it is the name Arthur that holds the magic. The magic first appeared in 1142, in the writings of William of Malmesbury's *De Gestis Regum*, which states that the ancient ballads maintained Arthur was not dead but merely sleeping on the island of Avalon in the Somerset marshes, waiting to be recalled to lead the nation when the time was ripe. This notion is perpetuated in works of Geoffrey of Monmouth (1147) and the *Chronicle of Roger of Wendover* (1191). The knightly king of chivalry, Arthur of the Round Table, became definitely established as a figure of romance in British literature by the compilation of *Le Morte d'Arthur*, completed in 1470 by Sir Thomas Malory, and in the nineteenth century, the legendary leader is celebrated by Tennyson's *The Idylls of the King*. In the twentieth century, the legend and its spin-offs went global, with theme parks and mock jousting tournaments galore. No other story could have reached both the pages of Richmal Crompton's charming 1930 book *William the Bad*, in which William

and his outlaws 'wrighted rongs', and the White House of President Jack
Kennedy, where friend and foe alike described Washington as the new
Camelot – with, by implication, the President standing as a truly great
historical figure, towering over his knights; a charismatic leader in an
enchanting and colourful setting.

It is this idea of a powerful leader, a King Arthur (or a President Kennedy), with their hand-picked band of personal followers meeting in
assembly at the Round Table (or the Oval Office), that gives a better
idea how the Privy Council started to evolve; a study of the Anglo-Saxon
Witenagemots may lead us down a blind alley. For there were many Witenagemots. There were many kings and assemblies held in Essex, Kent,
Mercia, Northumbria, Sussex and Wessex. The witans were believed to
have developed from the old sixth-century folkmoots. They had strong
local or regional concerns and interests. It is true that they had a say in
the choosing of their kings, and on at least two occasions they had a hand
in deposing kings – Sigeberht of Wessex in 757 and Alhred of Northumbria in 774. Local witans continued to meet until the Norman Conquest.
Both the witans and, later, the Privy Council certainly advised the king,
but to go further with any certainty is difficult, especially in view of the
different concepts of the divine right of kings, government and democracy
that have been held over the centuries. But it does seem possible to be
firm about three key factors: there were local concerns in the folkmoots
and witans that were not to be present in the Privy Council; members
served on the Privy Council only by royal appointment of the monarch;
and the Council did not really operate as an effective force until England had one monarch.

For a time in the tenth century, between the stability of Alfred's reign
and the conquest by William in 1066, there was much confusion. Alfred
had brought back learning and culture to the Anglo-Saxons. Monasteries were reconstructed and schools established. He codified a system

of laws, started to build a navy and encouraged trade. Much of this was dissipated by what *1066 and All That* describes as a 'wave of egg kings … Eggberd, Eggbreth, Eggfroth etc.' However, there were two developments in those years that clearly had an impact on the evolvement of the Privy Council. One was the introduction of the French language by Edward the Confessor (1005–66) into the protocols of court practice and procedure. Although born in Oxfordshire, Edward was the son of a Norman duke and almost all his courtiers were French. The other development affected the primitive local government arrangements of the Saxons. This was work started by Ethelred II (968–1016) – yes, the unready one, in this case showing a bit of foresight – and carried on by Edward. In order to combat the powerful position of the earls, the monarchy started to appoint shire reeves, later to be called sheriffs. Reeves were bailiffs of large estates, like the one in Chaucer's *Canterbury Tales*. They were responsible for the management of lands and the collection of rents. The king's sheriffs, who were recruited reeves, collected taxes for the king and dispensed justice. They also brought to the national treasury vital information about local wealth. Knowledge which, a few years later, made the *Domesday Book* a lot easier to compile. The king also appointed these new shire reeves to sit on witans, which by this time had become increasingly localised, meeting not only in cities such as London, Gloucester and Winchester, but also in smaller towns like Cheddar and Calne, as well as assembling in some areas in the open air, at prominent landmarks such as rocks and hills.

The victory of William the Conqueror at the Battle of Hastings in 1066 was one of the most decisive moments in British constitutional history. The squabbles about his legitimacy, the promises, half-promises and lies made and told before his succession will long be discussed. But one thing changed forever. From the moment of William's crowning by the Archbishop of Canterbury in Westminster Abbey on Christmas Day in

1066, England only ever had one monarch at a time – leaving the War of the Roses, and William and Mary, on one side for the moment. Sixty years earlier, England had been ruled by two kings, Cnut in the north and Edmund in the south. There had been many witans whose powers in relation to the king seem to have been unclear then and are certainly unclear now. Into that uncertainty came the Normans, led by a leader with the vision of establishing – by whatever force was needed – one nation. William's character is well summed up by Stephen Clarke in his book, *1,000 Years of Annoying the French*:

> William would pursue aggressors or anyone he felt like attacking until he either killed them or seized all their riches and rendered them totally powerless. Pretty soon, word had got round that it was not a good idea to annoy William unless you were sure of being able to take him out, which was a slim possibility given that he had a personal army of highly trained knights and was himself a fearsome fighter.

Here, like Arthur, was a leader supported by knights on a kingly quest. All he needed was a Round Table at which his advisers could assemble, and that was to appear in the form of the Curia Regis.

CHAPTER FOUR

THE CHIEF BUTLER OF ENGLAND AND OTHER GREAT OFFICERS OF STATE

I F, AMONG THE MANY assemblies, institutions and courts that have formed the basis of England's administration, there is one body from which the Privy Council evolved, it would be the personal household of William the Conqueror. To put this proposition at its simplest, if William wanted to impose his rule on England, he and his trusted followers had to physically ride around the country subduing, controlling and then ruling every part of the nation. Those who rode with him – loyal members of his household – became privy to his counsel. Some served on the Curia Regis, a name given to both a large and a smaller King's Council that evolved under the Norman kings. All household offices had grand names and titles. Some survive today either in the royal palaces or

in government posts. For instance, the correct constitutional names for
the government whips in the House of Lords are:

Chief Whip: Captain of the Gentlemen-at-Arms

Deputy Whip: Captain of the Yeomen of The Guard

Whips: Lords-in-Waiting

Some titles are conferred on office-holders only for special, and nearly
always brief, occasions. Prime Minister Winston Churchill was extremely
worried by the suggestion that on the accession of Queen Elizabeth II
the distinguished wartime leader Field Marshal Viscount Montgomery
should hold the post of Lord High Constable. As a historian, Churchill
knew of the sweeping powers that would give Montgomery. In the end, a
compromise of sorts was reached and the retired general was only Lord
High Constable for the actual day of the Queen's coronation. Some positions of vital importance to the Norman kings became less relevant as
the centuries went by, and they were – almost – quietly forgotten. This
might have been the fate of the Chief Butler of England, and although
there is still, in the early years of the twenty-first century, at least one
strong claimant to the post, it has virtually been extinct since 1902. This
is strange in a way, because if you had asked most Edwardian aristocratic
families – certainly the one living at Downton Abbey – who was the key
figure in their household, they would have replied that it was the butler.

This reputation of a loyal, committed, trusting servant, knowing everything that went on, impeccable in manner, behaviour and dress, didn't
just come out of thin air. It had been built up over the centuries based
on those who had successfully served the highest in the land. Arguably
the first King of England, William I, appointed as the first Chief Butler
of England Roger d'Ivry, who was also the Conqueror's Cup-Bearer – an
important post in the days when there was little knowledge of antidotes to

poisons. Henry I made the post a hereditary one, included in the deeds of the Manor of Kenninghall in Norfolk, which passed at one point to the Dukes of Norfolk. This caused a fuss in the early years of the twentieth century when cases were being prepared for presentation at the Court of Claims as to who was to be the Chief Butler to Edward VII. Like most of the great offices of state between the eleventh and twentieth centuries, the position of the Chief Butler of England was sometimes inherited and sometimes gifted by the monarch. There were some famous families in the list, including, between 1120 and 1397, eleven Dukes of Arundel. There were two other dukes – Northumberland and Cleveland – several earls and barons, many knights, a handful of commoners and a famous viscount – Francis Lovell, made famous by the poem written by William Collingham and pinned to the door of St Paul's Cathedral in 1413:

> *The Rat, the Cat and Lovell the Dog,*
> *Rule all England under the hog.*

The rat was Sir Richard Ratcliffe and the cat Sir William Catsby. With Lovell, they were three of the chief aides to Richard III, represented in the poem by the hog, which was part of his coat of arms. Unsurprisingly, Collingham was put to death for his ready wit. The lines have remained popular. Laurence Oliver added them to Shakespeare's play in his film adaptation of *Richard III*. As a true and faithful servant, Lovell, not only as the Chief Butler of England but now promoted to the office of Lord Chamberlain as well, played his part in supporting Richard at the king's fatal battle at Bosworth Field on 22 August 1485, and there are some reports that he was listed among the dead. But he is also reported as playing a part in the pretender Lambert Simnel's attempt to claim the throne two years later. He then seems to have disappeared from public life and, for the last fifteen years of the fifteenth century, Sir John Fortescue the younger served as the Chief Butler. But Lovell was to figure in history again when, in 1708, a skeleton was unearthed at the house in which his family had lived in Minster Lovell in Oxfordshire. The story was that after the trouncing of the Yorkists, of which he had been a leader, and having helped Simnel flee to Ireland, Lovell had gone into hiding in a secret chamber at his home and had stayed there and died. There is no hard evidence for this tale, but it gathered more interest when it was included in one of John Buchan's stories in the early part of the twentieth century.

Interestingly, the fathers of both Lovell and Fortescue had been involved in heated debates in the Privy Council at the start of the fifteenth century when Fortescue, author of *The Governance of England*, had complained that the oath of secrecy was ridiculous as all members of the Council talked to their families and servants. And Lovell was a participant in a case of 'brocage'. This was a practice whereby if a member of the Council had a vested interest in a plea because they were 'in quarrel' with one of the parties to the case, they could declare that and withdraw from the hearing. It took nearly 600 years before it was realised that Fortescue probably had a point and that counsellors probably did discuss Council business at home. A consideration of 'brocage' might well be useful in the many courts, tribunals and mediations going on today.

In the past few centuries, it was the main duty of the Chief Butler to arrange and preside at the coronation banquet organised for the incoming monarch. In 1902, there were three claimants for the title to serve Edward VII. One was a descendant of a previous Chief Butler, William de Albini. Another, a Mr Taylor of Norfolk, claimed the position as he was the current Lord of the Manor of Kenninghall and held the title from deeds granted by Henry I. The strongest claimant was Henry Fitzalan-Howard, the 15th Duke of Norfolk. He claimed that he held the post through one of his subsidiary titles, the Earl of Arundel. Ten of the first eleven Earls of Arundel had been Chief Butler of England,

and Fitzalan-Howard insisted that the Dukes of Norfolk had the title restored to them in 1856.

But the Court of Claims didn't get round to sitting before the 1902 coronation. The person responsible for calling the court, the Earl Marshal, was busy with other matters – mainly the fact that the new king was keen to limit the powers of the Earl Marshal in regard to the arrangements for the coronation. But, after much lobbying and arm twisting, the Earl Marshal held on to the prerogatives of his office established through the ages, and the Clerk of the Privy Council, Sir Almeric Fitzroy, wrote in his diary:

> 31 October 1902. The Coronation Committee met for the second time at St James's Palace with a complete attendance. The Earl Marshal has won his point and is to have his own office, secretary and staff as on the last occasion: in fact, the abatement of the claim to limit his liberty of action could hardly have been carried further. We spent an hour and a half discussing a variety of points, which might have been disposed of in half the time.

As the circulation of the Coronation Committee Privy Council minutes was restricted to members, we do not know the details discussed, but they may well have included a decision on who was to be the Chief Butler of England.

Anyway, whether the decision was made there or not, the Chief Butler of England is still included as one of the many hereditary titles held by the Dukes of Norfolk. The complete list is:

Earl of Arundel

Chief Butler of England

Earl of Surrey

Baron Beaumont

Baron Maltravers

Baron Fitzalan

Baron Clun

Baron Oswaldestre

Earl of Norfolk

Baron Howard of Glossop

Earl Marshal

Hereditary Marshal of England

You will notice that another of the titles held by the family is that of the Earl Marshal, so – you could be forgiven for wondering – perhaps that is why in 1902 the Fitzalan-Howards were able to retain the most ancient and honourable post of the Chief Butler of England. Whatever the reason, retain it they did – which gave much pleasure to the butler at Arundel Castle, the seat of the Norfolk family, when he was able to indulge in a 'butler to Chief Butler' public exchange with the Duke of Norfolk in the 1960s. Bernard, the 16th Duke, had recently returned from being manager of the 1962/63 MCC team on their tour of Australia. (Now there's a thought: if the Chief Butler of England had managed the English cricket team in their 2013/14 tour, would there have been all that fuss about Kevin Pietersen?) On the lovely cricket ground at the castle, Bernard, the Chief Butler of the nation, was batting. His own butler was umpiring. There was an appeal for LBW. The butler drew himself up to his full height and, in response to the cry of 'Howzat' from the bowler, came out with the great response, worthy of a line from *Downton Abbey*, 'Sadly ... His Grace is not in.'

*   *   *

Over the centuries, many of the posts established in the household of William I lost their function but, like that of the Chief Butler, retained their title. In some cases the titles were retained, though the

duties of the office changed significantly. This was true of the chamberlains. Their origins are obvious: to assist the monarch in his chamber;
to help and advise the monarch with his many duties. The greatest duty
of the monarch was that of government and so the chamberlains became
involved, first indirectly and then directly, with the government of the
nation. The term 'chamberlain' was generic. There were general chamberlains and those with specific duties. Some survive. The current Lord
Chamberlain is the most senior member of the Queen's household and
under him are the heads of six departments: the Private Secretary, the
Keeper of the Privy Purse, the Comptroller of the Lord Chamberlain's
Office, the Master of the Household, the Crown Equerry and the Director
of the Royal Collection. Another chamberlain, the Lord Great Chamberlain, is a really great officer of state. This is a hereditary office that is
jointly held by the Cholmondeley and Carrington families. The Lord
Great Chamberlain is responsible for the royal apartments, the Queen's
robing room and the royal gallery at the Palace of Westminster. He used,
on behalf of the monarch, to rule the whole palace. In conjunction with
the Lord Chancellor (a post now held by the Secretary of State for Justice) and the Speaker, he also looks after Westminster Hall. There often
seems no rhyme or reason, and perhaps there isn't, for the way in which
particular duties have become allocated to different officers. For example,
for many years the duty of acting as censor for stage plays in the UK was
undertaken by the Lord Chamberlain at Buckingham Palace. And the
Lord Great Chamberlain, although he has a flat in the Palace of Westminster and, with the Earl Marshal, is one of the two hereditary peers left with
permanent seats in the House of Lords, is certainly not a politician. But
the Vice-Chamberlain of Her Majesty's Household certainly is a politician, and whoever holds that position today must be an elected member
of the House of Commons and is appointed by the Prime Minister and
paid from parliamentary funds. At Westminster, the Vice-Chamberlain,

the Treasurer of Her Majesty's Household and the Comptroller of Her Majesty's Household are better known as the three senior government whips in the Commons. This is one of the many things that can be confusing to those outside the Westminster bubble. Much surrounding the whips is confusing, even for those inside the bubble. For instance, the correct constitutional title for the Chief Whip in the Commons is the Parliamentary Secretary to the Treasury ... and so on!

The Vice-Chamberlain plays as vital a role in the constitution of our country in the twenty-first century as the chamberlains' predecessors did in the eleventh century. Vital – but different. Vital because that post is one of the nuts and bolts that link a democratically elected government to the undemocratic and hereditary monarch who serves as head of state. The Vice-Chamberlain is involved in both helping to run the country and helping the monarchy. As a whip, they play their part in the black arts of Parliament. Getting in the vote. Counting the ambulances through New Palace Yard. In extremis, deciding with doctors and opposition whips whether an MP was alive or not when the vote was taken inside the Commons and the MP was 'nodded through' while lying on a stretcher. The most effective whips know not only where all the bodies are buried in Westminster and Whitehall but also who dug the graves. And then the whip who serves as Vice-Chamberlain has to switch from meddling in what many consider to be a dirty – but essential – part of politics to being a member of the dignified part of the constitution. Every day when the House is sitting, they have to write in a few hundred words on what has been happening in the Palace of Westminster and send the report to Buckingham Palace. They used to have to write it in their own hand and it was one of the sights of London when, in the early evening, the Vice-Chamberlain travelled through SW1 in a horse-drawn carriage to deliver their missive to their Queen. It now can go by messenger – no email allowed – and it is still one of the sights of the Houses of Parliament and its environ to see an anxious Vice-Chamberlain rushing around the Lords and Commons – tea rooms, bars, the terraces – picking up bits of gossip they think the Queen might enjoy. One of their other functions is to go to Buckingham Palace and stay hostage there while the monarch goes to open Parliament. This dates back to the 1600s and is a safeguard in case the MPs decide to arrest the Sovereign. One Vice-Chamberlain, settling down at the palace to watch the proceedings on television, wished the Duke of Edinburgh good luck and said he hoped it all went well. 'You're the one who should worry,' replied Prince Philip. 'If we don't get back, you're the one who gets shot first.'

But in the time of William I there were no nuts and bolts linking the monarch to Parliament. There was no Parliament. The members of the king's household, the chamberlains, chancellors, marshals, butlers and stewards, were busy with a different set of nuts and bolts: that of establishing a new kind of government. A national system for the start of a nation. It was always going to be difficult. England was made up of shires. After over a thousand years, the names of these shires are still apparent in our counties and still form some of the basis of our local government system. Each shire was divided into hundreds and a sheriff was appointed by the king to collect taxes and administer justice. William was determined to impose on this system the methods he had inherited from the Dukes of Normandy, whereby the key institution was the ducal household. The household ruled and if that meant almost continual travelling to impose their national will on the Saxon regions then so be it.

A symbol of these methods that has lasted through the ages is the Tower of London. This was constructed as the Conqueror's stronghold in the capital, from which his armies would march out to subdue the native population. Where there was rebellion, as in Cambridge, Gloucester, Exeter, Warwick, York, Huntingdon and Chepstow, buildings were demolished and local castles were built. Where there was prolonged resistance, villages were torched and people made homeless. About 20 per cent of the population was slaughtered or died of starvation. Northumberland was destroyed, soldiers confiscating ploughs and farm tools so that it was not even possible to scratch a living from the land. When the last rebel, Hereward the Wake, was betrayed after valiantly fighting in the fenlands of the Isle of Ely, the Conqueror could justly claim that he had laid the foundations for one nation. He had used the members of his household – rewarding them with land, money and castles – to oversee the production of the *Domesday Book* and to impose his will on the country. This gave his successors both knowledge and power, but it also gave England a system of government strong enough to survive the problems that arose when he died. The fights between his sons Robert and William lost the family much of their authority in Normandy but had little impact on Norman rule in England, and after William II's much questioned death following a hunting accident in the New Forest in 1100, the Conqueror's third son, Henry, was able to carry on his father's work. Both Professor Albert Dicey of All Souls, in his award-winning essay on the Privy Council in 1860, and Sir Almeric Fitzroy, in his 1928 book *The History of The Privy Council*, agree that during this period it was the monarch who was the absolute centre and key component of government. But, as John Gillingham writes in *The Oxford Illustrated History of Britain* (edited by Kenneth O. Morgan):

> Naturally the king could not govern alone. Wherever he went he was followed by a great crowd; courtiers, officials, servants, traders, petitioners, and hangers-on … At the centre was the king's household … cooks, butlers, grooms. The men whose work was political and administrative as well as domestic. The Chancellor was responsible for the king's seal. Treasurer and chamberlains. Constables and marshals. The household was omnicompetent.

It was understandable how and why this method of government had developed under the Norman kings. But it was unwieldy. Many of the members of William I's original household had got fed up with the travelling around essential if the king was to stamp his authority on the country. They wanted to settle down and, as the business of government became more complex, permanent institutions were needed. This was a piecemeal process – the Treasury at Winchester and the Chancery at Westminster. One of the most important acts at this time was the organisation of the Curia Regis as the royal court of law administered by trained lawyers. Henry also appointed itinerant justices whose courts periodically supervised the administration of justice in the provinces.

The 300 years following the Norman Conquest saw the shaping of the great institutions of government, administration and justice that are still evolving today, but when we look back at the work of historians trying to make sense of these developments, we see confusion and not clarity. For instance, the nobles who deposed Richard II and conspired against Edward II had no belief in the theory or practice of the divine right of kings. Yet the historians of the Stuart period pictured the 'divine right' as a general assumption of Plantagenet England, along with the belief that the monarch would rule for the general good. Later, some liberal constitutional writers of Victorian times tried to see in the workings of the king's household (which developed into the various and differing meetings of the King's Council) the start of a growing desire by those with influence, the feudal barons, to bring power to the people. It was of course nothing of the kind. Kings needed money. Money to support their lavish lifestyles and those of their household. Money to support foreign adventures and overseas wars. And money to try to curb rebellion. What better way to bring in revenue than to bring on board those who both had money and could raise and collect taxes from their land? They could be flattered by being asked their advice and given posts of limited power. Many of these people with powerful local positions had served on regional witans. Their knowledge could be channelled and controlled. The power of the Church could be harnessed in the same way. It was a classic case of keeping your friends close but your enemies closer. Dicey maintained that these changes were not planned: they were a pragmatic response to circumstances. In his essay, he writes that

> the early Norman kings may be considered as the greatest family among the nobility. No statutes curbed the prerogative of the Conqueror or of William Rufus. Their power was bounded by customs supported by the swords of an aristocracy in arms. Among those usages was one found in every feudal monarchy – that of the interchange of advice between the king and his nobles.

It was the slow formalisation of that advice between monarch, household, barons and Church that led to the setting up of two councils around the king. There was a great council, consisting of the main officers of the household and anyone else whom the king liked to appoint, along with the two Archbishops. The Church had now reached such a powerful position that it would only have been a very foolish king who would have stopped them attending. Then there was the much wider council, known as the Curia Regis. This term was sometimes also used to describe the smaller council, leading to much confusion among later historians, who offered the speculation that – at the time – the people involved did not appreciate that this separation of powers and duties was taking place. The Curia Regis grew into being an executive body with legal powers. This was in fact, in its widest sense, the Court of the king, when the term 'court' could either mean status, honour, banquets and dancing with the monarch, or the majesty and severity of the law. The expression 'Curia Regis' was also used as a more general term for regional meetings where the king was present. From these council meetings, both great and small, specific bodies were formed to deal with particular matters, and so the Exchequer and the Law Courts came into being, the Court of King's Bench and the Court of Common Pleas separating from the Curia Regis in 1174.

There is much that is uncertain in the history of government between 1066 and 1367, but one thing is clear: that by the time of Richard II's reign, three major institutions of English life had been established to be added to the monarchy:

Two Houses of Parliament (Lords and Commons)

The Law Courts

The King's Council (later to be called the Privy Council)

Parliament originally meant a parley – nothing more. The word is found in French early in the twelfth century and its use became common in England during the thirteenth. It meant any kind of conference, but its official use was restricted to a full meeting of the larger King's Council, summoned by the monarch four times a year. As land was the chief source of revenue for the king, the greatest tenants-in-chief, whether bishops or barons, were required to attend by individual writ. For lesser tenants, a system was devised which eventually led to our having a popularly elected legislative body as a tax-raising institution. In Anglo-Saxon times, the reeve and four important men of each town were required to attend the shire moot. The same principle was then extended to the King's Council and, if the local lord of the manor decided not to go to the Council, the community had to send the reeve and the four 'best' men. The boon of this representation was not that so few had to attend – an expensive business for the persons concerned – but that all the rest were allowed to stay at home.

Most of the work – financial, legal or the presentation and consideration of petitions – was done in sub-committees, with the assembly forming working groups based on their particular vested interests. Originally, the King's Council met in Westminster Hall, built by William Rufus. This is one of the most evocative parts of the Palace of Westminster, particularly at dusk on a December's evening with the fog swirling around the rafters. Later, when the king called Parliament, they met in the Painted Chamber, where the Lord Chamberlain announced the reasons for Parliament being summoned. Because of their seniority, when the Council split into groups, the prelates, earls and barons either stayed in the hall or withdrew to the White Chamber. Their group gradually became known as the House of Lords. The lesser clergy went off to convocation in Westminster Abbey and lived up to their name by becoming less and less important in the business of the Council, while the knights of the shires and burgesses united to form what became the House of Commons. They met wherever they could, eventually finding a home in a no-longer-used chapel that had been built for Edward I in 1229. The members sat in the choir stalls on the north and south walls, with the Speaker's Chair placed where the altar had been. When fire destroyed the old chapel in 1834, the new Commons chamber was designed by E. M. Barry along the same lines. Over time, the separate activities of these two groups, the House of Lords and the House of Commons, grew more important than their work in common session, and the general council ceased to meet.

CHAPTER FIVE

FROM KING'S COUNCIL TO PRIVY COUNCIL

THE PRIVY COUNCIL EVOLVED from the rump of the smaller King's Council of Norman and Plantagenet times while the larger council was forming part of the basis of a developing parliament. Inevitably, tensions grew between the two bodies – tensions which are still present in modern times. Especially in the ways in which the United Kingdom declares war on, or enters into armed conflict with, other countries. Until comparatively recently, the question of 'how' the UK declared war, as opposed to 'whether the UK should declare war', was mainly an academic one, in the proper sense of the word. By and large, public opinion supported the First and Second World Wars and also British involvement in the Korean War. It was the Suez Crisis of 1956 that provoked questions in both the common room and the pub along the lines of 'What on earth does Britain think it is doing?' Serious debate on whether there should be co-ordinated international action to protect the shipping lane through the Suez Canal after its seizure by the Egyptian government was completely overshadowed by overlapping arguments about legality; conspiracy between Britain, France and Israel; the possible madness of the Prime Minister, Sir Anthony Eden; and the senseless policy of putting at risk the lives of teenage national servicemen.

Among those national servicemen was Anthony Howard, later to become one of our most distinguished political commentators, presenter of BBC Radio 4's *The World at One*, and editor of the *New Statesman*. He was a 2nd Lieutenant in the Royal Fusiliers, luckily unharmed when a bullet went through the sleeve of his battledress. Howard maintained that one of the reasons there was so much public outcry was that so many families were affected by national service. This fed the mood for debate, which was also reflected in the media. The mood in those post-war years from the mid-1950s to the mid-1960s was well summed up by the American senator Dean Acheson in a speech at the Military Academy, West Point, in December 1962: 'Great Britain has lost an Empire and has not yet found a role.'

In the debates in Parliament during the Suez conflict, the Labour opposition first supported the landing of British troops on Egyptian soil and then opposed it. There were heated discussions, and fisticuffs in the Members' washroom. Overshadowing the debates, demonstrations and protests was a sense that somehow the government was conspiring to keep all the facts both from Parliament and from the general public. This was later found to be true – in a remarkable way. While researching her book *Chequers* in the early 1990s, the Prime Minister's wife, Norma Major, discovered that, away from the public gaze and with no one signing the visitors' book for that day, a secret meeting had been

held at the Prime Minister's country home, where the PM, Sir Anthony
Eden, had made plans with the Acting French Foreign Minister Albert
Gazier and the Deputy Chief of Staff of the French Air Force General
Maurice Challe. She wrote that Harold Wilson was also convinced
that another secret meeting had been held at Chequers with a high-
ranking Israeli officer. The plan being worked on was that following
Egypt's denial of the Suez Canal to Israeli shipping, Israel would attack
to regain the Sinai Peninsula. Britain and France would then launch
an invasion (as they did) to separate the combatants and take charge
of negotiating a settlement.

Leaving America in the dark as it did, and ignoring any United Nations
route towards peace, the plan hadn't got a chance. The result, after a run
on the pound and the threat of sanctions from the UN, was a humiliating
withdrawal by Britain and France. This fuelled the feeling, both in Westminster and among the general public, that the government was taking
action in foreign policy without any due accountability either to Parliament or to the voters. This feeling surfaced again when Tony Blair was
Prime Minister and the UK joined in the American bombing of Iraq in
December 1998 – and again with the start of the war against the Taliban
in Afghanistan in 2001.

There were of course other wars and armed conflicts between 1953
and 2001 in which the UK was involved, notably in Aden, the Falklands,
the Gulf (mark I), Bosnia and Kosovo, but on the whole the government
had the support of both Parliament and the electorate in these matters.
It was in the cases of Suez, Iraq and Afghanistan that there was a feeling of impotence, a feeling that if you opposed these actions there was
nothing effective that you could do. Some Members of Parliament especially became frustrated and angry. They blamed their impotence on the
Privy Council.

Only the Queen in the Privy Council using the royal prerogative can declare war and peace. This power has rested with the monarch since 'remote antiquity'. There seems no sign of the power switching from the Queen in Council to Parliament now. Parliament tried to debate a Bill in 1991 on this matter with the intention of giving to Parliament and especially to the House of Commons the right to declare war. This was the Military Action Against Iraq (Parliamentary Approval) Bill. The Queen, acting as always on the advice of her government, refused to allow the debate to take place.

In Norman and Plantagenet times, tensions between the Council and the newly developing Parliament were not nearly so clear cut. Both bodies overlapped and competing interest groups were more concerned to advance their own concerns and status rather than establish formally defined institutions. All the functions of the state were being organised in two different forms, distinguished from each other only by the size and manner of meeting. This system had the merit of being elastic in character and adaptable in practice. It also gave great scope for mischief-making and in-fighting. The monarchy, the king's household, the officers of state, the barons, the Church, and a new and growing group of clerks and lawyers all took great delight in jostling for position. In retrospect, this activity is very difficult to chart. In *The History of The Privy Council*, Sir Almeric Fitzroy writes:

> Throughout the stormy episodes of the time when the size and composition of the Council was the bone of contention between the different parties to the struggle for supremacy in the king's government each was concerned, in order to establish its own pre-eminence, to play tricks with the nomenclature of the past by the use of terms which justified their own pretensions. Thus historical pundits have fallen into the habit of fighting with shadows and, in the desire to give symmetry to the evolution of events, have allowed their bewilderment at

the want of precision characteristic of our ancestors' use of language
to obscure their judgement.

After the monarchy, the most dominant element in the thirteenth-century
struggle for constitutional power were the barons, in particular when
they worked together. They united against the king in 1215, forcing John
to sign the Magna Carta, and again in 1263, when Simon de Montfort
was successful in forcing Henry III to sign letters patent establishing a
Council of Barons that would take precedence over the King's Council and report directly to Parliament, which would sit three times a year
irrespective of the wishes of the monarch. But having been of one mind
in their stand against the king, the barons then split into many diverse
groups when it came to deciding on the actual composition of the Commons in Parliament. They fought one another at Evesham and, following
de Montfort's death on the battlefield, the King's Council reversed de
Montfort's plan; the Council once again took precedence over, and did
not have to report to, Parliament.

It is impossible to judge whether those involved at the time saw these
as years of constitutional experiment. Probably not. No more than we
consider the 100 years from 1914 to 2014 as a time when we deliberately
experimented with reforming the House of Lords. We would probably
use other words.

It was not only the composition of the Council that depended on
the ideas and character of the monarch. It was also largely in the gift of
the monarch as to how the Council actually worked. Henry II loved the
whole business of planning and administration. He divided the Council
into groups with different responsibilities and functions. This work was
carried on under the advisers to his grandson, Henry III, and later the
king himself. As Henry came to the throne at the age of nine, he ruled
via a regency, of which one figure, Hubert de Burgh, became the most

important. De Burgh established an executive on the Council of which he was the head. The executive attended all meetings. This caused some disquiet among the barons, who thought de Burgh was becoming too powerful and, in 1239, had him first isolated and then removed.

The Plantagenet barons knew all about how to work committees. The existence and work of the King's Council, which was a body unique in Europe, was recognised by Pope Gregory IX, who wrote to Henry asking that the bishops be allowed attendance at Council meetings. It was around this time, during what was then the longest reign in British history (1216–72), that counsellors started to swear allegiance to the king on the Bible and, perhaps somewhat surprisingly, the king also swore to follow their advice. In some cases, no doubt with fingers firmly crossed behind his back. From this came the formation of the Privy Council oath, given in its entirety in Chapter One. And that caused trouble. Many of the barons felt that by virtue of their position they had already expressed loyalty to the monarch. In 1386, the Archbishop of Canterbury was unwilling to be sworn, claiming as a general privilege of the Church of Canterbury the right to be present at all councils and parliaments, secret or otherwise.

During the reign of the first three Edwards there were three factors at work which were more clearly identifying the nature of the Privy Council. The king's finances were being separated from those of the country. The Chancellor gradually withdrew from the Council to concentrate on the revenue and expenses of the royal household and his place was taken on the Exchequer by his chief clerk, who became the Chancellor of the Exchequer. The courts and those institutions concerned with justice and the legal system became separate in working practice, though still under the auspices of the whole Privy Council as a body of appeal. This was to cause much fuss at later dates, especially with the Church and the Court of Arches. Under Edward I, the Council was beginning to become a more professional and workmanlike group. This of course upset the barons, who rebelled during the reign of Edward II in an attempt to both define and limit the number of counsellors who could serve at any one time. They felt extremely challenged by lawyers and clerks with specialised knowledge. Edward III, who could not afford to have the barons as enemies, was forced to make big cuts in the professional officers on the Council, though when Richard II came to the throne he was able to reappoint the Chamberlain and the Steward.

No precise records of the work of the Council were kept. Much of their activity was carried out against the backdrop of momentous events in British history. But if you studied our past solely by looking at the life and times of the Council, you would find, for instance, little mention of Magna Carta. Today, of course, you can read or go and see a production of Shakespeare's *King John* and discover that the Bard completely ignores Magna Carta. When Michael Hordern played the part of John at the Old Vic in 1953, this led him to pose the question: 'Do people living through great events really appreciate that they are doing so?' Similarly with the Edwards. Apart from raising revenue, the Council as a body (as opposed to individual barons) seem untouched by questions of policy concerning the hammering of the Scots by Edward I, or the battles of Crécy, Calais and Poitiers fought by Edward III. Perhaps the court and advisers were too busy with other matters. There was a romantic streak running through the Edwards. They loved dressing up and fanatisising. In *A Short History of England*, Sir Simon Jenkins tells us that Edward I 'adopted the "crown" of King Arthur and claimed to have found and reburied the remains of Arthur and Guinevere at Glastonbury'. As we saw earlier in connection with President Kennedy in the 1960s (and also *Just William* and his outlaws), there are elements about the Camelot story that make it a particularly attractive setting for a leader and their advisers. These fantasies emerged again in the reign of Edward III, when the king's relatives, friends and advisers dressed up in what they thought to be clothes of King Arthur's period. The king, no doubt getting ready for the Hundred Years War, acted out the part of Sir Lancelot. This left serious members of his Council to get on with work, the most significant development being that the Chancellor increasingly began to operate at one remove from the Council, especially in legal matters. It became established that anyone presenting a petition to the king had to do so through one of his counsellors. But, as Bishop William Stubbs points out in his *Constitutional History* of 1873 (much quoted by both Dicey and Fitzroy), most comment on the work of the Council before the time of Richard II has to be assumption because there is so little written material available.

In the fourteenth century, that began to change. The Privy Council was now sufficiently well established to decide who should be members of the regency to govern until Richard II, who inherited the crown at the age of ten, came of age. They used their power to deny a place on the regency to the kingmaker, Richard's uncle, John of Gaunt. These were difficult times for any form of government, with the Peasants' Revolt and the Black Death, and indeed for a time there was no effective government. However, there was one historic footnote. The Privy Council was obviously now recognised to have its own functioning identity, as it began to record its own meetings. These show that the business of the Council and the work that it did was broadly the same from the reign of Richard II (1377–99) to the ascension of Henry VII in 1485. A flavour of the Council meetings is given by this note from *Proceedings of the Privy Council 1389*:

> The Council is to meet between eight and nine o'clock. Business of the king's and of the realm's is to have precedence over all other matters. Matters relating to the common law are to be determined before the justices. What relates to the Chancellor is to be decided before him. What to the office of the Treasurer before him in the Exchequer.

The king's pleasure is to be ascertained on all matters, which cannot
be decided without his special grace. No grants to the detriment of
the revenue are to pass without the advice of the Council.

From the decisions and rulings of the Council that can be read, it can be
seen that at most times it was a body made up by royal appointment for
the pleasure and advantage of the monarch. It was not an independent
body and could be considered as no more than a group of royal officials.
This was how it saw itself. During the next regency it had a paternal role,
making Henry VI at the age of five years put on record to the Chancellor:

If we are negligent in learning or commit any fault we give our cousin,
the Earl of Warwick, full power, authority and licence, and direction
to chastise us, from time to time, according to his discretion, without being impeded or molested by us or any other person, in future,
for so doing.

When Henry was thirteen he received further guidance from his Privy
Council:

It is far from our intention to advise anything prejudicial to the king's
prerogative, or might be a restraint on his liberty or power; and temper their reproof with the flattering assurance that while knowledge
and experience are needed for affairs of State this knowledge and feeling the king is like, by God's grace, to reach as soon as possible by
nature, and as has been seen in any person before his time.

The king was not entirely free in making his appointments to the Privy
Council. Since Norman times, some positions, such as the Chief Butler, the Marshal and the Chamberlain, had been held by families with

an inherited right. In the twenty-first century this is still the case. Some-times it was a matter of practical politics to allow relatives, Parliament and, later, the government of the day to have a say in appointing coun-sellors. Over the centuries the pendulum of appointing has swung from monarch to Prime Minister. But in the Middle Ages, appointments were the prerogative of the monarch, though often the king had to compromise in appointing members, as there were powerful nobles and bishops who would cause great trouble if they were left out. Some kings found ways round this. When the Merciless Parliament of 1388 attempted to bring an end to the anarchy of the regency by establishing a Continual Council in which the Lords Appellant of Gloucester, Arundel and Derby (later Henry IV) were given prominent places, the young Richard II decided to act. He burst into the Council Chamber and declared that he had now come of age and that there may well be a Continual Council but he was king and would summon his counsellors when he saw fit. Which, in the early years of his reign, was not very often. He found that the best way of avoiding any critical comments.

After Richard had been forced to abdicate, the hold on the throne by the Lancastrians was tenuous and Henry IV was sensitive to parlia-mentary opinion. When, in 1406, he had a dispute with Parliament over the spending of public money and stated that 'kings do not have to give account of their spending', he did not resist when Parliament insisted, 'Then their officers must' and set about reforming the Privy Council – as it was now to be called – by defining its powers and naming its mem-bers. There is an interesting description of this in Fitzroy's *History of The Privy Council*:

> The insistence of the Commons was endorsed by Henry, who went
> so far to meet their wishes as to enforce the oath, which was taken
> as stated 'at the instance of the Commons and by command of the

king', and led to the parliamentary plan achieving a success unknown to previous efforts.

He follows this with a few pertinent lines about the Prince of Wales; Sir Almeric was Clerk to the Privy Council in Queen Victoria's reign and had views, expressed in his *Memoirs*, about the activities of her Prince of Wales. What he writes about the future Henry V may seem odd to those whose opinions are garnered from Shakespeare's plays. Sir Almeric writes: 'No small measure of this result was due to the tactful intervention of the Prince of Wales, an unusual instance of an heir apparent in active support of his father's government. His popularity was no doubt of great use in making sure of public confidence in the dynasty.'

The credit for the drawing up of these reforms, in which some historians have seen the germ of the Cabinet structure of government, must go to the man with the apt surname of Prophet. John Prophet, who had been trained in Council work during Richard's rule, and was then Dean of Hereford, was appointed Clerk of the Council later to become King's Secretary and Keeper of the Privy Seal.

* * *

The next big development in the history of the Privy Council came with the premature death of Henry V. The Council now enjoyed a good working relationship with Parliament, which was content for them to amend Acts of Parliament by Orders without seeking statutory permission. This allowed the Duke of Gloucester to act as Lord Commissioner, issuing writs on behalf of the Privy Council to summon Parliament during the new regency, and also charged the Lords with the duty of naming the new Council. This had the effect of removing from membership some of the old and established circle of court favourites.

The counsellors took advantage of the regency to award themselves pay and allowances. In many cases these were munificent on a large scale, dwarfing the recent scandals of parliamentary allowances. In fact, so much money was involved that the Treasury found itself over twelve years in arrears with back pay. The Council for the period of the regency was:

> Duke of Bedford, Protector
> Duke of Gloucester, Deputy Protector
> Archbishop of Canterbury
> Bishop of Durham, Chancellor
> William Kinwelmersh, Treasurer
> John Stafford, Keeper of the Privy Seal
> Bishops of: London, Worcester, Norwich, Winchester
> Duke of Exeter
> Earls of: March, Warwick, Northumberland, Westmorland
> The Earl Marshal
> Lord FitzHugh, Chamberlain
> Knights: Ralph Cromwell, Walter Hungerford, John Tiptoft, Walter
>   Beauchamp
> Henry Beaufort

The payments they received were £200 each per annum for dukes, the Archbishop, the Chancellor and Henry Beaufort. The Treasurer, the bishops and earls got 200 marks each and the barons and knights £100. (A mark was around eight ounces of silver.) In addition – and oh, shades of modern times – they were allowed to claim expenses, and the Exchequer was instructed to pay them without questioning the counsellors' accounts. For historical record, it should be noted that today members of the Privy Council are not paid and that Members of Parliament did not receive any salary until the twentieth century. Members of

the House of Lords can draw expenses and allowances but have never
been paid a salary.

It is not surprising that Jack Cade noted these salaries as one of the
reasons for the heavy taxation affecting a downtrodden nation when he
launched his rebellion in 1450 with a demand that the king no longer
surround himself with such evil counsellors. This rebellion caused little trouble for the Privy Council, but there was a greater test to come for
the survival of the institution five years later, with the start of the Wars
of the Roses.

CHAPTER SIX

THE PRIVY SEAL, THE GREAT
SEAL, AND THEIR KEEPERS

THE DIFFERENCES BETWEEN THE Privy Seal of England
and the Great Seal of the Realm go back to the twelfth century. There is a consensus of opinion that in the early days of
monarchy the Privy Seal accompanied the king on his travels while the Great Seal remained in the Chancery. The Keeper of the
Privy Seal was nominally the Lord Privy Seal, a position about which
more jokes have been told than probably any other post in the British
Cabinet. Ted Heath is said to have turned it down on the very reasonable
grounds that he wasn't a privy, nor yet a lord and he certainly couldn't
– by any stretch of the imagination – be considered a seal. But stories
about Ted and Cabinet jobs are legion. He got his first appointment as a
whip in Winston Churchill's last administration in an amazing sequence

of events. Sir Walter Bromley-Davenport, the Conservative Member for
Knutsford, was on duty as a regional whip to ensure that all his MPs
voted in the 'aye' lobby. Seeing one of them sneaking down the steps
towards the St Stephen's entrance, he yelled after the miscreant – who
took no notice. That was too much for Sir Walter, who as well as being
an archetypal Tory knight of the shires was also an extremely active member of the British Boxing Board of Control. He knocked – some people
say kicked – the MP to the ground. It later turned out that the victim of
the whip's wrath was not a Conservative MP but the Belgian ambassador. Reluctantly, Winston agreed that Sir Walter would have to resign
as a whip. So there was a vacancy in the government and Heath got his
first foot on the ladder. The government Chief Whip, officially the Parliamentary Secretary to the Treasury, Sir Patrick Buchan-Hepburn, told the
Prime Minister that the new whip, officially a Lord Commissioner of the
Treasury, was 'sensitive, a good listener, ready to argue with recalcitrant
members rather than kick them', as Heath's biographer Philip Ziegler
recounts. But Westminster watchers beware. The trouble with many
political stories is that while the substance remains the same, the names
of the characters can change. In Jerry Hayes's recollections, *An Unexpected MP*, he writes about Conservative whip, Spencer Le Marchant:

> One evening out of the corner of his eye he spotted a Tory MP creep-
> ing down the steps to slink out of a vote. This seriously angered the
> old boy and he aimed a kick which sent the MP flying … However,
> there was a slight problem. The kickee wasn't a Tory at all. Nor an MP.
> It was the Peruvian ambassador on his way home from a drinks party.

But to return to jokes about the Lord Privy Seal. There is one which has
now become legendary. If you Google 'Lord Privy Seal', you will find
brief mentions of the history of the office and details of the Seal, but most

space will be given to this story, which has become an essential part of the repertoire of any Westminster after-dinner speaker trying to explain the mysteries of the parliamentary system to the uninitiated. The name of the actual Lord Privy Seal is rarely mentioned. The Prime Minister involved is always Winston Churchill.

The Lord Privy Seal turns up on the door of No. 10 at an early hour in the morning demanding to see the Prime Minister on a very urgent and important matter. The PM's staff are reluctant to disturb Winston, suspecting that until he has had breakfast he will not wish to talk to anybody officially. The Lord Privy Seal insists. A message goes up to the private flat on the top floor of No. 10. A message comes back: 'Pray inform the Lord Privy Seal that at this hour the Prime Minister is sealed in his own privy and can only deal with one shit at a time.'

The original duties of the Lord Privy Seal are now obsolete, but because it is the fifth most important position in the land, it is a part of the most useful patronage for any Prime Minister to have and can be given to a senior politician whose actual job may not have a constitutional basis. This is how many of the old Officers of State titles are used. For instance, there is no official post of Deputy Prime Minister, so to reflect Nick Clegg's rank in the Conservative–Liberal coalition of 2010–15, in which he served as deputy to Prime Minister David Cameron, he was appointed Lord President of the Privy Council. The Lord Privy Seal is the deputy in the Privy Council to the Lord President. In that coalition, the Lord Privy Seal was the Leader of the House of Commons, Andrew Lansley. There is no constitutional title of Leader of the House of Commons. In the same way, the Leader of the House of Lords, Lord Hill, was given the post of the Chancellor of the Duchy of Lancaster.

The Privy Seal was attached to documents by the monarch as proof that he had made a decision. It was then passed to the Chancellor, who could act on those royal instructions. The Chancellor then attached the

Great Seal to the papers to show that they had the approval of the Council. This is a simplified explanation; it often wasn't as clear cut as that.
For instance, when Richard II was anxious to conclude a bargain with
the Earl Marshal for the defence of Berwick, the Privy Council refused to
give their consent and insisted that the Great Seal be not attached. They
thought that the demands of Berwick – who could always argue that their
position on the Scottish Borders made them a special case – were too
costly. They were also worried that Parliament would charge them with
'having wantonly burdened the revenue'. The king went off in a huff to
his palace in Kennington. Eventually a compromise was reached and the
Great Seal was attached to the indentures. This was an early example of
how a system of checks and balances became built into our unwritten
constitution. No legislation could be enacted by having the Great Seal
attached unless it had first been authorised by the king's Privy Seal. No
writing expressed the king's command without having the impress of
the seal. In an age when communications of any kind were difficult, this
was a vital method of ensuring that writs, bills and laws were genuine.
There were often many barons close to the monarch who would be only
too happy if he signed away parts of his prerogative, so it was essential
from the king's point of view that he always appointed a Chancellor he
could trust completely and who would stop him doing something silly.

As the distinction grew between the Privy Council and Parliament,
so too did the ownership of the two official seals. This happened as our
system of government was evolving, the Privy Seal becoming an instrument of the Privy Council, safeguarded by the Lord Privy Seal, and the
Great Seal being given to the Lord Chancellor to hold on behalf of Parliament. The monarchs, who obviously did not want to be left out of
the process of law-making, decided that all official warrants etc. must be
sealed with wax by their own signet rings.

The seals were signs of authority. Tangible evidence of the law. With few being able to read, people could see and understand that the seal in the form of a royal portrait was indeed a command of the king. This practice was started by Edward the Confessor when he had a cast of his own face made in wax to signify that the document to which it was attached was an expression of his will. Since then, most British sovereigns have designed their own emblem – in cases of a long reign, more than once, as the wax used for the seal has a high melting point and the silver plates used in casting wear out. During Oliver Cromwell's Commonwealth, a seal was devised showing a map of England, Ireland, Jersey and Guernsey on one side and the arms of England and Ireland on the other.

The changing wording on the Great Seal marks historical changes, but it also hints at how different monarchs and their advisers thought about themselves. Thus, Edward the Confessor is simply 'Seal of Edward, Sovereign of the English'. Richard I was still 'King of the English', but also 'by the Grace of God, Duke of the Normans and of the Aquitanians and Count of the Angevins'. By the time of Henry III, the monarchs had become 'King of England' rather than 'King of the English', and Henry was also 'Lord of Ireland and Duke of Aquitaine'. Henry IV, of course, was also 'King of France' and Henry VIII had the imposingly long title of 'Henry VIII by the grace of God, of England and France and Ireland, King, Defender of the Faith, and on Earth, of the English and Irish Church, Supreme Head'. Queen Mary made the point on her seal that she was the 'first of her name'. Elizabeth I didn't think that necessary in her own case. There is a story that James II considered his seal had become an unlucky charm, and one dark night he threw it into the Thames in the hope that would stop the activities of Parliament. It didn't. William and Mary were quite lyrical on their seal: 'By the grace of God, of England, France and Ireland, King and Queen, Defenders of the Faith/Golden Apples grow in flowering rosebushes; the security of Britain restored'. When Mary died and William III ruled alone, he deleted 'England' and

inserted 'Great Britain'. George I continued to claim that the King of
England was also the King of France and, not unnaturally, included
some German titles too. The wording read: 'George, by the grace of
God, of Great Britain, France and Ireland, King, Defender of the Faith;
of Brunswick and Luneburg, Duke; of the Holy Roman Empire, Arch-
Treasurer and Prince-Elector'. George III became the first king to be
named as 'of the United Kingdom', and he dropped the pretence that
the King of England was also automatically the King of France.

George IV reverted to the idea that he was the king of the people,
rather than the country, becoming 'King of the Britons' – a claim maintained by William IV, Victoria and Edward VII. Edward wrote rather a
long narrative for his seal: 'Edward VII, by the grace of God, of the Britons and of the lands across the sea which are in the British Dominion,
King, Defender of the Faith, Emperor of India'. Elizabeth II, recognising
the move from Empire to Commonwealth, had her last seal inscribed:
'Elizabeth II, by the grace of God, of the Britons and her other Realms,
Queen, Head of the Commonwealth of Nations, Defender of the Faith'.

The inscriptions on the seals are in an abbreviated form of Latin which,
when translated into English, accounts for some of the odd grammar. The
Great Seal of 2015 was designed by James Butler and authorised by the
Privy Council in July 2001. It is 6 inches in diameter and the weight of
both sides of the matrix exceeds 270 troy ounces. One side shows the
Queen enthroned and robed. In her right hand is a sceptre; in her left,
the orb. On the other side, for the first time on a Great Seal, the full royal
arms are portrayed, including crest, mantling and supporters. For nearly
1,000 years the Great Seal has been affixed to official documents of state,
royal papers, letters patent, proclamations and the summons to Parliament. All the current uses of the seal were codified under the Great Seal
of the Realm Act in 1884.

The Great Seal of the Realm is in the custody of the Lord Keeper of the Great Seal, who is also the Lord Chancellor. The affixing of Great Seal is the responsibility of the Clerk of the Crown in Chancery. He is helped by a deputy and one Sealer and two Scribes to Her Majesty's Crown Office. The seal is guarded by the Queen's Bodyguard of the Yeoman of the Guard and until the mid-nineteenth century was protected by the office of the Gentlemen Servants in Attendance. They included the Clerk of the Hanaper (a hamper which carried documents waiting to be sealed), who lived in the Palace of Westminster; the Spigurnel, who escorted the Great Seal when it left the Palace of Westminster; the Chaffwax, who prepared the wax for the seal; and the Portjorie, who looked after the sumpter-horse that carried the books and parchment rolls.

That sounds tremendously colourful and many of the titles are still used today. But very often they are used by politicians and civil servants with much more prosaic working jobs. For example:

> The Lord Chancellor and Keeper of the Great Seal = Secretary of State for Justice
>
> The Clerk of the Crown in Chancery = Permanent Secretary at the Ministry of Justice
>
> Captain Yeoman of the Guard = Government Whip in House of Lords

There is still, though, a great sense of history, of drama and comedy, at many of the events involving members of the Privy Council. Especially those which, as the former Clerk Sir Almeric Fitzroy put it, carry 'the inheritance of ages'. One such event is the breaking of an old Great Seal after the death of a monarch. This is done in the presence of the new Sovereign, who then has in their gift the pieces to keep or present to others as they think fit. No minutes of these occasions are published and details are meant to be kept secret, but sometimes word gets out. Charles

Greville's words caused an outrage. He was a nineteenth-century diarist and an insider to Court life. His grandfather, the Duke of Portland, had been a Whig Prime Minister for a short time between 1807 and 1809. His mother is believed to have had a long-running affair with the Duke of Wellington. Charles had been a page at the coronation of George IV. After Eton, Oxford and various jobs as a private secretary, he became Clerk to the Privy Council in 1821. In 1837, his horse, Mango, won the St Leger Stakes. His prize money of £9,000 enabled him have an independent lifestyle, careless of the opinion of others. He recorded his views in a set of three diaries, which were published after his death. When it became known that the first diary was going to be printed, Queen Victoria was 'horrified and indignant at this dreadful and really scandalous book. Mr Greville's indiscretion, indelicacy, ingratitude, betrayal of confidence and shameful disloyalty towards his Sovereign make it very important that the book should be severely censored and discredited.' Here, Greville, as Clerk to the Privy Council, describes the behaviour of William IV at the ceremony of the breaking of the seal of the previous Sovereign, George IV:

> This King is a queer fellow. Our Council was principally for a new Great Seal and to deface the old seal. The Chancellor claims the old one as his perquisite. I had forgotten the hammer, so the King said: 'My Lord, the best thing I can do is to give you the seal and tell you to take it and do what you please with it.'
>
> The Chancellor said: 'I believe there is some doubt whether Lord Lyndhurst ought not to have half of it as he was Chancellor at the time of Your Majesty's accession.'
>
> 'Well,' said the King, 'then I will judge between you like Solomon; here' (turning the seal round and round) 'now do you cry heads or tails?'
>
> We all laughed and the Chancellor said: 'Sir, I take the bottom part.'

The King opened the two compartments of the seal and said: 'Now, then, I employ you as ministers of taste. You will send for Bridge, my silversmith, and desire him to convert the two halves each into a salver, with my arms on one side and yours on the other, and Lord Lyndhurst's the same, and you will take one and give him the other, and both keep them as presents from me.'

Viscount Kilmuir, who was Lord President in the 1950s, said that this was one of the two most difficult tasks for elderly chancellors to perform, as clutching both the old and new seals safely to one's chest meant you were carrying over half a hundredweight of silver and at the same time performing the traditional royal genuflexions. The other task fraught with opportunities for mistakes was walking backwards down the steps from the throne in the House of Lords after delivering the Opening of Parliament speech to the monarch. But, said Kilmuir, it did bring variety into the more mundane duties of serving on the Privy Council.

CHAPTER SEVEN

PAWNING THE CROWN JEWELS – AND OTHER MEDIEVAL WORKING PRACTICES

THE WORKING PRACTICES OF the medieval Privy Council were myriad but not especially complex. Ideas of relevance and appropriateness were subsumed into straightforward questions of power and control in relation to both the monarch and the fledging parliament. Concepts of 'due process', 'fit for purpose' and 'compliance' were centuries away. Albert Dicey wrote that 'in modern days, legislative and judicial, administrative and political functions have been separated from each other to an extent which would have seemed unnatural to statesmen of the fifteenth century'. Thus, in the spring of 1401 a Privy Council meeting was concerned with matters as

various and diverse as granting annual pensions to the sons of the Lords
Salisbury and Oxford and enquiring into a dispute between the Abbot
of Cirencester and the citizens of that town. They also discussed a new
treaty with Scotland. At another meeting they decided who should be
Lord-Lieutenant of Ireland, and made arrangements for a new embassy
in France. Much of the business of the Council was concerned with the
ever-growing number of petitions directed to the king and with the ad
hoc dealing with disputes between towns, organisations and individuals.
Records show that they especially loved getting involved in arguments
where members of the aristocracy were concerned. Their other work can
be grouped into five overlapping sections: finance; trade; the treatment
of aliens; the Church; and keeping the king's peace.

Over time, the vast majority of financial work passed to the Exchequer, the Treasury and Parliament, but up to and during the 1400s, all
items of royal and national expenditure and income were considered
by the Privy Council. In 1421, the national income was £55,743 and
expenditure was £52,235. Small enough. But getting the money in and
settling accounts was hell. Henry V was reluctant to repay loans. And
when he did so, it was always late. For over seventy years, our soldiers stationed at Calais often had to seize the wool meant for export
in lieu of wages that didn't arrive. From time to time the Council had
to summon rich men before them and extort them to give money by
playing on a mixture of their loyalty to the king and their fear of dis-
pleasing him. Ready cash was extracted from foreign residents living
in England on the grounds that their tenure here gave them protection
from troubles in their home countries. In 1415, admittedly after a spell
in prison, several rich merchants from Venice, Florence and Lucca
gave the Privy Council substantial loans which they had little hope of
ever getting back. This met with the general approval of the public,
but what was not approved of, particularly in the coastal towns, was

the commandeering with no recompense of merchant ships to ferry troops to France.

At a meeting on 27 May 1415, faced with an ever-rising national debt, the Privy Council remembered the actions of Edward III when he pawned the Crown Jewels to pay his army during an overseas campaign, and made the decision to raise funds by pawning some of the jewels again. This collection of ceremonial treasures dates back to the regalia Edward the Confessor deposited in Westminster Abbey in the eleventh century. Over the years, the precious stones, the crowns, the banqueting plate, the robes, the various medals and insignia, the sceptres and the orb have had many adventures. King John, so the story goes, lost some of his jewels in The Wash in 1216. Oliver Cromwell broke up the collection, in every sense of the phrase, but Charles II restored the jewels, at a cost of £12,185, for his coronation in 1661. Since then there have been many additions, some stones only being lent to the monarch for special events. Some pieces have been sold; some lost. In spite of many films suggesting otherwise, there has only been one actual serious attempt to steal the Crown Jewels, in 1671 by Colonel Thomas Blood. He was caught at the East Gate of the Tower of London and was released without trial and with a state pension after he made the king laugh by allegedly replying to the monarch's question 'Why did you try to steal them?' with the statement: 'Because I was hard up, Sir.'

The Privy Council realised that, in extremis, the pawning of the Crown Jewels could be a problem-solving act of fiscal policy, and between 1300 and 1650 the jewels were put into hock at least four times – the last time not by the Council but by independent action of the wife of Charles I, Queen Henrietta. There is no narrative that gives a clear account of the actual logistics of the processes used, but it seems that on at least three occasions, one of the precious stones involved was the famous, colourful and legendary Sancy Diamond. In 1415, this stone was owned by

Duke John the Fearless, Duke of Burgundy. He was a friend of Henry V and his armies had helped Henry defeat the official French forces at Agincourt. With the consent of the Privy Council, Henry had a meeting with the Duke of Burgundy, and there are grounds for believing that the duke offered the Sancy Diamond as surety for the Privy Council's pawning of the Crown Jewels in Amsterdam.

If true, it was just one more incident in the long and notorious history of this illustrious diamond. The stone is believed to have been mined at Sambalpur on the banks of the River Mahanadi in India and, having been cut in Venice, in 1389 it came into the possession of the Duke of Milan, who gave it to his daughter when she married the brother of the King of France, Charles VI. From the French royal family it passed to Philip, Duke of Burgundy, who was regent of France in the 1390s, and was then inherited by his son, John the Fearless. The diamond, which is over fifty-five carats and shield-shaped, is white with a green/yellow tint. Until the seventeenth century it was the largest known white diamond in Europe. The jewel acquired its name in 1570 when it became the property of Nicholas de Harlay de Sancy, a financial adviser to King Henry IV of France. It was owned at various times by, among others, the Kings of France and Portugal; the Queen of Spain; Prince Demidov of Russia; Elizabeth I, Queen of England; and by James I and Charles I, Kings of Great Britain.

The Sancy Diamond became part of the English Crown Jewels when Elizabeth I bought it from the Portuguese, and, it is believed, had her portrait painted wearing it. When the Privy Council needed funds for the army, the Earl of Leicester was sent to Holland to pawn the diamond through the offices of Francesco Rodriguez. The Privy Council never claimed it back but James I bought it privately in 1603 and returned it to the royal collection. Charles I pawned the diamond again in 1625 but redeemed it twenty years later, when his wife, Henrietta, managed to get hold of it, only to pawn it once again to raise money for the royalist cause in the Civil War. After King Charles I was executed, his wife was in no position to redeem the stone. The Prime Minister of France, Cardinal Mazarin, took over the queen's debts and claimed the diamond, which then passed out of the British Crown Jewel collection for ever. The stone reappeared in public in 1867 as the property of an Indian merchant, Sir Jamsetee Jeejeebhoy, and was on show in Paris, having been given a value of 1,000,000 French francs by the jeweller G. Bapst. In 1906, the 1st Viscount Astor bought the Sancy as a wedding present for his daughter-in-law, the American Nancy Langhorne. As Nancy Astor, she became the first woman Member of Parliament and wore the diamond in her tiara on state occasions at Westminster. In 1976, the Astor family sold the Sancy to the Louvre for an undisclosed price in a deal financed by the Banque de Paris.

Although there were struggles between Parliament and the Privy Council over which body held responsibility for which activities, Parliament at this time seemed happy for the Council to administer and decide policy on trade. This the Council did – on behalf of the Crown – with gusto. Here is an account from Albert Dicey's *The Privy Council* of how the Council dealt with the matter of staples: 'No prerogative was more cherished and more constantly exercised by the Crown than the privilege of appointing certain places as staples, i.e. as the sole towns whither it was permitted to bring particular articles for sale.' The staple most frequently mentioned in the Council's records is Calais. This town was held by the British from 1347 to 1558 as an English colony, represented in the British Parliament at Westminster, and having an English Mayor. In 1407, the Mayor was the Privy Counsellor Richard Whittington, who was also Lord Mayor of London. Not a lot of pantomime producers know that. The reason England hung on to Calais was not just to annoy the French. The answer is given very clearly in Stephen Clarke's book,

1,000 Years of Annoying the French: 'Calais was a self-financing market-place for English wool. The town had a monopoly on exporting English wool. Merchants had to give a cut of their profits to the government. At one point it provided a third of government income.' Clarke also went on to explain that what really upset the French was that packages could pass through Calais unopened, so some poor trader in another part of Europe might eagerly open his box of fine-quality English wool only to find it contained sand or stones.

There was keen competition among English cities to become one of the handful of staple towns and have links with the merchants who belonged to the Company of the Staple at Calais. Among the fortunate ones were Newcastle, and – often because of the interest of the bishops in mercantile affairs – many of the great cathedral cities: Canterbury, York, Lincoln, Exeter etc. The power to regulate the use of staples and to grant exemption from them often seemed to be used capriciously. No doubt in many cases there were personal agendas now hidden by the mists of time. In 1422, for example, a licence was granted to the Earl of Westmoreland to export to Bruges 500 sacks of wool grown in northern England without sending it to the staple at Calais.

Often, the Council's power over trade matters coincided with their power over 'aliens', the official name for foreigners who were resident in this country. In 1441, a complaint was made by the Lord Mayor of London that British traders in Pruce, the Dansk and Hansk were not being treated fairly. This was passed by Parliament to the Privy Council and the *Proceedings of the Privy Council* record that 'the complaint before them read so it seemed to the Council was that the complaint which the Englishmen made was of more likeliness true', and the Council therefore decided to write 'to the said Master and Governors of Pruce etc. showing unto them the said Englishmen's complaints and desiring the wrongs to be redressed'. Otherwise it was threatened that action would be taken against Prucian merchants living in London. This was entirely in accordance with how the Privy Council, and indeed everybody else, saw its duties. The idea that aliens living here had the same rights as a freeborn English person was completely unthinkable in medieval times. They only had such rights as from time to time the Crown might grant them. This was entirely the monarch's prerogative. Dicey writes: 'In theory the prerogative had no limits. In practice it was limited, as regarded Englishmen, by the existence of certain rights on their side, which it is hardly an inaccuracy to say were gained from the Crown by bargain. Rights so obtained could in no way affect foreigners.' Any rights that aliens enjoyed other than those granted by the king were the result of special treaties with other countries. All letters written by aliens and sent abroad had to be in English.

Our history never leaves us, and political debate and public discussion on how we should regard immigration and settlement is a continuous theme now lasting well into the twenty-first century.

So too is the relationship between Church and state. In the medieval years there was a good understanding between the Privy Council and Rome. This was largely due to the prominence on the Council of Cardinal Beaufort, a half-brother of Henry IV who became Bishop of Winchester and three times Chancellor. He had won the gratitude of the Vatican at the Council of Constance in 1417 by urging the compromise that resulted in the election of Martin V as Pope. In appreciation, he had been made a Cardinal, and he personally put the crown on the head of the young Henry VI in Paris, proclaiming him King of France. He and the Privy Council were content to let the Papal See decide appeals from English clergy, and in return the Council could make some ecclesiastical appointments and offer comment on the distribution of Papal Bulls.

The Council had oversight on matters of heresy and sorcery and could chase up bishops if they thought they were being too slack in this regard.

Thus, the *Proceedings of the Privy Council* on 2 January 1406 exhorts the Bishop of Lincoln to 'bring before him certain persons accused of practising magic, sorcery, necromancer etc. to the scandal of the Catholic Church'. Often the persons accused were not informed of the exact charges against them or allowed the benefit of counsel. Sometimes torture was used, as in 1441, when Roger Bolingbroke was charged, along with the Duchess of Gloucester, on several counts of witchcraft. This was one of the great scandals of the age. Eleanor, Duchess of Gloucester, had been a lady-in-waiting to Jacqueline, the first wife of Humphrey, Duke of Gloucester, the youngest son of King Henry IV. Eleanor became the duke's mistress and married him when the duke had his marriage to Jacqueline annulled. The couple lived at La Pleasaunce in Greenwich and set up a court of artists, musicians, writers and pleasure-loving friends including astrologers and a woman known locally as the Witch of Eye. When the duke's elder brother died and Humphrey became heir presumptive, Eleanor enlisted the help of her secretary, Roger Bolingbroke, to work with astrologers to try to predict the date that the throne would become vacant. Understandably, when the king found out about this, he was not pleased, and had Bolingbroke arrested on several charges, including treason, sorcery and conspiring to kill the king with necromancy. Bolingbroke blamed Eleanor, and she and the witch, Margery Jourdemayne, were arrested. All were found guilty. Eleanor had to do public penance and was imprisoned in various castles for the rest of her life. The Witch of Eye was burnt at the stake. After his trial by the Privy Council on 18 November, Bolingbroke was brought from the Tower and exhibited before the people, with the instruments of torture hung about him. He was then taken to Tyburn, where he was hanged, drawn and quartered. His body was then distributed to different towns around the country.

In the 'Keeping of the King's Peace', the Privy Council is using the monarch's prerogative in a manner which combines elements of policing and making judicial judgments. Since the conquest, the option that some nobles thought they enjoyed to settle their quarrels by force of arms had been frowned upon by kings and councils, but they had not made protection under the law a right for citizens. Rather, it was considered a privilege. So much so that when Edward I could not get money from the clergy, he withdrew from them the right to be protected by law. When disturbances got out of hand, the Council sent in the sheriffs, as they did in Norwich and Coventry. Sometimes the law courts themselves were the scenes of violence. On one occasion, the supporters of the Earl of Devon and Sir W. Bonville were only prevented from fighting by the arrest of the two nobles, who were then summoned to the bar of the Privy Council.

Nobles were not infrequently hauled before the Council. In 1492, Sir James Berkeley used his servants to prevent the Countess of Warwick entering Wotton Manor. The Council frowned on this behaviour, and used its own unchallenged power to call and interview witnesses. In spite of the freedom granted to the Privy Council with regard to trade and aliens, Parliament took a dim view of this display of authority, as the Privy Council's actions undermined the Commons, which supported greater development in the separation of judicial and executive powers. This was a trend that had been growing since the reign of Edward I and, at this stage, as Professor James Baldwin pointed out in his book *The King's Council of England during The Middle Ages* (1913), 'the King's Bench was … not fully a court of common law, but it was rapidly being drawn away from the Privy Council into the prevailing judicial current'.

This, then, was the position of the Privy Council in the middle of the fifteenth century. There was no great discussion taking place on how it should continue to evolve, any more than there was sustained debate on how Parliament or the legal and judicial systems should develop. This seems to be a constant factor throughout history. Although some leaders and politicians may plan ahead, it is nearly always short-term, and one generation cannot make realistic plans for future generations. Looking back, Professor Dicey's warning from All Souls about exercising caution in making assumptions about cause and effect must be borne in mind. But it is fascinating to trace the possible pathways.

It helps if there are records to consult, and this makes it difficult to speculate on the activities of the Privy Council between 1460 and 1520. There are no records. From the collapse of government under the Lancastrians to the strength of the Tudors – nothing. There are, of course, other historical records: rolls of Parliament, patent rolls, warrants under the Privy Seal, letters, accounts, bills, wills, transactions etc. But nothing affecting the Privy Council. On this, the great historians of the period agree. Sir Harris Nicolas writes in *Proceedings and Ordinances of the Privy Council, 1834-37*: 'Of the Privy Council under these monarchs [Edward IV, Edward V, Richard III, Henry VII] nothing appears to be known.' Dicey writes in *The Privy Council*: 'The effect produced by this gap is to place side by side two most different eras in English history.' Professor Baldwin, in *The King's Council in England during the Middle Ages*, wonders why this state of affairs came about: 'There are series considerations which give colour to the view that there was for a time a failure in the operations of the Council itself.' He goes on to explain that there were no fixed appointments, no membership of the Privy Council, but that 'men were employed or retained as they were needed'. Sir Almeric Fitzroy puts forward the argument in his book, *The History of the Privy Council*, that 'the cessation is due to the absence of any Council activity'. Some historians maintain that if the lack of records was due to a cessation of Council, this was only part of the much wider lack of parliamentary and government activity as a consequence of a quarter of the population being killed by the Black Death. Another explanation offered is that for part of that time, especially between the Battle of St Albans in 1455 and Henry Tudor's defeat of Richard III at Bosworth in 1485, the very nobles who should have been the life and soul of the Privy Council were busily engaged in the War of the Cousins, an utterly pointless exercise in personal ambition better known as the War of the Roses. But the continual evolution of our (albeit unwritten) constitution was still taking place, and very markedly so in the treatment of petitions and in the growth of Chancery and other courts.

CHAPTER EIGHT

THE COUNCIL, THE COURTS AND THE ORIGINS OF THE STAR CHAMBER

B Y THE MID-FIFTEENTH CENTURY, the number of petitions being presented to the Privy Council was growing enormously. Some petitioners tried to approach the king or the Privy Council directly; others went to the Keeper of the Great Seal. Others wrote or tried to meet with the Chancellor, the Treasurer, or Members of Parliament – the Lords and the Commons. Officers of both the Exchequer and the Chancery were solicited. It must be remembered that the Exchequer was not only an office for collecting revenue: it was also a law court, the Exchequer of Pleas. The name came from a cloth with squares like a chess board which was laid across a table during financial transactions, different squares being used for different amounts of money. The

name Chancery simply comes from its being the office of the assistants
to the Chancellor. The pleas were many and various. Most people had
no idea of the appropriate place to send petitions or claims, and the various bodies and officials had no real idea of whether or not it was within
their remit to deal with them. Most had no remit of detail anyway. It was a
lottery, with the constitution being worked out by trial and error. In Baldwin's *The King's Council in England during the Middle Ages*, he writes of
a widow claiming custody of a manor as the heir of her late husband. She
made direct petition to the Privy Council. This was sent to Parliament
and they referred her to the office of the Treasurer. After some delay, the
Treasurer was told by Parliament to 'call the justices and others of the
Council to render speedy justice'. It all sounds very modern.

Sometimes there was friction between the workings of the Council and
of Parliament. Parliament had to have their Acts entered in the rolls of Parliament, while the Council had recourse to the machinery of the Privy Seal.
By this means, Acts of the Council were not subject to scrutiny and therefore
escaped publicity. At other times, particularly with regard to dealing with
petitions, the activities of both bodies were so close that there was little distinction between them. They certainly attempted to work together to reach
agreement on how to cope with the ever-increasing problem of petitions. A
scheme was tried whereby the officials of both bodies dealt with the bulk of
cases and only passed the more important on to actual Privy Counsellors or
Members of the Lords or Commons. That failed. There were just too many
petitioners. Another method considered was that all petitions went first to
the Chancery. Then a Commission of Receivers was established to decide
to which body pleas should be sent. Local Committees of Hearers were set
up to try to deal with the problem geographically. Again, if one thinks of the
different ways of organising and reorganising education or the NHS in the
twentieth century, it all seems very modern. Here is the situation at this time
as described by Sir Almeric Fitzroy in *The History of The Privy Council*:

Hence a great variety in the forms and elaboration of the petitions sprang up, which sometimes even took the shape of appealing to different authorities in the hope, sometimes realised, that if it failed with one it might succeed with another, no strict co-ordination appearing to subsist between them, and there were obvious attempts to coach the courts with unctuous and flattering phrases. Others by their irregularity and hesitancy reflected the doubt and anxiety of the petitioner, whether for instance he should address himself to the Privy Council and Parliament – or should include the king.

Out of that confusion a working infrastructure did grow and eventually emerge – overlapping in some areas – of monarchy, Parliament, the judiciary and the Privy Council. Some people, on occasions wearing different hats (sometimes quite literally), were and, in the twenty-first century, still are either members of or closely associated with all four bodies. The Lord Chancellor, for example, was until recently the most senior member of the House of Lords, sat on the Woolsack and acted in many ways as the Speaker of the second chamber. He worked with the Speaker under the authority of the Lord Chamberlain to manage the Palace of Westminster on behalf of the Queen. He was the head of our legal system, a member of the Cabinet and the Privy Council, and, fully robed, had the duty of handing the Queen's Speech to her at the State Opening of Parliament. The last governments of the twentieth century changed that. The Lords started electing their own Speaker(s) and there was an attempt made to abolish the office of the Lord Chancellor. Because of the complexities of our unwritten constitution, this proved to be impossible and the job and position of the Lord Chancellor became a secondary role for the newly created post of Justice Secretary, who sat in the House of Commons.

Hopefully, having two Cabinet ministers in the Commons who can both be called Chancellor will not result in the same muddles of centuries back, described above by Fitzroy, when among the many ways in which citizens could seek redress at law were at least two courts run by different Chancellors, the Chancery and the Exchequer. At least there is now no great office of the Lord High Treasurer to make the situation more complicated. This was 'put into commission' in the seventeenth century and merged into the offices of the Lords Commissioners of the Treasury (now known as the government whips), with the First Lord always being the Prime Minister and the Second being the Chancellor of the Exchequer – when there is one. On some occasions the Prime Minister decides to be his own Chancellor of the Exchequer. This was the case for some of William Gladstone's premiership and was last done by Stanley Baldwin in 1923.

Of the two chancellorships, the Exchequer and the Lord Chancellor, it was the latter that was the most important, going back to the rule of Edward the Confessor, whereas the first Chancellor of the Exchequer was not formally appointed until 1221 when Eustace Fauconberg, Bishop of London, was given the job. Before then the work of the Exchequer was overseen by the Treasurer. The work was split into two parts: the collection of revenue from the county sheriffs (the old shire reeves) and the judicial court (the Exchequer of Pleas). It was largely these two courts that came under the authority of the Privy Council and were responsible for overloading the Council with so much work in the fifteenth and sixteenth centuries.

The Court of Chancery had grown out of the Council itself and records are often unclear as to whether the members of the court are sitting as part of the Privy Council or as a separate court. As it came under the jurisdiction of the Lord Chancellor it had one specific duty which did not come under the remit of either the Exchequer of Pleas or the courts of common law. The Lord Chancellor, having taking over many of the functions of a previous high office holder, the Justiciar, was also the Keeper of the King's Conscience. The Chancery operated this conscience in dealing with matters of contracts, and trusts so that, for example, poverty could be accepted as a reason a contract had not been honoured. For this reason, petitioners who understood the law were keen to direct their cases towards the Chancery rather than the common courts of law, the Exchequer, or directly to the Privy Council. What made it difficult for such petitioners was that the Chancellor was often required to accompany the monarch on his travels. And so the work piled up.

The Lord Chancellor was ultimately responsible for the judiciary system operated through the Privy Council. There were other courts of law as well as Chancery and the Exchequer in the fifteenth century, and they grew in later years. At the start of the thirteenth century, a new Court of Common Pleas had split from the Exchequer of Pleas. The Court of Common Pleas dealt with disputes between individuals or organisations which did not concern the king in the matter to be decided. The king, represented by a lawyer (or lawyers), acted as the judge. The court sat in Westminster Hall for about 600 years, being joined at later dates by the Exchequer of Pleas and the King's Bench. Until its merger with other courts by the Supreme Court of Judicature Act of 1873, and its complete abolition by Order of the Privy Council three years later, this court was considered to be, in the words of Sir Edward Coke, 'the lock and key of the common law'. And people and kings listened seriously to what Sir Edward said. He was in his time the celebrity lawyer of the Privy Council and, like many celebrities of all ages, he came to a sticky end – though unlike some of those he prosecuted he did keep his head. In 1600, as Attorney General, he prosecuted Essex and Southampton for rebellion. He led the case against Sir Walter Raleigh in 1603, and the gunpowder plotters in 1605. In each case, his 'verbal violence' was conspicuous, and his language to Raleigh was infamous. But he was proved right in a prediction that the Court of Common Pleas would last for hundreds of years.

This was in spite of the illegal poaching of their cases by the Court of the King's Bench. This was the court of common law that followed the monarch on his travels around the country and lasted from around 1190 to 1420, when it joined the Court of Common Pleas and the Exchequer Pleas in Westminster Hall. The King's Bench took its cases from wherever it could and tried to operate as a court of appeal, though it was not a court of last resort, as its decisions had to be signed off by Parliament. It worked two scams. It took cases from other courts by claiming, but not proving, that the defendant or plaintiff came from or lived in Middlesex – the home of the King's Bench – and it also poached cases under a writ whereby a defendant could claim non-payment of debts by offering a legal fiction that the money concerned was already owed and pledged to the king. The king was a great supporter of this writ.

Then there was the Court of Requests. This operated under the Privy Seal; the Lord Privy Seal had to appoint two Masters of Requests Ordinary to help the poor, and specifically the very poor, servants of the king to obtain justice. Later, two Masters of Requests Extraordinary were added to allow judges to accompany the monarchs on their travels around their kingdom. Over the years, extra courts were added to the responsibilities of the Privy Council, for which they acted as the final court of appeal. These will figure in other chapters and include the Prize Court, which was concerned with the just distribution of the rewards for piracy on the high seas, and the Court of Arches, which was, and still is, a disciplinary body of the Church and plays a role in the defrocking of clergy. 'Defrocking' is a technical term used when a vicar or rector has to be sacked, and already there is a body at work trying to pick the right phrase to be used when the first woman priest has to be removed. The cases passed up from the Court of Arches to the Privy Council can be both extremely sad and, in retrospect, very funny, as in the case of a rector in the twentieth century who became both the first parson to be banned from visiting tea shops and cafés in the West End of London – he had a penchant for the bottoms of young waitresses – and the only Christian in this country to be killed by a lion when proclaiming his faith.

When we move into the eras of British colonisation, Empire and Commonwealth, the legal role of the Privy Council grows enormously. But before that, the most prominent development in the judicial aspect of the functioning of the Privy Council was in the establishment and growth of the Star Chamber. This was a body so powerful in its impact that the name lives on in politics long after the Chamber was closed in 1641. In the twenty-first century, the process that takes place before each Budget whereby departmental ministers argue their case for more money from the Treasury each year is known as going before the Star Chamber. In some years, an independent Cabinet minister from a non-public spending office, such as the Lord Privy Seal or the Chancellor of the Duchy of Lancaster, is appointed to chair this body. In the fifteenth and sixteenth centuries, it was chaired by the most powerful person on the Privy Council, normally the Lord Chancellor. It is believed that the court took its name because it met in a chamber where 'all the roofe thereof was decked with imagines of stares gilted'. Court sessions were held in secret with no indictments and no witnesses. Evidence had to be presented in writing. It evolved into a political weapon, and increasingly many lawyers saw it as a symbol of the misuse and abuse of power by the English monarchy and courts. To delve into its history, it is necessary to go back to the enquiries of Albert Dicey and his award-winning Arnold essay of 1860:

> It is with something of astonishment that the enquirer discovers that this august tribunal [the Star Chamber] was merely the Council under another name; and that the court, whose overgrown power the patriots of 1640 cast to the ground, was the same body whose early encroachments had alarmed the parliamentary leaders under Edward III and

Richard II. The process by which the judicial authority of the Council passed into the form of the Court of the Star Chamber admits of
some dispute and is involved in no little obscurity. No one need feel
ashamed to avow their ignorance when they find that even in the time
of James I, when the Star Chamber was in full activity, men learned
in the law could dispute no less as to its origin than as to its power.

Professor Dicey shows his mastery of polite scholarship – something not
always readily apparent among historians – with that phrase to describe
the institutionalised confusion concerning the origins of the Star Chamber: 'admits of some dispute and is involved in no little obscurity'. This
institutionalised confusion was but one factor linking all the developments
of our courts at that time, and it lasted until well into the nineteenth century. No wonder that in *Bleak House* Charles Dickens could write with
such feeling that 'Jarndyce and Jarndyce still drags its dreary length before
the court, perennially hopeless', and makes Mr Bumble say, more sharply,
in *Oliver Twist*: 'The law is an ass.' At a later date, readers were delighted
by the accounts of J. B. Morton (Beachcomber of the *Daily Express*) of
Mr Justice Cocklecarrot presiding over the Court of Uncommon Pleas
in such trials as the Case of the Talking Horse. But at the height of the
activity of the Star Chamber, getting caught up in its tentacles was no
laughing matter, particularly for the nobility.

CHAPTER NINE

PRIVY COUNSELLORS PLOTTING AND COUNTERPLOTTING

N HIS BOOK *A Short History of England*, Sir Simon Jenkins, an expert on our historic country houses, describes the mid-sixteenth century as 'a time of codes and secret societies, of the "five symbols at your door", false walls and Jesuit priests' holes'. He goes on to describe one house, Harvington in Worcestershire, as having as many holes as a Dutch cheese, and the designer Nicholas Owen 'being so cunning that he was eventually caught only by the house in which he was hiding being burned to the ground'. In this atmosphere, treason and plotting flourished and Nicholas Owen, a Jesuit lay brother who became – and still is – the patron saint of illusionists and escapologists, excelled. He is remembered today as a character in Robert Benson's novel *Come*

Rack, Come Rope, and one of the priest holes he built plays a pivotal part in the Catherine Aird mystery *A Most Contagious Game*. He was a considerable Catholic thorn in the side of the Privy Council, and they were out to get him.

Before becoming a Jesuit, Owen had been trained as a carpenter and, under the name of Little John, travelled the country constructing hiding places and secret panels in the houses of wealthy Catholic families. Some are believed to be still undiscovered. Working undercover, he masterminded the escape of many prisoners, including the famous exploit of getting Father John Gerald out of the Tower of London in 1597. He was arrested several times before eventually giving himself up to the authorities. The house where he was concealing some Catholics who were on the run was put to the fire. By offering himself as a hostage, he enabled them to escape. He died under torture in 1606.

When Owen had finally been captured, the Lord Privy Seal, Robert Cecil, later to become the Earl of Salisbury, expressed the relief and delight of the Privy Council: 'It is incredible, how great was the joy caused by his arrest, knowing the great skill of Owen in constructing hiding places, and the innumerable quantity of dark holes which he had schemed for hiding priests all over England.'

Salisbury himself was no stranger to strategies and schemes. It runs deep in the blood of the Cecil family. Even as I write, there is a Cecil sitting on the Privy Council and in the House of Lords, a former Lord Privy Seal in John Major's government, who was sacked for disloyalty by Major's successor as Conservative leader, William Hague. As the Conservative Leader of the Opposition in the Lords in 1997, he was closely involved in the negotiations for the reform of the second chamber being put forward by the new Labour Prime Minister Tony Blair. Seizing an opportunity for at least ninety-two hereditary peers to keep their seats in the Lords, he went to 10 Downing Street and suggested a plan which was acceptable to both the Prime Minister and the majority of members of the House of Lords. He neglected to consult William Hague, who learnt of the plans from a friendly journalist. It was too much for the new Tory leader to be treated in this way by a member of a family with a background of over 500 years of political ducking and diving, and Salisbury had to go. (However, as with all former Leaders of the House of Lords, he was given a life peerage and sits in the Lords as Baron Gascoyne-Cecil of Essendon in the County of Rutland – and, just to keep the family record straight, when he was in the Lords as a hereditary peer he didn't use the name Salisbury but sat under his courtesy title, Viscount Cranbourne.)

Gascoyne-Cecil was the grandson of the 5th Marquess, who shared the same Christian name, Robert, which means care is needed with reference indexing. The earlier Gascoyne-Cecil also served in high office in government and in the Privy Council, where he was for a time the Lord President. And he too ran into trouble with the leadership of his party, most notably when he attacked the Conservative Prime Minister Harold Macmillan and Colonial Secretary Iain Macleod for their plans to give independence to the newly emerging African states in the 1950s. Salisbury claimed that he 'spoke for the white people' and famously called Macleod 'too clever – too clever by half'. Salisbury eventually resigned over Macmillan's policy on Cyprus. Macmillan's biographer, Charles Williams, writes that in his diary, Macmillan comments: 'All through history the Cecils, when any friend or colleague has been in real trouble, have stabbed him in the back.'

Robert's father, the 4th Marquess, also served in the Cabinet and was sworn to the Privy Council, where he too, like so many of his family, was Lord Privy Seal. He also played a vital role in the Conservative Party in the selection of their leader. Until 1964, the Conservative leader emerged

from a magic circle of the Tory political establishment. The Chief Whip
of the party, with former members of the Cabinet, took soundings and
then advised the monarch whom to invite to form an administration. The
Cecils were always firmly in the magic circle.

Tracing the family still further backwards to the Tudors, the 3rd
Marquess was Prime Minister twice between 1885 and 1892. His father
served as both Lord President of the Privy Council and the Lord Privy
Seal, and was the Cecil in post when the title was upgraded in 1789
from earl to marquess. A note in passing about this title, as it can also
appear as 'marquis'. According to *Titles and Forms of Addresses: A
Guide to Their Correct Use*, a supplement produced in 1918 by Adam
and Charles Black, the publishers of *Who's Who*: 'This title is rendered in two ways, marquess or marquis. The former is the older
and purely British. Peers of this rank use which form they prefer.' It
is probably fair to say that throughout history the Cecil family not
only had a pretty good idea of where the political bodies were buried,
they probably dug a lot of the graves themselves. Not that the plotting started with Robert Cecil in the sixteenth century. His ancestors
include the kingmaker Richard Neville, Earl of Warwick. So it is in
the blood, and, although the competition is stiff, the Robert Cecil of
1565–1612 can probably claim to be the leading mover and shaker of
their family tree.

In *Tudor England*, Professor John Guy writes: 'Few would claim
that Robert Cecil was a man of integrity. He enjoyed intrigue as well
as wealth and power; he liked secrecy, and preferred to join rather than
restrain the scramble for profits.' Sworn to the Privy Council at the
age of twenty-eight, he found himself scrambling for profit among fellow counsellors including a lifelong enemy of the Cecil family, Robert
Devereux, Earl of Essex. This is their positioning in regard to their relationship with Elizabeth I, as described by John Guy: 'It was, however,

the dazzling but paranoid Essex, Elizabeth's third and last favourite, who self-consciously rivalled the Cecils for patronage and power. By the late 1590s their feud had escalated into a factional battle to control her policy.'

Essex's career had certainly been dazzling. Born in 1566, the eldest son of the 1st Earl of Essex, he was introduced at Court when he was eleven, and at nineteen was appointed a general of horse under his stepfather in the Netherlands, being knighted for gallantry at Zutphen. He became a great favourite of the queen, though his lack of self-control led to frequent quarrels, and his marriage to the widow of poet and soldier Sir Philip Sidney especially angered her.

His exploits have captured the imagination of romantic writers, not least his prowess as a soldier at Cádiz and his success in tracking down and securing a conviction of Roderigo López for conspiracy against the queen. Many of life's glittering prizes came his way. He became Master of Ordinance, Earl Marshal, Chancellor of Cambridge. He was tall and handsome. He argued with Elizabeth and she loved it – sometimes. Once, she boxed his ears and, to the horror of one of her ladies-in-waiting, his hand strayed to his sword. (No doubt she was also mistress of the innuendo.) Or so the stories told to Robert Cecil suggested. When these stories reached other members of the Privy Council and the royal establishment – probably somewhat embellished – it confirmed their belief that while Essex was a suitable plaything to amuse the queen for an idle hour, he must be kept away from serious policy-making.

Cecil, while not having any of Essex's physical attributes or charm, was a smooth operator. In 1599, Essex was appointed Governor-General of Ireland, many miles from Court. He was keen to go. This was a chance to win back the favour of the queen, to prove to his enemies that he was no dilettante, and to strengthen his supporters. He failed both militarily and diplomatically. Cecil was not surprised. He knew

that Essex had a reputation as a brave soldier but doubted his ability as a commander, and Essex's capricious temperament meant he
was entirely out of his depths dealing with the Irish problems. Essex
failed to suppress the rebellion of Hugh O'Neill, Earl of Tyrone, and
was accused of attempting to make an illegal and dishonourable treaty
with him. In an attempt to salvage his position, Essex deserted his
post as Governor-General and dashed to London to see Elizabeth.
Unthinkingly, he forced his way into her bedchamber at the Palace of
Nunsuch as she was in the process of being dressed. The queen had
him thrown out and later that day he was arrested. Brought before
the Star Chamber of the Privy Council, he was found guilty of malad-
ministration and abandoning his command, and was suspended from
the Privy Council and sacked from most of his public offices. Placed
under house arrest, Essex began to plan an act of treason, a revolt in
which he would lead his followers in an armed attack to take control
of both the Palace of Westminster and the Tower of London. The few
rebels had no money – Essex was completely broke, with many debts
– and no basis of support outside of London. It was a crazy scheme
and doomed to end, as it did, in fiasco. Once again, Essex, together
with his chief supporter the Earl of Southampton, was brought before
the Privy Council.

In *Our Island Story*, H. E. Marshall tells the once popular story that
Queen Elizabeth gave Essex a ring in their happier days. If he was ever
in trouble and returned the ring to her, so the story goes, she would recognise that he needed help and was looking to her to save him. Essex
tried to get the ring to Elizabeth but failed. This would fit into his life's
pattern. This story is now largely discredited, though a 'reputed' ring,
with doubtful provenance, was sold at Christie's on 9 May 1911 for £3,412.
Bearing that in mind, there is an interesting account in *Acts of the Privy
Council* entitled 'Lord Essex to be searched':

16 February 1600

At Hause's House in Westminster.

Mr Secretary of State, Robert Cecil; Lord Keeper; Lord Admiral; Lord Chamberlain;

Edward Busshell, Sir Gilly Merryck and Henry Cuffe were examined

A letter to Sir John Peyton, Knight, Leiutennante of the Tower of London. Her Majesty is informed by the confession of divers of the confederates of the Earle of Essex that he hath as yet about him some paper in a blacke cover fitte for her Majesty's sight, and so much the rather because divers of his followers have confessed now that he told them when he should be found eyther dead or alive yt should appeare that he had bin betrayed by the cyttie. Now forasmuch as yt is conceaved that notwithstanding his denial to me, the lord Admirall, that he had it not, that yet doth remaine about him, wee are commanded by her Majesty to require you in decent sorte to seek for yt, but so assuredly as that it may not be unfound yf it be there, but being recovered by you may be sent unto us for her Majesty to see. Wee thinke this fittest to be done in the morninge early before he be up if this come time enough but if it do not then to take your owne time.

Could the black paper be covering a ring? Who knows? The result of the Privy Council trial was that Essex was found guilty and the verdict was conveyed to the queen for her to sign the proclamation of death, which was the one and only punishment the Star Chamber was not allowed to impose. Elizabeth, somewhat reluctantly, we are told, duly signed, and Essex was beheaded on 25 February 1601.

One of those judging the case against Essex was his former friend, chief adviser and confidant Francis Bacon. Bacon is one of the many politicians throughout history to switch sides, form different allegiances and abandon friendships. In every case, it is difficult in retrospect to decide which reasons were the most responsible for this mercurial tendency, whether awareness of new principles, the desire for public advancement, or some personal agenda not known to others at the time. Certainly, Bacon's early friendship with Essex did him no good. Essex tried to influence the queen to appoint Bacon Attorney General, then Solicitor-General, then Master of the Rolls. All attempts failed. After Essex was arrested, Bacon switched his friendship to, among others, some of the Cecil family. His relationship with the queen improved dramatically and Elizabeth asked him personally if he would write the official report of Essex's trial. He then prospered under both Elizabeth I and James I, becoming Attorney General, Keeper of the Great Seal and Lord Chancellor.

Bacon was a man of many parts: scientist, philosopher, writer and now a successful and prominent public figure. But nemesis was waiting. As Bacon had been climbing the greasy pole, like many (then and now), he had flirted with debt, bribery and corruption. Most got away with it, and in Tudor times much of this activity would not have been regarded as criminal. For Bacon, retribution awaited in the form of Sir Edward Coke, who had conducted the successful prosecution against Essex. He and Bacon had clashed before. As a young, struggling lawyer, Bacon had wanted to marry a rich young widow, Mrs Elizabeth Hatton. She turned him down and married the older, and very wealthy, Sir Edward Coke. Then, when Essex had tried to persuade the queen to offer Bacon the post of Attorney General, she gave it instead to Coke. There was bad blood between them.

Coke ensured the downfall of Bacon by using his position to have charges of corruption and bribery brought against him. Bacon was found guilty, heavily fined and held in the Tower at the king's pleasure. Eventually the king remitted the fine and allowed him to retire from public life and live quietly at home in Highgate. Here, he continued his writing and scientific experiments, one of which caused his death in a most unusual way. Probably a unique ending of life even for a member of the Privy Council, whose roll call of deaths over the years would include dying under torture, hanging, beheading, burning at the stake and being shot. Bacon, while pursing an idea to keep meat fresh by stuffing the insides of chicken with snow, developed such a severe cold from using so much snow that he died of pneumonia.

Sir Edward Coke was promoted from Attorney General to become the Lord Chief Justice and must have been pretty satisfied with his position. But, like his victim Sir Francis Bacon, nemesis was waiting for him too, and the consequences of disagreements with James I and startlingly public family disputes led to him being stripped of public office, including losing his membership of the Privy Council. In *The History of The Privy Council*, Sir Almeric Fitzroy blames his downfall on innate character defects:

> His whole course of conduct in this affair gives emphatic expression to the alternate arrogance and servility which he never failed to display. Great as was his genius as a jurist, his reputation as a man was compact of meanness and cowardice; his only stimulus to political action an overweening vanity.

Coke was already in dispute with the king when, as Chief Justice of the Common Pleas in 1606, he had opposed James I's 'aggeration of the royal prerogative'. Then what was described as a most extraordinary case was introduced into the Star Chamber of the Privy Council by Mr Secretary Lake, whereby Sir Edward Coke was charged with an unseemly act of

high-handed violence towards his daughter by his marriage with Elizabeth (the daughter of Thomas Cecil, 1st Earl of Exeter), widow of Lord
Hatton. Mr Secretary Lake read out a letter which had been sent from
the Privy Council to Sir Edward:

> Whereas complaint hath been made unto us by your wife that her
> youngest daughter being gone a little into the country to take the air
> for a day or two, you followed after and with great violence broke open
> the door, dragged out your daughter with such violence and fury as
> she is fallen desperately sick. In regard thereof she humbly pray she
> may presently be brought to London where she may have the help
> of phisicke for the recovery of her health. And ... forasmuch as this
> cause is appointed to be heard and examined by this Board ... where
> we desire you to be present, these are therefore to will and require
> you to deliver the person of your said daughter unto this bearer, the
> Clarke of the Privy Council.

When Lady Elizabeth heard that such had been the immediate reaction
from the Privy Council to her petition, she thought that the Council did
not understand the seriousness of the situation. She burst into a Privy
Council meeting one afternoon and regaled the members with the urgency
of the matter. She explained that having become extremely anxious about
the amount of violence that Sir Edward was inflicting on their daughter, Frances, she had arranged for her to go and stay with friends at the
house of Sir Edmunde Wythipole. In response, her husband, 'pretending
warrant from the Council with his son and ten or eleven servants weap-
oned in a violent manner, repaired to the house where their daughter was
remaining and with a piece of timber broke open the door and dragged
her along to his coach'.

The Council decided that in view of Lady Elizabeth's pleas, Frances should be delivered by Sir Edward to the house of the Clerk of the Council and reside there until the case came before the court. Two ladies of quality would also stay there, one chosen by Frances's mother and one by her father. Lady Elizabeth nominated Lady Burleigh, and Sir Edward, Lady Compton. Such a high-profile case was heard by the Lord Archbishop, Lord Keeper, Lord Treasurer, Lord Privy Seal, Lord Viscount Wallingford, Mr Secretary Winwoode and Mr Chancellor of the Exchequer. The first session was concerned with the character and reputation of one Sir John Villiers. This was a nobleman Sir Edward was determined should marry his daughter. His wife disagreed, arguing that the wedding would be one of 'forced consent' and that she doubted that Sir John would act in a 'noble and religious fashion'. There was dispute as to whether these were actually Lady Elizabeth's words or the comments of one of her lady servants.

Sir Edward thought that his wife was planning to remove his daughter to France, out of his and Sir John's way. Eventually, the court found that Sir John was a noble gentlemen certainly worthy of marrying Sir Edward's daughter but gave an order that 'the Attorney General should prefer an information into the Court of the Star Chamber against Sir Edward Coke for the force and riot he used upon the house of Sir Edmund Withipole, to be in that court heard and sentenced as to justice doth appertain'. The court also ruled that in order to avoid any more breaches of the peace Sir Edward's daughter should go to live 'in some convenient place agreeable to her worth and quality until further order were taken'. This seems to have brought the Coke family into a frame of mind where they could consider reconciliation and, after lengthy talks between the Attorney General and Sir Edward, it was decided that no further action be taken but that the matter remain on the table at His Majesty's pleasure.

For Frances, the story ended with her marriage to Sir John Villiers – the brother of James I's favourite the Duke of Buckingham. Whether or not this was a happy marriage must be explored outside of a remit on the Privy Council. For Sir Edward, his troubles with the Privy Council were far from over. He had many enemies and this case created the climate they could use to bring other offences to light. He was charged with: making a fraudulent transaction when he was Attorney General by 'misusing' a debt owed to the Crown by the Chancellor, Sir Christopher Hatton; making speeches of 'high contempt' in court; and allowing his footman to ride bareheaded on his carriage when in the presence of the king. He was also accused of using the title 'Lord Chief Justice of England', when the correct wording was 'Lord Chief Justice of the King's Bench'. All these were matters no one would have dared to bring against Sir Edward when he was at the height of his powers. He would simply have swept such trivial matters aside. Now, in spite of crawling to the king, he was suspended from the Privy Council, and retired to Stoke Poges.

This was an age of plots and counterplots, but in studies of the Privy Council, two of the greatest and best-remembered figures of the age (N. B. *1066 and All That* – 'history is what you remember'), Thomas More (1478–1535) and Thomas Wolsey (1475–1530) hardly figure. Both were Lord Chancellors, both were close to the king, and both were charged with high treason, Wolsey dying before his trial could begin and More being beheaded. Yet Fitzroy, in *The History of The Privy Council*, only mentions More and Wolsey four times each, and then mainly in the context of lists of Privy Counsellors. I think the reason probably is that the narrative of both men is well documented and that in both cases their impact on the development of the English Privy Council was marginal. It is true that Wolsey was responsible for moving a great deal of work from the King's Bench to the Star Chamber, but a look at the records would suggest that this would have happened anyway. Wolsey and More's main sphere of influence was in Europe: More's with the Pope in Rome, whereas Wolsey wanted to be the arbiter of European politics, especially concerning the French.

For a tangible, physical feel of the politics of this age, of the cut and thrust of personal ambition and the religious persecutions, visit the house mentioned at the start of this chapter, Harvington Hall, near Kidderminster in Worcestershire, and experience the priest holes, secret passages and illusions described by Sir Simon Jenkins. In another of his books, *England's Thousand Best Houses*, he writes of a room which 'looks as if a monk has been disturbed while writing and vanished into the wall. He has, since even the fireplace is a fake, concealing another hole. An axonometric drawing shows the location of various hides, *at least of those so far discovered*.'

CHAPTER TEN

RECORDS OF THE PRIVY COUNCIL

THE EARLY RECORDS OF a body which historians agree had its origins in the mists of remote antiquity are by that definition going to be difficult to access with any reliability. The problem is made harder in this case because, as Professor Baldwin writes in *The King's Council in England during the Middle Ages*, 'The Council was never a court of record in the same sense as the King's Bench or the Exchequer. It was under no obligation to record its actions and did so only so far as the utility of the moment required.' Sir Harris Nicolas published an account in 1837 on the *Proceedings and Ordinances of the Privy Council of England*, which included entries from *The Book of the Council* containing details of some of the Council's work until 1435. Then there was the gap in records already referred to from

1460 to 1540. But from that date onwards, things looked up when it was
decided to keep a register of all Privy Council meetings,

> with the names of those present and the topics which engaged their
> attention and for the convenience of public business a book shall in
> future be kept, in which the Clerk of the Council shall, after each meet-
> ing, enter such matters of business as in the opinion of the Council
> ought to be put on record.

The first of these was published for the general public in *Acts of The
Privy Council of England*, by the authority of the Lords Commissioners
of Her Majesty's Treasury, under the direction of the Master of the Rolls
in 1890. They were edited by the lawyer John Roche Dasent, who was
also an examiner in the education department of the Privy Council. In
his introduction he sounds a warning note about the qualification that
the Council had of deciding for themselves what items should be put
on public record:

> It is obvious that a record made under such limitations must naturally
> observe a most disappointing silence as to many topics of absorb-
> ing interest which could not be safely set forth in a formal Register
> intended to be handed down to posterity through a succession of
> officials, and that the deliberations of a body which was practically
> the predecessor of the modern Cabinet of Ministers must often have
> been too confidential a nature to be entrusted even to a sworn officer
> of the Council.

Davent goes on to give one example: 'We may search the Register in vain
for any record of the proceedings in connexion with the disgrace and
execution of Catherine Howard.'

The first Privy Council meeting to be recorded in this manner was held at Greenwich on 10 August 1540. There were present:

Thomas Cranmer, Archbishop of Canterbury

Lord Audley, Lord Chancellor

The Duke of Norfolk, Lord High Treasurer of England

The Duke of Suffolk, Great Master of the Household and President
    of the Council

The Earl of Southampton, Lord Privy Seal

The Earl of Sussex, Great Chamberlain of England

Lord Russell, Great Admiral of England

Lord Sandes, Lord Chamberlain

Sir Thomas Cheyne, Lord Warden of the Cinque Ports and
    Treasurer of the Household

Sir Anthony Browne, Master of the Horse

Sir Anthony Wingfield, Vice-Chamberlain

Sir Richard Rich, Chancellor of the Augmentations of the
    Revenues of the Crown

Sir John Baker, Chancellor of the First Fruits and Tenths

The Earl of Hertford

Bishops: Durham, Winchester

Secretaries: Sir Thomas Wriothesley, Sir Ralph Sadler

In *Proceedings and Ordinances of the Privy Council*, Sir Harris Nicolas writes that 'there appears to have been no point of domestic or public life in England which was not subject to the interference of the Council'.

Because the powers of the Council were not limited by protocol or statute, they could use their laws to summon anyone to appear before them as either defendant or witness. They could use any method, including torture, to obtain evidence and they could also impose any punishment except the death penalty. The records show that they were often cruelly imaginative in their choice of punishment, once imposing a sentence on a man who refused to eat pig on religious grounds that he should be imprisoned and fed only on pork.

The Council loved to meddle and were especially keen to compete with both the evolving parliament and the law courts. If other bodies were unclear as to whether or not there was a situation that needed to be examined, the Council would plunge right in. At no time would the question be asked, 'Is this anything to do with us?'

So the interpretation of the scriptures by clergy or laity, the owner-ship of property, the legal rights of a university, disputes between traders or shopkeepers, licences to sell goods, arguments with city corporations (both internal and external), individual cases of libel or slander, all were grist to the Council's mill. Financial problems were especially popular. The Exchequer, the Privy Chamber, the Treasury of Augmentations of Revenues of the Crown and that of First Fruits and Tenths were all called to account, as was the Mint, where the possibility of the debasement of the coinage was a regular topic for debate.

There were many mundane matters. In the first few of these newly recorded meetings, the time of such people as the Archbishop of Canterbury, the Lord Chamberlain and the Lord High Admiral was given over to deciding whether the Treasurer of Calais should be chased up for not paying a bill for some bricks; writing to the Governor of the Fleet Prison, telling him to allow the wife of one of his prisoners, Robert Belson, regular visits; and settling a dispute between a citizen of York, Reginald Beseley, and the Sheriff of York, Sir H. Savill, as to what should happen to the profits from the office of the Clerk of York Castle. One function the Council seemed to take particular delight in carrying out was punishing those found guilty of eating meat in Lent. At St James's Palace on 1 April 1542, the Earl of Surrey was brought

before the Lord Chancellor, the Lord Privy Seal, the Bishop of Westminster and other Privy Counsellors, charged with this offence. The
example illustrates Dicey's point that on occasion the Council acted
as the Star Chamber but didn't actually convene itself as such. The
Earl of Surrey had obviously had a good day on 31 March, because
not only was he sentenced for 'certeyne misdemeanoures and abuses
accustumably used within the Cite towching eating off flesshe in the
Lent', he was also accused of 'the breaking off sondrye wyndowes in
the nights in diverse places off the sayde Cite, and the licentiows manner of playours'. The earl had no defence and admitted 'he could not
denye butt he had verye evil done therein submitting himself therefore to such ponisshement as should to them be thought good'. The
Council committed him to the Fleet Prison. Several other offenders
suffered the same fate, with some being sent to the Fleet and some to
the Tower. A Mr Arundel had his sentence postponed until 'he do
first repayre until the Mayor and Recorder of London humblye asking them forgiveness for the certain lewd words spoken off them and
give his daily attendance upon the Council until he be by them dismissed ... or else etc'.

This was a busy week for the Council at St James's: they deported
some gypsies, paid a sea captain for a group of French prisoners and
licensed another captain in these terms: 'It has pleased the King's Majesty
to licence John Burgh to go to seas at his own adventure for reprisailes
to be taken off the Frenchmen.' Burgh was instructed to keep the Council informed of all his activities.

The Council could, as we have seen, authorise torture and, according to their lights (but not, of course, in tune with modern views), they
tried to be fair about its application. Following a meeting at Cecil House
in February 1589, the Lord Chancellor sent a letter to the Governor of
the Tower of London:

A letter to sett Tristam Winslade at liberty, for that he hath not only
been often examined by Sir George Carey, Sir Walter Rauleighe, Sir
Richard Grenevile, knights, Mr Atturney General and Justice Young
and others, as by their hands appeareth, but has also been on the rack
to draw for him his knowledge of the intended invasion and being
found by his examinacions and the reports of other men taken at
the same time with him and in the shippe of Don Pedro, that he was
brought hither against his will, and so taken bondes of him for his
appearance at all tymes upon ten days warning to answer any things
this shall be his warrant to discharge him. [Another N. B. from *1066
and All That*: 'People in history didn't care how they spelt things.']

Many of the functions of the Privy Council in Tudor times have now
devolved into responsibilities of today's government departments.
Between 1542 and 1547, the Council issued over 200 passports, including some for the Scottish Lords Cassillis and Maxwell, who had been
held prisoners on charges against the state, to return to Scotland. They
also issued one to the Scottish Pursuivant-at-Arms to travel with them
to make sure that they had 'horsses and syche other necessaries as they
sholde need by the way'. There are fascinating stories behind many of
the reasons for granting passports. In April 1546, one Arthur Kellans,
described as a king's servant, was given a passport to 'repayre into Flaun-
ders for the doing of certein his owne affayres'. This is thought to be
coded Tudor language for spying. The duty of issuing passports eventually passed to the Foreign and Commonwealth Office and now resides
in the Passport Office.

Not surprisingly for an island nation, the registering and naming of
ships occupied many columns of the records of the Council. This was
especially the case for naval ships, and remained the responsibility of
the Privy Council until the setting up of the Board of the Admiralty in

1629. Before that, the authority was vested in one of the great officers of state, the Lord High Admiral, who was a major figure on the Council and attended most of their meetings. Ships and passports, together with the issuing of warrants for payments and licences for trading and storing goods, took up a large part of the regular work of the Council. Most of this would not cause comment at any time by an observer studying a country's import and export of wool, wine, wood etc. And it would also be no surprise to learn that two of the inevitable consequences of trade regulations were piracy and smuggling. The records of the Privy Council are full of such incidents. Letters were dispatched to naval commanders and sea captains to act on information received and sail at once to specific coastal towns where it had been learnt that French or Spanish pirates were set to attack our merchant ships. At one meeting of the Council at Greenwich on 10 September 1542, a letter had to be composed to be sent to the French ambassador, who asked if two French pirate ships captured off Yarmouth could be returned to France. This took the Archbishop of Canterbury, the Lord High Admiral, the Controller of the Household and Mr Secretary Sir John Gage some time, as the reply had to be 'devised in Frenche'.

One activity that took up a great deal of the Council's time and is covered by many column inches in the records is the listing of 'Recognisances', which are the conditions of release imposed on wrongdoers by the Council. Some names, especially for drunk and disorderly conduct, occur regularly.

Another function that, according to the early records, occupied much time was the overseeing of the Court of Augmentations. This had been set up in 1536 after the dissolution of the monasteries. (Friaries were dissolved the following year.) Its main duty was to hear cases arising out of the disposal of monastic lands, the object being to augment the revenues of the Crown. All religious establishments with incomes of less than

£200 per year were finally abolished by 1540, when Waltham Abbey in Essex was closed, and there were many legal disputes. Some buildings were allowed to remain in religious use, with some being bought from the Crown by wealthy lay people to serve as their local parish church. The Court of Augmentation dealt with the income thus raised. In 1554, the court became part of the Exchequer, and references to its work disappear from the index of the proceedings of the Privy Council.

Another subsidiary court of the Privy Council that figured in the first index of the records and has now vanished from our lives – unlike, for instance, the Court of Arches and the Prize Court – was the delightfully named Court of First Fruits and Tenths. This was a tax on the clergy initiated by Henry VIII in 1534 to put pressure on the Pope to grant him an annulment from his marriage to Catherine of Aragon. Priests had to pay a proportion of their first year's income and thereafter one-tenth of their salaries to the Papacy in Rome. The Lord Chancellor of the Privy Council, Thomas Cromwell, introduced new legislation to divert this money to the Exchequer. It was a difficult piece of legislation to both devise and enforce, resulting in legal disputes. Eventually, tax collected in this way formed the basis of Queen Anne's Bounty for poor clergy, which was instituted in 1703.

Over the years, new methods of indexing Privy Council records were introduced and, in 1571, a new classification appeared, under the heading of 'Complaints'. Of course, people and institutions had complained before, but these had been listed under other entries in the records. The complaints were as diverse as might be expected:

Against one Tusser, for cutting off a man's ear;
Of Lord Thomond against Lord Clanricarde;
Of one, Ball, a widow;
Of a Scotsman against certain of Hull;

A false, against the Dean and Chapter of Durham;

Of the inhabitants of Worcestershire as to the enclosure of a

    common (four different complaints);

French of piracy;

Against Henry Chauncey for seditious speaking;

Of the Countess of Cumberland for deer stealing;

Of the Undertakers in Ireland of the prohibition of the transport of

    grain;

Of the inhabitants of Blackfriars.

And many, many more – and as Dicey, Fitzroy and Baldwin have all pointed out, when the reference for what seems a promising story is looked up, there is so little detail. Just take the last example given above. What are the good people of Blackfriars protesting about? The bare facts are that

> one, Henry Naylor, who hath late erected smale cottages within the parcel of the Cloister of the Fryers, which he has pestered with sundry poore people upon whom he exactethe excessive charges and thereby makethe their povertie verie burdensome unto the inhabitants of the precente, besides the danger that may followe if the infection of the Plage or other desease might come among them.

Naylor is also accused of 'making a highway through the Cloister yarde'. Naylor was called before the Privy Council on 4 June 1581. The Lord Chancellor and four other counsellors instructed him to 'reform the defaultes and disorders in some sorte as iy the case require, not only may the cottages be put down and the highways barred up but also Naylor may be bound hereafter not to errecte or practise anything to the offence of the inhabitants aforside'. Obviously a marvellous story full of human interest being condensed into a small paragraph. How frustrating!

A major function of the Privy Council, which it still carries out today, is inquiring both for Parliament and for the general good under royal mandate. At the time of writing, the most recent commission has been into the press, and this will be examined in a later chapter. In the sixteenth century there was wide scope to commission subjects of inquiry. Some of these were simply examinations of the facts and a submission of evidence to the Council to establish what had occurred, such as an incident indexed 'as to innkeeper's charges' to follow up a complaint by a traveller of being overcharged for horsemeat. Others, for example a request to the Bishop of Rochester to inquire into the state of religion in Kent, were lengthier affairs. Many just listed a commodity, e.g.:

> For cheese;
> For wheat;
> For malt.

Others were more specific:

> To oversee the Sussex iron mines;
> As to gold in a Spanish ship.

It is often difficult to cross-reference a decision to set up a commission with any results that might be obtained. For instance, in September 1542: 'A commission was directed to the Byshop of Chichester, the Mayor of Chichester, Master Knight and Mr Whight off Sowthwyke, for the trial owt off an author off a certayne seditious bill fownde in the open felde beside Chichester.' Not surprisingly, no further comment was ever recorded. At Greenwich on 15 May 1582, before the Lord Treasurer, Mr

Secretary Walsingham and two others, Edward Bell and James Hapten, were examined following a violent dispute: 'Bell castethe the cause of his quarrel with Hapten atte some falling out atte a foot balle play more than a month before at the town of Writtell.' A decision is taken to refer the matter to Essex County Assizes, but nothing else is recorded, so perhaps the phrase 'kicking the ball into the long grass' goes back at least as far as Tudor times.

The size of the Privy Council has always varied. In 2015, it has over 600 members. At the start of the sixteenth century there were about 200 counsellors and this dropped steadily throughout the next hundred years. In 1600, there were around twenty; the fifty or so who held office under Queen Mary either retired or were withdrawn by Elizabeth at the beginning of her reign in 1558. The new queen preferred a small inner circle of trusted friends with whom she could work. In *The History of the Privy Council*, Sir Almeric Fitzroy describes the arrangement in these slightly non-politically correct terms:

> Taking their relations as a whole, it will be found that, in spite of some outbursts of womanly impatience, Crown and Council preserved throughout the reign a mutual confidence and amity that realised to the full the promise of the Queen's accession. Indeed, she listened to their remonstrances, not only with attention, but in the latter case with a genuine effort at accommodation no doubt emphasised by the conviction that in Burghley and later in his son she had the best advisers in the service of the state.

Throughout the Tudor period, the Council worked extremely hard. This was partly because the monarchs loved travelling and required their counsellors to be on hand so that official Privy Council meetings could be held wherever the Sovereign happened to be staying. For instance,

in the last five years of the reign of Henry VIII, 1542–47, there were frequent sessions held not only at Westminster (over 150), Greenwich (over
130), and Hampton Court (over 100), but also at over twenty other places,
including Windsor, Portsmouth, Titchfield, Nonsuch and Havering.
Although records are not strictly accurate and give no reasons why certain
counsellors attended specific meetings, one can guess from information
elsewhere at a combination of public duty, request from the monarch,
vested interest and personal agenda. In this period, when Henry was king,
the assiduous attendees were led by Lord Russell, the Great Admiral of
England and, later, Lord Privy Seal, with over 400 appearances, and Stephen Gardiner, the Bishop of Winchester, with 350. The Archbishop of
Canterbury Thomas Cranmer has 121 ticks.

CHAPTER ELEVEN

THE MAN WITH NO EARS AND OTHER STORIES FROM THE STAR CHAMBER

F ROM THE 250 YEARS of the Star Chamber's existence, many bizarre stories have emerged. Some of them show the behaviour of the Privy Counsellors sitting in judgment to have been outrageously cruel. It is the only body in England ever to have been responsible for torturing a woman and then having her burnt at the stake. Officially, the Star Chamber could not impose the death penalty, but its parent body, the Privy Council, had ways of getting round that. Because of the lack of detailed information in many of these stories, there are only fascinating snippets on which to wonder. In his essay on the Privy Council, Albert Dicey gives an example when the Council took it upon itself to intervene 'in the interests of morality when an individual acted in such a way which the law could not punish but moral feeling condemned'. In that spirit, a woman is severely punished 'for the practising to have her husband whipped. This punishment is rendered the more strange by the discovery that the injured husband was dead, and that his father performed the part of prosecutor.' In another instance, the Star Chamber passed judgment on one, John Bulmer, whose wife had left him to live with his brother. The verdict was that she should stay with the brother for a year and then Bulmer 'should resort to his wife and use her after such a sort as it behoveth an honest man to use his wife'.

As with the law courts today, many of the cases that were brought before the Star Chamber concerned squabbles within families, often the details of the dispute simply being a cover for much deeper enmity. Thus, in 1615, Sir Thomas Cheney, a Privy Counsellor of some standing, and not only Warden of the Cinque Ports but also Treasurer of the King's Council, was accused by his own son of treason. After a thorough examination by other Privy Counsellors, the Chamber decided that Sir Thomas's son had been wasting their time. As an example to others not to try the same approach to settling family problems, the son was committed to the Tower of London.

One of the most gruesome stories from the Star Chamber centred around a prominent lawyer of very extreme puritanical views. William Prynne was a Christian who hated Christmas, couldn't stand plays, and, in November 1632, published a book, *Histriomastix*, denouncing all dramatic productions as the work of the Devil and against the law of God as set out in the scriptures. This came out just after the wife of Charles I, Queen Henrietta – she who later pawned some of the Crown Jewels – and her ladies-in-waiting had taken part in a Court performance of Walter Montagu's *The Shepherd's Paradise*. Prynne's book was taken by many to be an attack not only on the queen but also on the king for allowing such decadent revelry. Prynne was no stranger to religious controversy.

Since leaving Oriel College, Oxford, in 1621 and being called to the Bar at Lincoln's Inn seven years later, he had denounced the policy of the Archbishop of Canterbury and written tracts maintaining that the custom of drinking health was sinful and that men should wear their hair short – but not women, for that would be unnatural, impudent and unchristian. So he knew that by attacking the royal family and the Archbishop, the two heads of the Church of England, he was courting danger. In particular, he flirted with disaster by making references to Nero and other tyrants seem like a criticism of the character of the king. The Privy Council asked the Attorney General to start proceedings in the Star Chamber, and Prynne was held in the Tower of London for almost a year before his trial began. On 17 February 1634, he received a horrendous punishment which also showed the powers that the Star Chamber took upon itself. With no explanation of where their authority came from, they stripped him of his Oxford degree and his membership of Lincoln's Inn. He was fined £5,000 and imprisoned for life. Most dreadful of all, he was sent to the pillory and had both ears cut off.

William Prynne was a fighter, and this action by the Star Chamber only stirred him to respond. Perhaps somewhat foolishly, he wrote a letter to the Archbishop of Canterbury, William Laud, accusing him of illegal actions and lack of judicial understanding. Laud handed the letter to the Attorney General with a request to prepare for another case against Prynne. The letter was handed to Prynne and he was asked to agree that he wrote it. Prynne tore it up. Which didn't endear him to the authorities. As a footnote to the spirit of the times, it is worth noting that Archbishop Laud was himself later impeached and beheaded at the Tower of London, by which time Prynne's fortunes had significantly changed and he was an official observer of this execution.

Back in prison, Prynne launched attack after attack on the established Church. Many of the tracts he wrote were published anonymously, but

by now Prynne's views and style were so well known that he was easily
identified. After one vicious piece about the Bishop of Norwich, Matthew Wren, Prynne was again brought before the Star Chamber. Once
again he was fined £5,000 and his life imprisonment was confirmed.
He was returned to the pillory to lose what was left of his ears. From
then on he was always known as 'the man with no ears'. The Chief Justice, John Finch, also insisted that he had the letters 'S. L.' branded on
his cheeks – standing for 'Seditious Libeller'. This time, the conditions
under which he was kept at the Tower were much harsher. No pens or
ink or any books other than the Bible and his own prayer book were
allowed. To remove him from any contact with his friends and supporters, he was transferred first to Wales and then to Mont Orgueil Castle in
Jersey, where no doubt the prison doctor subjected him to examination
by their 'Wheel of Urine'. If you want to learn more about this medieval
medical practice, the wheel is still in one of the castle's turrets. Here,
he was befriended by Sir Philip Carteret, who, as Seigneur of Sark and,
later, Bailiff of Jersey, had considerable powers in the Channel Islands
in regard to the interpretation of Orders of the Privy Council. Powers,
as later chapters will show, that the bailiffs still have. Carteret used these
powers to give Prynne as pleasant a life as he could and the prisoner
occupied his time in some comfort, writing poetry until he was eventually released by the Long Parliament in 1640.

The man with no ears spent the last thirty years of his life arguing with
the bishops, opposing the right of the clergy, as opposed to the state, to
practise excommunication and ban people from taking communion. He
successfully reclaimed his degree and was appointed a Commissioner for
the Visitation of the University of Oxford. He was inexhaustible in his
public disputes, clashing in print with John Milton, becoming a Member of Parliament and being barred from the Chamber, upon which his
friends smuggled him in and the authorities could only remove him by

formally adjourning the House. Imprisoned again, this time for a refusal to pay his taxes, Prynne was released on appeal and probably got most satisfaction by manipulating himself into the position of being the Overseer for the trial and execution of his old enemy, Archbishop Laud. He managed to end his days as Keeper of the Records in the Tower of London and a parliamentary adviser to Charles II. A remarkable career.

Many and varied were the amazing figures who clashed with the Privy Council, and none more so than the seventeenth-century fantasist Titus Oates. As pictured by Professor David Starkey in his book *Monarchy: England and Her Rulers from the Tudors to the Windsors*, Oates was 'lame, stunted, homosexual and extraordinarily ugly (his mouth was described as being in the middle of his face)'. Not only that, says Starkey, but 'he had failed at everything'. Matthew Parris, in *The Great Unfrocked*, quotes Roger North's summary of Oates: 'He was a most consummate cheat, blasphemer, vicious, perjured, impudent, and saucy, foul-mouthed wretch.' Yet for a few months he was responsible for over thirty men being executed as he persuaded Charles II and the Privy Council that England was in one of the greatest dangers it had ever faced – a Popish plot of tremendous proportions.

A natural conspirator and habitual perjurer, Oates was expelled from the Merchant Taylors' School for cheating, He went up to Cambridge and was sent down twice, from Gonville and Caius for lack of work and from St John's for an undisclosed scandal. He had no degree but still managed to become ordained in the Church. He had an unhappy time in several parishes – or rather the parishioners had unhappy times, many losing money and livestock to Oates, and some, to deflect attention from his own misdeeds, being publicly accused by him of sodomy and treason. In his family's hometown of Hastings, he overstepped this activity when he reported a local schoolmaster to the Privy Council for unnatural acts, and was fined for slander and imprisoned in Dover Castle. He escaped and ran away to sea as a naval chaplain, where he was unmasked and returned to Dover Castle. He escaped again and his strange and singular career continued when he obtained a clerical appointment at Arundel Castle to look after the Protestant Christians employed in the household of one of the most senior members of the Privy Council, the Earl Marshal, the Duke of Norfolk, and the leader of the Roman Catholics in England.

This was a time when England was awash with stories of religious plots and rumours of rebellion. It was over fifty years since the failed attempt by Guy Fawkes to blow up the Houses of Parliament but the famous line 'I see no reason why gunpowder and treason should ever be forgot' still echoed throughout the land. Oates was now mixing with a broad cross-section, both religiously and socially. He lived with highly placed Catholics and indeed in 1677 he entered the Roman Catholic Church and went to the English Jesuit College at Valladolid. Whether he did this to further his freelance spying activities is open to question. Unsurprisingly, he was expelled. As a natural go-between – or spy, or whatever – he still kept his Church of England connections. A homosexual, he had a life among friends which transcended the normal social barriers and depended on trust and secrecy. There has been much written about Oates's state of mind and how far this way of life fuelled his undoubted inborn tendency to fantasise, but no consensus has been reached. Did he really believe anything of the plots he was about to bring forward to the Privy Council, or was it all deliberately and consciously made up, for reasons no one will ever fully understand?

Certainly, his allegations were believed. One reason for this was that in 1677 he became friendly with the rector of St Mary Staining, Israel Tonge, described by Parris as 'obsessed with Catholicism to a degree unusual even for that febrile time. That he was in some degree mad is beyond doubt.' Tonge inspired Oates to put forward increasingly wild and imaginative stories of papist plots against the king. Oates persuaded a sufficient number of low church, Protestant Whigs on the Privy Council that the king's brother, James, Duke of York – a Catholic and heir to the throne – was a party to this treachery, and Oates was called before the Council to give evidence to a justice of the peace, Sir Edmund Godfrey, who was found dead shortly afterwards. Oates had revealed to Godfrey the full details of his invented Roman Catholic plot to kill the king, invade Ireland and indulge in a general massacre of Protestants. For a time, Oates became a popular public hero. Strong rumours suggested that the Catholics had murdered Godfrey. There were many executions of Catholics, including three Privy Counsellors. The Tories, high church Catholic friends of King Charles, responded with stories that the Protestants had killed the JP themselves to add credence to their outlandish stories of plots. In time, opinion turned against Oates, and in May 1784 he was arrested for calling the Duke of York a traitor. He was held in prison until the duke was enthroned as King James II, after which he was found guilty under Judge Jeffreys of perjury, and was fined and sentenced to an unusual but, for the seventeenth century, typically imaginative punishment.

This is how it is summarised by Matthew Parris in *The Great Unfrocked*:

> On the Monday morning following his conviction he was to be set in a pillory in Westminster Hall. On Tuesday he was to be pilloried in the Royal Exchange. On Wednesday he was to be flogged from Aldgate to Newgate. Thursday was a day off. On Friday the whip was to be picked up again at Newgate, and dropped at Tyburn ... For the remainder of his life Oates was to be annually pilloried on four days in April and August.

Different times and different circumstances produce different methods and practices in public life so it would be unreasonable to say that the Star Chamber was undemocratic, but some of its activities were breathtakingly despotic. For instance, the Sovereign could attend any session and take charge of the proceedings. If short of money, the monarch could sell a pardon. In *The Privy Council*, Dicey writes of cases where 'criminals escaped justice by bribing the monarch. There are entries in the minutes, such as 'Earl of Derby, for his pardon, £6,000; for the pardon of William Harper for treasons, felonies, escapes and other offences, 200 marks.' At various times the Star Chamber acted as censor of both plays and printed material, a duty that the Privy Council carried on with much enthusiasm when the Star Chamber was abolished. The best example of the futility of making modern-day judgements on the work of the Star Chamber is probably in consideration of its use of torture, which although many lawyers claim was illegal, was used in England until 1640 and was generally held to be a valid prerogative of the Crown. The most shameful example of its use must be in the case of Anne Askew, an English poet and Protestant who was tried and found guilty of being a heretic. She is the only woman to have been both tortured at the Tower of London and burnt at the stake.

Anne was born in 1520 into a rich, well-connected and influential family. Her father, William, was a wealthy Lincolnshire landowner who was often at the court at Henry VIII. He had arranged a marriage between his eldest daughter, Martha, and Thomas Kyme, who was an active and prominent Catholic. When Martha died, William immediately substituted young Anne, aged fifteen, as a wife for Thomas. The trouble was that Anne was a highly intelligent self-taught young lady who, through rational thought, had very firmly decided to become a Protestant. They fought. Anne left home and moved to London, becoming a gospeller. In accordance with family law at that time, Thomas had her arrested and forcibly returned to Lincolnshire. She escaped and the process was repeated. When she escaped yet again, she was re-arrested and taken to the Tower of London, where she steadfastly refused either to confess or to recant.

In other years, Anne may well have been released on the grounds that it was too much bother to continue to hold her imprisoned. But this was 1545, the approaching climax of the battle between the traditionalist Catholics and the Protestant reformers to win over Henry VIII to their cause. Because of Anne's friendships with some of the ladies-in-waiting to the queen, Catherine Parr, who were known to have Protestant sympathies, she became a pawn in this battle. The pressure on her intensified when her uncle, the Revd Edward Askew, was appointed curate to the Archbishop of Canterbury, Thomas Cranmer. By now, Cranmer lacked influence and many of his friends were being arrested. The traditionalists were in the ascendancy in the Privy Council and Anne was imprisoned. On 10 March, she was taken from the Tower to be examined by the aldermen of the City of London, where she was found guilty of heresy under the Six Articles Act. She was then questioned by Edmund Bonner, the Bishop of London, who ordered her to undergo further investigation by the Lord Chancellor, Sir Thomas Wriotheseley; Stephen Gardiner, Chief Secretary to the King; the Bishop of Winchester; and the Solicitor-General, Sir Richard Rich. Anne refused to give any names of Protestants close to, or connected with, the queen. She was then taken to the White Tower and made to climb onto the rack. The gaolers were instructed to begin the torture. According to Anne's own account, written from prison, she was raised 5 inches above the table and very slowly stretched before she fainted from the pain. The officials gaolers, failing to make Anne speak, then gave up and the wheels of the rack were seized by the Lord Chancellor and the Solicitor-General, who, as this account in *The Examinations of Anne Askew* by Elaine V. Beilin shows, were merciless: 'They turned the handles so hard that Anne was drawn apart, her shoulders and hips were pulled from their sockets and her elbows and knees were dislocated. Askew's cries could be heard in the garden next to the White Tower where the Lieutenant's wife and daughter were walking.'

Anne refused to talk. She was executed by being burnt slowly at the stake at Smithfield on 16 July 1546, in the last year of Henry VIII's reign. She was twenty-six years old.

Towards the end of the sixteenth century, there was an acceleration of the feeling that the Star Chamber had grown too powerful. This came partly from the general public, who had become extremely resentful at the omnipotent attitude of Privy Counsellors, who used the Star Chamber to interfere in any aspect of their lives in which they chose to do so. However, it also came from a growing number of lawyers, who, in a report published in 1594, questioned the whole validity on which the Chamber was based. They argued that it had not been founded on statute or law but on a pragmatic misuse of the prerogative of the Crown. As Fitzroy writes in *The History of the Privy Council*, 'It had become the flexible and aggressive instrument of tyranny, the symbol, as it were, of the abuse of power in its most offensive form.'

The time had come for the Star Chamber to be abolished. The means by which this happened was the Habeas Corpus Act of 1640. This was one of the first measures of the Long Parliament. The official government reason was that 'the conditions that led to the establishment of the Star Chamber no longer exist'. A hundred and fifty years later, the actual building was demolished, the famous 'ceiling of stars' moving to Leasowe Castle in Cheshire and the main door going to nearby Westminster School.

CHAPTER TWELVE

THE STUART SUCCESSION AND THE POSSIBLE PREGNANCY OF LADY ARABELLA

A S WELL AS THE ruthless development of the Star Chamber, the Tudors – more quietly – also carried out a wholesale reorganisation of the structure of the Privy Council. By the start of the seventeenth century, there were three clear divisions of membership. There were the monarch's counsellors, who consisted of the hereditary nobles upholding their traditional right to be members; below them in status was a group which came to be known as the Ordinary Council and was largely made up of highly competent professional men who took on the administrative and much of the legal work of the Council; then there were 'the others', made up of many of the justices and described by Fitzroy as 'the relic of medieval times still occasionally invoked to give legal advice'. It was the middle group of professionals that managed to steer a course through the demands of the monarchy, and the growing aspirations of those involved in parliamentary government that ensured the survival, if not the power, of the Privy Council through all the crisis and civil war of the Stuart period. This was summarised by Professor Dicey in *The Privy Council*:

> The king talked in a new strain about the prerogative. The Parliament assumed a new tone about its privileges. As certainly as each Parliament met, so regularly the illegal acts of the Crown were denounced. If James had held parliaments and kept within the law, the Council might have passed through a process of gradual change. He did neither. The Treasury was empty. The Tudors had gained little by having plundered the Church, for before James's accession the plunder was spent. The old sources of revenue from feudal rights were running dry. Hence James was driven to Parliament; but he had not the vigour to rule legally, and his whole reign was a series of encroachments which were checked, and acts of tyranny even more useless than oppressive. It took no great acuteness to foresee that the assembly which the Crown found it necessary to cajole was on the point of becoming the sovereign power of the state. A revolution, it was manifest, drew near.

James used his belief in the divine right of kings to tell Parliament that 'kings are appointed by God and answerable only to God'. Apart from not being the most tactful way to ask for money, this was a doctrine split between those who believed the grace of divinity was given at birth and those who insisted that it was only conferred by sacrament at coronation. Besides this, there were voices raised in public pamphlets asking why, in the matter of appointing monarchs, God kept making so many mistakes. To bolster the family belief that God was the top of the hereditary system, followed by kings, dukes, marquesses etc. (See Appendix C: Order of Precedence), Charles I reconstructed his Privy Council with a heavy emphasis on those he considered his loyal nobles. In 1630, the key members were:

> The Lord Keeper – Sir Thomas Coventry
>
> Lord Treasurer – Lord Weston
>
> Lord Chamberlain – Earl of Pembroke
>
> Lord Privy Seal – Earl of Manchester
>
> Earl Marshal – Earl of Arundel
>
> Earls: Bridgewater, Danby, Kelley
>
> Viscounts: Wimbledon, Dorchester, Falkland, Grandison
>
> Baron Newburgh
>
> Bishop of London
>
> Sir T. Edmunds
>
> Sir H. May

Gone were the highly efficient administrators of Tudor times. There were no Cromwells, Cecils or Walsinghams. Those were the people the Stuarts had to thank for constructing a machinery around the monarch that allowed them even to think of taking on Parliament in debate and battle. By the accession of Charles I, the Ordinary Council had divided the work of the Privy Council into twelve separate committees. In some of these can be seen the origins of various government departments now headed by Cabinet ministers:

1. The Booke of Rates, Imposycions, Exportacion and Importacion.
2. Putting Lawes into execution and concerning straingers.
3. Debtes.

4. The Household. In respect of which it was intimated to those concerned that His Majesty [King James I] desired to reduce the charge to £50,000, excepting the stable.

5. The Navy.

6. Fishinge.

7. Enfranchisinge Copyholders and Improvinge of Rentes.

8. Giftes, Graunts etc.

9. The State of Ireland.

10. Wardrobe and Robes.

11. Workes, Castles and Fortes.

12. Grievances in Generall.

These administrative reforms show that, even though the Privy Council could still not resist meddling in any aspect of life to which it took a fancy, it had developed a collective responsibility for national duties. This might have evolved much further if James I had not insisted that much of the Council's time was devoted to dealing with offences touching the person or property of the Crown. A typical example of that is an instruction issued by the king on 25 April 1614 to the Attorney General in respect of a serious complaint 'of riotous entry into a coppes called Newland for the preservation of His Majesty's game in that part of the forest of Windsor by pulling up and overthrowing a hedge and ditch and to proceed against the culprits'. To be absolutely fair, this was very much in the spirit of the day. Hunting affrays, which affected many Privy Counsellors directly, occupied what some would think to be a disproportionate amount of the Council's time. One such incident shows not only the seriousness with which such matters were considered but also the lengths to which the Council would go to find a reasonable and equitable settlement between the various parties. Lord Compton brought before the Lord Chancellor, the Lord Treasurer, the Duke of Lennox, the Earl of Worcester and the Earl of Pembroke, by the express wish of the king, a case against two Northampton landowners, George Catesby and Henry Lane, for indulging in 'particularly riotous hunting by night in Lord Compton's park at Yardly'. The defendants were examined and

> did upon their answers contradict and falsify one another and have since promoted seven severall riotous huntings in the purlew, whereof some of the very greate and outrageous as well in respect of the greate number and unlawful weapons as gunnes and suchlike, as also in respect of divers unfitted words and speeches uttered by them tending to contempt.

Yet, in spite of this, the Lord Chancellor and his four noble colleagues entreated Lord Compton 'with a wish that enmity and unkindness might cease between the parties and such neighbourly correspondence be held and settled between them as the deer may hereafter be preserved'. After some discussion, Lord Compton agreed to hold his complaint over until the end of the Trinity and Michaelmas law terms to see if Catesby and Lane and their servants had kept off his lands. This they did and the matter was resolved, much to the delight of King James, who wrote to the Lord Chancellor praising his efforts in successfully bringing the parties together.

Many of these disputes involved work and evidence given by the justices of the peace, who were at that time the sole agents of local administration for the Council. Many of them and the traders in their communities were concerned with far more pressing matters in which they needed the help of the Privy Council. One such matter was wool. Here was an illustration of how the new Council committee dealing with imports and exports was being really effective in its work. In *The History of the Privy Council*, Fitzroy writes, 'Nothing exhibits the

energies of the Council in a more attractive light than the vigilance
it displayed in shaping the production of wool and its utilisation to
the national advantage according to the economic notions of the day.'
When the clothiers of Shrewsbury, Oswestry and Whitchurch complained that French merchants were buying up hundreds of pieces of
wool and shipping them to France, the Council issued an Order to
stop them. When that had little effect and the committee saw the 'utter
impoverishing of many thousands and the decay of the said ancient
staple and market at Oswestry', they immediately referred the case to
a judge in assize, who legally enforced the Order, adding the rebuke
that 'merchants and drapers who were foreigners should rest content with doing their business in London where the trade would be
authorised by the Customs'.

It wasn't just wool. This committee was energetic. They supported the
Company of Silkweavers of London 'against the importation by merchant
strangers of sondry wares of silk, lace, ribbons and suchlike contrary to
an Act of nineteen Henry VII'. This was directed against the increasing trade of the Dutch in Norwich and Colchester, an ongoing problem
for our east coast satirised at a later date in a poem by the nineteenth-
century Prime Minister George Canning:

> In matters of commerce the fault of the Dutch
> Is giving too little and asking too much.

Imagine saying that – publicly, in verse – about another European country in Brussels today.

The Council also dealt with problems caused 'by the importation into
this realm by merchant strangers of foreign commodities of an exceeding
great value, more than is exported by them of the native commodities of
their Kingdom, whereby the money and coin of this realm goes to the

exhaustion of its treasure'. A very neat way of summing up the perpetual trouble in trying to maintain a balance of trade.

Another Privy Council committee that was extremely active was that of 'Fishinge'. This is a classic example of a department of government that grew directly from its roots in the Privy Council, flourished for a time as a major concern of government – and then faded. Indeed, the title 'Fisheries' was kept as a ministerial description until comparatively recently. Although merged with other interests, there was a Cabinet post in Sir Anthony Eden's 1955 government of Minister of Agriculture, Fisheries and Food, with three junior ministers given the rank of parliamentary secretaries to be in charge of the different divisions. This status was maintained for almost another fifty years. Then, in 2001, Tony Blair's reorganisation of Cabinet duties resulted in a newly named department called Environment, Food and Rural Affairs, which became commonly known as DEFRA. By the time David Cameron formed his first Cabinet in 2010, DEFRA had become a wide-ranging department in which fishing was relegated to the responsibility of a parliamentary under-secretary. It is interesting to note the change in national importance and recognition given to the fishing industry. From being one of the key concerns of government, it was now part of a sub-department of a ministry. For the record, it is worth noting the other matters which were the responsibility of that sub-department and – importantly – the order in which these duties were listed by DEFRA:

National Environment, Ecosystem Services, Biodiversity, National Parks and Areas of Outstanding Beauty, Wildlife, JNCC, Flooding and Water including Nitrates, Inland Waterways, including British Waterways, Land Management, including Commons and Contaminated Land and Soil, Rural Affairs, Cultural Erosion, Marine and Coastal Access Act and Implementation, Marine Management Organisation,

Coastal and Wider Access, Countryside and Rights of Way, Marine
Environment, Fisheries including CFP, EU Fisheries Council, Departmental Administration, Apprenticeships.

In the early seventeenth century, fishing had a very different priority. In
order to protect the herring fleet operating out of Yarmouth, the Privy
Council threatened the French government that, if they continued the
practice of trying to import herrings to East Anglia in French ships, the
Council would put into execution the statute of 5 Eliz, banning them
from all trade in herring. This was as much to do with the protection of
the established rights of merchant shipping as it was to do with fishing
– a precursor of the future Cod Wars. The Council took a similar action
against the French for attempting to use French ships to export their
wine through Southampton.

The Mercantile Marine was especially looked after by the Privy
Council. They had exercised their rights to establish Royal Charters
by persuading James I to incorporate by Royal Charter the Company
of Shipwrights to maintain the proper provision for the building, repair
and servicing of ships. They even gave the Warden and Masters power
to conscript craftsmen and apprentices into work in the dockyards when
needed. The Council fought fiercely to insist on their historic right for
their ships to operate in the coastal waters of those parts of the world
where the Crown had established 'first rights' as discoverers or settlers.
There was a dispute with Holland about Greenland. The Dutch ambassador had complained that Holland had been prevented from fishing
around Greenland, yet Holland had been the first to discover the country in 1596. The Council replied as follows:

Answer was made by their Lordships that the country of Greenland, together with the fishing of whale upon that coast and all other

commodities arisen from thence to properly belong to His Majesty, *jure domini*, his subjects having been the first discoverers thereof, as was made manifest unto their Lordships, and possession taken in the name and on behalf of His Majestie by erecting His Highness' Standard upon the place.

The Council argued their case well. They produced evidence that the object of the Dutch excursions around Greenland was to try to discover a north-east shipping passage to Nova Zembla and that at no time had they occupied or settled in any part of the country. The ambassador having seemingly failed to make any positive case, the Council then showed, as they did on many occasions, a degree of magnanimity, and assured him that 'their Lordships would then do their endeavour to procure the Ambassador suche honourable satisfaction as shall reasonably content him'.

Trade and shipping disputes and quite often problems of piracy took up much of Council business and the records show that those involved developed a good reputation for diplomatic success, on many occasions managing to isolate individual incidents and prevent them from escalating into more serious international trouble. Thus, in 1616, the Privy Council asked the king's ambassador in France to make representation to the Governor of Dieppe to prevent two French ships from sailing to the East Indies because they feared that the ships' aim was to establish a pirate base there from which to attack British citizens. This was successfully done and, following an exchange of information, two registered British ships bound for the seas around the Cabo da Boa Esperança were arrested off Cowes and held on suspicion of engaging in unlawful activity on the high seas.

When, in the twenty-first century, there is indignation that some foreign diplomats in London refuse to pay their parking fines, it is worth noting that in the 1620s, when the Venetian ambassador was preparing to return to Italy, there were complaints to the Council from some merchants and shopkeepers in the City that 'he doth refuse to satisfy and pay such debts and sums of money as he doth owe them'. The Council then issued an Order that if the petitioners were not immediately satisfied they could seize the ambassador's goods for 'the satisfaction of their due debts'.

As always, the counsellors were very keen to meddle in matters that, for one reason or another, took their fancy. Many of these concerned the activities of their fellow counsellors and much time was taken in arranging the trial of the Earl of Somerset and his wife, who were indicted of felony for the murder and poisoning of Sir Thomas Overbury. Nor were comparatively ordinary people immune to the attentions of the Privy Council. In 1621, one John Roope was ordered by the Council to appear before the Lord-Lieutenant of Devon for failing to keep a hedge and ditch in good condition at Gallion's Bower near Dartmouth.

But it was during this period that one of the most extraordinary investigations ever undertaken by the Privy Council occurred. It was set up after the death, on 25 September 1615, of Lady Arabella Stuart, who for a time had been considered a successor to Elizabeth I. She died a prisoner in the Tower of London at the age of forty, having been captured while fleeing to France disguised as a man. She was found hiding on a ship stopped and boarded by the Privy Council's militia just before it reached Calais. Even for an age when there was a high degree of paranoia surrounding possible claims to the throne, the terms of the Privy Council's inquiry seem remarkable:

> Whereas a report was given out amongst divers persons that the
> Lady Arabella Seymour, late wife of Sir William Seymour, daughter
> of Charles Steward, and grandchild to Matthew, Earl of Lennox, had

a child born during her confinement in Sir Thomas Parrie's house
at Lambeth, in the year of our Lord 1610, His Majesty commanded
us whose names are underwritten (George Canterbury, Thomas Suffolk, Treasurer, Ralph Winwood, Secretary of State, Francis Bacon,
Attorney General) to take notice thereof and to proceed as should be
expedient of the manifestation of the truth of this report.

Arabella Stuart was the great-great-granddaughter of Henry VII. Her
uncle was Lord Darnley, the second husband of Mary Queen of Scots,
and her cousin James I. Another relative in an interesting family tree
was her maternal grandmother, Elizabeth, Countess of Shrewsbury, now
more commonly known as Bess of Hardwick. Her father died when she
was a baby and her mother when she was aged seven, and it was this
grandmother who brought her up well away from other young people
at Hardwick Hall in Derbyshire. There is a story that one of her tutors
was a university student called Christopher Marlowe. She attracted the
interest of the Cecils – Lord Burghley and his son, the Secretary of State
Sir Robert Cecil – as the person to follow Elizabeth as queen, but Arabella showed little interest in either the Crown or the Court, and both
the Cecils then championed her cousin James.

   While Arabella quietly pursued her interests in learning foreign lan-
guages and playing the lute, others tried to use her as a pawn in the battles
for the throne. There was a failed plot to marry her to the King of Spain
and use Spanish support to gain her the English crown. There were
rumours that the Pope wanted her to marry his brother, a defrocked cardinal, in an effort to bring back a Roman Catholic to the English throne.
This was always going to be unlikely as Arabella publicly took Protestant communion. Then she ran into trouble with Queen Elizabeth. As
fourth in line, she needed the monarch's permission to marry. The Earl
of Hertford informed the queen that Arabella was planning to elope with

his grandson, Edward Seymour. Nothing came of that, but the queen had Arabella hauled before the Privy Council to be questioned. Then the King of Poland sent envoys asking for her hand in marriage. She said no. The Privy Council were keeping a close eye on Arabella and her growing relationship with another Seymour, William, the grandson of Lady Catherine Grey, the sister of Lady Jane Grey, and when they discovered that in spite of earlier denials the couple had married in secret at Greenwich Palace on 22 June 1610, they were both imprisoned for marrying without seeking the consent of the monarch, now King James I. Sadly for them, they were sent to different prisons, Seymour to the Tower and Arabella to the custody of Sir Thomas Parrie in his large house at Lambeth. She was allowed a degree of freedom, including that of sending letters to friends. When the Council found out that some of this correspondence was to Seymour, they ordered Arabella to be taken to Durham and placed under the guard and protection of the Bishop of Durham, William James.

This was too late. They had already made plans to escape. Arabella, dressed as a man, reached their meeting place at the village of Lee, on the edge of Blackheath in Kent. Seymour was delayed and so Arabella rode to the coast and set sail for France. (This story is believed to have been the inspiration for the cross-dressing heroine Imogen in Shakespeare's play *Cymbeline*.) Seymour got a later boat to Flanders, but by then Arabella had already been caught. She was sent to the Tower and never saw William Seymour again.

Arabella had been fourth in line to the throne. Seymour, later to inherit the title of the 2nd Duke of Somerset, was the sixth in line. Many factions in England and Scotland would be concerned if they had produced a legitimate child and there had been rumours that a girl, some said called Mary, had been born in 1611 or 1612. Seymour was the first witness to appear before the Privy Council inquiry, followed by the attendants of

Lady Arabella and the servants at Sir Thomas Parrie's house, where it was believed the birth – if there had been one – must have taken place. They all pleaded ignorance, but there was a general agreement that if Lady Arabella had given birth, the one person who would know was 'Mrs Ann Bradshawe, a gentlewoman attending at that time neare the person of the said Lady Arabella and the best able to clear that doubt'. There was, however, a problem. Ann Bradshawe was extremely ill and had moved to Duffield in Derbyshire, and 'such was her weakness and indisposicion of boddie, that she could not take so great a jorney at soe unseasonnable tyme of the yeare without danger of her life'. So the Council told Mr Edmondes, one of their clerks, 'to make his repaire unto her at her dwelling-house in Duffield in the countie of Derby and to examine her upon such interrogatories, as by our instructions were delivered unto him'.

Mr Edmondes reported that Mrs Bradshaw's evidence was concise: three months after her marriage, 'Lady Arabella let fall some words as though she thought herself with child ... Lady Arabella was somewhat distempered in her boddie which caused her to swelle, so that her gowne was let out ... There was never any midwife bespoken for the Lady Arabella.' The report concluded, 'For any report that the Lady Arabella be with child this examinaunt knows none and well knoweth that Lady Arabella never had a child. And this is the truth of this examinaunt's knowledge touching this matter as she will answer the same upon her duty and allegiance.' It was signed by Ann Bradshaw and Examiner C. Edmondes. So the rumours were all due to a distemper of the blood. The report was endorsed by the Privy Council committee. But, as Sir Almeric Fitzroy writes in *The History of the Privy Council*,

> For directness and pertinacity of intention to arrive at the truth this examination could hardly have been surpassed, but it would have

fallen strangely on modern ears [1928] if it were announced that the
Archbishop, the Prime Minister, a Secretary of State, and the greatest intellects to be found in the ranks of the Privy Council, were to be
charged with such an Inquiry.

Fear no more the heat o' the sun,
Nor the furious winter's rages:
Thou they worldly task has done,
Home art gone and ta'en thy wages;
Golden lads and girls all must,
As chimney-sweepers, come to dust.

> *Cymbeline*, William Shakespeare, Act IV, Scene ii

CHAPTER THIRTEEN

THE CABAL: 'GREAT WITS ARE SURE TO MADNESS NEAR ALLIED'

N HIS SECTION ON the Stuarts in *The Oxford Illustrated History of Britain*, John Morrill writes:

> The Stuarts were one of England's least successful dynasties. Charles I was put on trial for treason and was publicly beheaded; James II fled the country fearing a similar fate, and abandoned his kingdom and throne. James I and Charles II died peacefully in their beds, but James I lived to see all his hopes fade and ambitions thwarted, while Charles II, although he had the trappings of success, was a curiously unambitious man, whose desire for a quiet life was not achieved until it was too late for him to enjoy it.

It was against this background that the Privy Council found itself in competition with Parliament, and the Council was becoming unequal in its work. As new requirements arose, it became apparent that the Council was simply not fit to deal with them. In *The Privy Council*, Professor Albert Dicey identified one of these new measures:

> There was a need for a regular army. In earlier times the necessity had not existed. But by the beginning of the reign of Charles I, it must have been evident to keen observers that it was impossible for much longer to stave off the formation of a regular army; that when one was created either the King or the Parliament must extend their power; and whether the authority of the Crown or the liberties of the people were augmented, the form of government that had previously existed must come to an end.

The military force in England had developed very much as a commercial concern. The attempt by William I to introduce a system of knight-service to the Crown had failed and in most cases the feudal duties of landowners to provide militias was replaced by payment to the Privy Council, the money being used to hire soldiers from private contractors. War was regarded as a profitable business, involving risks but promising large rewards from ransom or plunder. Cash was invested in a military company much as merchants might invest in a private man-of-war, holding control in it in proportion to the amount of their venture. Under this system, commissions were bought in the army until 1870.

By the end of the fifteenth century, civil strife and the introduction of firearms had weakened the organisation of the national militia. Hitherto, every man had been required to bring his own weapons to muster; but firearms were beyond the reach of ordinary men and so the burden of providing weapons shifted from the individual to the state. In each county, the state operated in the person of a Lord-Lieutenant, a figure of some dignity in the order of precedence, being the Sovereign's officially appointed chief representative of that county. Until 1907, the Lords-Lieutenant were responsible for finding soldiers for the national militia and also for raising forces when needed to combat and deal with local disorders. They were constantly chivvied by the Privy Council. In 1613, the Council rebuked Lord Cumberland, noting that men have never been 'ordered into bandes or companies, nor mustered nor trained as in other places'. They must now 'assure suitable and sufficient persons as shall be meete to find either horse, armour or other furniture for the service of His Majestie ... and to see the same bandes from time to time to be viewed, mustered and trained'. A similar letter was written to the Lord-Lieutenant of Middlesex, with – to rub the point home – copies to the Chancellor of the Exchequer, the Chancellor of the Duchy of Lancaster and the High Sheriff, wanting to know of the men listed in their bandes how many were actually dead and unable to fight. In May 1616, a stern and urgent communication was sent to the Lord Mayor of London:

> All gentlemen and other persons of what quality whatsoever under
> the degree of *a Lord of Parliament or Privy Counsellor* should in
> regard of the houses they there hold, contribute upon all occasions
> to the finding of men and arms and weapons in all assessments made
> for such or other like services.

The Civil War showed that the entire military system of England was chaotic, and in 1645 Parliament created the New Model Army of around 24,000 trained men, which, when supplemented by Oliver Cromwell's military constabulary, became known as the Terror of Europe. Though largely swept away at the Restoration, one regiment of foot was saved and a regiment of horse was formed by enlisting discharged troopers. These, with the foot-guards and the king's horse-guards, formed the nucleus of a standing army. The Privy Council tried to reorganise county militia along the old lines, with soldiers funded by local landowners. It was a shambles. The relationship between the monarch and the army, and also between the Sovereign and the Royal Navy, was exercised and operated through the finances of Parliament and not the Privy Council. The old county landowners just weren't interested in providing either the money or the troops. However, it did seem fitting that, in 1907, when the Lords-Lieutenant were discharged of these responsibilities, they were also formally appointed as presidents of their counties' territorial forces associations.

Not surprisingly, given our geographical place in the world, there has always been a strong connection between the monarch and the navy, which continues into the twenty-first century, with the Queen having appointed Prince Philip to the highest post in the Royal Navy, that of Lord High Admiral. Queen Elizabeth herself launched a new Royal Naval aircraft carrier on 4 July 2014 – the biggest ship ever built in Britain. The nuts and bolts of that relationship had its origins in the Privy Council, with the Lord High Admiral always being one of its most senior positions. The Privy Council had funded the navy by a tax on imports. At the time of Henry VII we had five warships; this number was increased by twenty-seven when the Council had access to the money gained from the sale of monasteries in the reign of Henry VIII. At the time of the Restoration, England had over forty ships and 3,500 sailors and a monarch who, in the words of Professor Callender of the Royal Naval College at Greenwich (1920), 'was more than any other ruler of England since Henry VIII the true friend and well wisher of the service'. Later centuries have been generous with praise of both Charles II and James II. In the early twentieth century, Hilaire Belloc wrote in *James II*:

Charles II was strongly interested in the art of naval design, and for an amateur not unskilled in it. He and James were perhaps the two men in the kingdom who most appreciated what a strong navy meant to England and how necessary it was to furnish one; not only by sufficient expenditures to secure quality, but by attention and intelligent application to secure quality.

Perhaps because of his eagerness to get things done, Charles had no concept of what today we would call 'due process' in his treatment of the Privy Council. Here, he followed in the cavalier footsteps of his father, who had left the Council completely foxed by his attempts to raise money for a new fleet to be sent to give succour to Rochelle in the French wars. With peers and many counties refusing to contribute to a forced loan, one of the strongest and most treacherous members of the Privy Council, the Duke of Buckingham, broke ranks and advised the king to recall Parliament. Sir Almeric Fitzroy writes in *The History of The Privy Council*: 'When Buckingham to the astonishment of the Council advocated the calling of a Parliament the bewildered counsellors supported the king in his refusal, but were at a loss when the alternative means of raising money came to be considered.' Like father, like son. No doubt in his treatment of the Privy Council Charles II gave little thought to the long-term weakening that would take place following the methods he adopted. As membership of the Council – in spite of efforts from Parliament to nominate members – was solely by royal appointment, the king had much scope for manoeuvre and he used this to appoint small committees with selected members who did what he wanted. This, as Samuel Pepys showed in his diary when describing his meetings with the Lord Privy Seal to obtain timber for the ships, was a very effective way of working. But it left the Privy Council as a whole with a decreasing aura of authority. Real power was passing to its committees, which, for the purposes of obtaining money, had to turn to Parliament. When the Council objected to the king about this way of

working, Charles replied curtly that it was his right to employ who he
wanted and to call them ministers if he wished and that he was 'always
proposing to employ persons of ability and integrity'. The Privy Council had used committees and commissions before, but there had always
been a direct line of devolved responsibility and accountability. These
new committees were in a powerful limbo: although nominally under
the umbrella of the Council, they would in practice become much more
an adjunct of parliamentary government. Again, Fitzroy writes, 'Nothing
could have been more complete than the sudden collapse of the whole
machinery of government known to a generation.'

The most famous of these committees was one made up of some of
the most colourful characters of the Stuart period and was given a name
that has lasted throughout history – the cabal. There is no real agreement on what the original meaning of this word was. It seems to have
something to do with the secret and exclusive study of Hebrew scriptural
texts. Certainly, the concept of secret discussions is now firmly associated with any small group described as a cabal. One reason for the name
being remembered is that at some point some scholar (or not) explained
that it was because it was made up of the first letters of the surnames of
its members. Thus:

> Thomas Clifford (1st Baron of Chudleigh)
> Lord Arlington
> 2nd Duke of Buckingham
> Lord Ashley
> Lord Lauderdale

Of these, the most notorious was George Villiers, the 2nd Duke of Buckingham. In that respect, he took after his father, the 1st Duke, also called
George Villiers, whose good looks had brought him to the notice of

James I. He became firm friends with the king's son Charles, the Prince of Wales, who was eight years his junior. George Villiers, with his flamboyant and bizarre behaviour, was allowed by the king to dazzle the Court. He was given the nickname Steenie while the Prince of Wales was known as Baby Charles. James indulged many of Villiers's mad schemes, letting him take Charles to Madrid to seek a marriage for the prince with the Spanish Infanta. The two proposed to do this by telling the King of Spain that they would convert England back to Catholicism. The result of this venture is put succinctly in Sir Simon Jenkins's book *A Short History of England*: 'The Infanta took an instant dislike to Charles. The two Englishmen fled.'

In 1623, Villiers, now a duke and Lord High Admiral, narrowly escaped being impeached by Parliament for naval failures against the French at Rochelle and Cadiz. He loved being involved with the navy and spent much time at Portsmouth, where, in the Greyhound pub on 23 August 1628, he was stabbed to death by a renegade naval officer called George Felton. There is a footnote to this story. Villiers often brought the Prince of Wales to Portsmouth. Much to the amusement of the boys of Portsmouth Grammar School, until the early part of the twentieth century there was a plaque on the wall of a nearby pathway proudly proclaiming, 'King Charles I, as Prince of Wales, often walked here twenty-five years after his head was cut off.' I am told it figured in their lessons on English punctuation.

If the first Duke of Buckingham achieved notoriety, his son outshone him. He was regarded at the time as one of the most impressive Restoration rakes and has figured in many romantic novels and films of that period, most notably in Alexandre Dumas's Musketeer novels. He was seven when his father had been assassinated and Charles I insisted that he be brought up with his own children and sent to Trinity College, Cambridge. Fighting, naturally, on the royalist side in the Civil War, he acquitted himself well but ran into a great deal of political trouble after his lands were sequestered in 1651, and then six years later he married the daughter of the parliamentary general, Fairfax, to whom most of his estates had been assigned under the Commonwealth. This particularly caused anger among a group of peers led by Edward Hyde, the Earl of Clarendon, who managed to estrange Buckingham from the favour of the king and prevent his appointment to the Privy Council. By a series of adroit political measures in both the Commons and the Lords, Buckingham completely outplayed Clarendon and became once again a favourite of the king, joining the Privy Council and the cabal. He was one of Charles II's strongest, politically wisest and richest supporters. But it was not to last. In 1673, he fell out with another member of the cabal, Lord Arlington, and then spent ten years dabbling with the Whig dissenters, even supporting Titus Oates's fantasy of a Popish plot.

But his fame was not primarily due to high-level intrigue but to aristocratic scandal, indulged in with wit, good humour and toleration from the readers of the news sheets. As a young man in 1661, he had been charged with escorting the king's daughter, Princess Henrietta, to Paris for her wedding to the Duke of Orleans, but had to be recalled because of his persistent advances to her. He had a long-running affair with the Countess of Shrewsbury – whose husband he eventually killed in a duel – and rumour had it that they had a child who died and was buried in Westminster Abbey with the name 'the Earl of Coventry' on his tombstone. Often in fights, he had served time in the Tower of London for pulling off a peer's wig and knocking him out in the House of Lords. A life well summed up by Dryden as Zimri in *Absalom and Achitophel*:

> *A man so various that he seemed to be*
> *Not one, but all man's epitome:*
> *Stiff in opinions, always in the wrong,*

Was everything by starts and nothing long;
But in the course of one revolving moon
Was chemist, fiddler, statesman and buffon;
[…]
Then all for women, painting, rhyming, drinking;
So over violent or over civil
That every man with him was God or Devil.

Anyone who wanders around the London streets to the east of Charing Cross Station can be aware of a lasting memorial to George Villiers, Duke of Buckingham. The first road running south from the Strand towards the river is Villiers Street, with the George pub being a prominent landmark. The next road is Buckingham Street, on the site of the former mansion that was the home of the Dukes of Buckingham. Once, there was a Duke Street, and to complete the name and title there was even a narrow passageway called Of Alley until it was renamed by the old London County Council.

The Privy Counsellor whose name leads the cabal, Sir Thomas Clifford (who became the first Baron Chudleigh), could not have been more different than Buckingham. A member of the House of Commons who distinguished himself in naval battles in the Dutch wars, he rose through hard work to become in turn Comptroller of the Household, Secretary of State and Lord Treasurer. In the frenetic atmosphere in which the cabal worked, he was probably the only member trusted by all the others. It was said that the most interesting thing about his life was his death. He was reported to have died 'by his own hand', but perhaps accidentally, when he became strangled with his cravat on the bed-tester.

Lord Arlington, if not the joker in the cabal pack, certainly inspired others at court to imitate his strutting around with stick and scarf, which they did knowing it caused the king much amusement. This Malvolio figure seemed an odd choice to be a member of a group concerned with secret plotting. Although Arlington desperately wanted to be Treasurer, the king told him that he wouldn't embarrass him by offering him the job as he simply wasn't up to it. And Lord Clarendon, always bearing a grudge because he had not been invited to join the group, declared that 'Arlington has as much interest and knowledge in our constitution as he has in the history of China'.

With Sir Thomas Clifford, Lord Lauderdale was perhaps the only other member of the cabal on whom the king could completely rely. He had brought fifty of his own troops from Scotland to support Charles I at Nunsuch Palace and had discussed details of the Restoration with Charles II at Breda in the Netherlands. His interests were almost wholly Scottish and the king rewarded him by making him Secretary of State for Scotland. Created Duke of Lauderdale in 1672, he ruled Scotland for the next eight years with a ferocity that has made his name execrated. There was a demand from many Privy Councillors for him to be sacked, but Charles used his personal influence to defeat the agitation for the removal of one of his favourites, and Lauderdale retained his power in Scotland almost to the end of his life in 1682.

Anthony Ashley Cooper, who became the first Earl of Shaftesbury, was a politician of great capacity and versatility, as exemplified by the way in which, in 1680, he managed to arrange the judicial murder of his personal enemy, Lord Stafford. He was never averse to changing sides. In the Civil War, he first served with the royalists and then joined the parliamentary forces. He was cunning, with outstanding diligence and ability, if not integrity, and served in many parliaments in both the Commons and the Lords. During the Commonwealth parliaments, he moved from government to opposition and went to Europe to discuss the Restoration with Charles, who, when on the throne, appointed him Lord Chancellor and a member of the cabal in 1672. A year later, he crossed the floor and joined the opposition to speak in the cause of Protestantism. Like Buckingham, to whom by one of his marriages – he had three – he was related, he was imprisoned in the Tower of London for fighting. He fell in and out of favour with the king, who, in 1679, had appointed him Lord President of the Privy Council, and then sacked him for trying to exclude James from the succession in favour of Monmouth. Shaftesbury attempted to foment rebellion and was again imprisoned in the Tower, but was acquitted of treason by a jury loaded with Whigs. He fled to Holland and died in Amsterdam on 22 January 1683. Like Buckingham, he was a prize subject for John Dryden and is Achitophel in the poem *Absalom and Achitophel*:

> *The false Achitophel was first,*
> *A name to all succeeding ages curst;*
> *For close designs and crooked councils fit,*
> *Sagacious, bold, and turbulent of wit,*
> *Restless, unfixed in principles and place,*
> *[…]*
> *Would steer to near the sands to boast his wit,*
> *[…]*
> *Great wits are near to madness sure allied.*

CHAPTER FOURTEEN

THE PRIVY COUNCIL'S
TIPPING POINT: 30 JULY 1714

AFTER CHARLES II'S DEATH from a stroke in 1685, John
Dryden's view of his successor, James II, was:

A plain good man, whose name is understood,
(So few deserve the name of plain and good.)
That unsuspected plainness he believed;
He looked into himself and was deceived.

James, a Roman Catholic, wanted to introduce legislation that would
start a movement towards giving equal status to his Church. Although
warned by a weakened Privy Council that only a policy of moderation
would secure national loyalty, he deliberately drove both Anglican and

constitutional sentiment into opposition by arbitrarily dispensing, in individual cases, with the disabilities imposed by law on Roman Catholics – and Protestant Non-Conformists. James also outraged the Tory Anglicans with his efforts to reorganise local government, which involved calling in the Royal Charters of Towns and encouraging the appointment of Catholics and dissenters to replace the Tory squirearchy in the counties. The Privy Council in the form established by the early Stuarts was too ineffective to prevent most of the existing Lords-Lieutenant and JPs from being sacked. The Privy Council as a body was institutionally confused. As an organisation whose members were only there by royal appointment, there was an obvious tacit agreement that they supported the Crown. But some of them were not only Privy Counsellors, they were also becoming effective members of either the House of Lords or the House of Commons. This was not so much because they looked into the future and saw where future power would be; it was more a natural evolution, which would manifest itself in the Glorious Revolution. The Privy Council was bound to support the monarch, but, as before in the history of England, there was the question: 'Which monarch, the current one or an aspiring one?'

Privy Counsellors were involved in the revolution both individually and as members of other bodies – some of them actually wrote seeking help from the leaders of another country – but the Council as such played no part in the process and thus its proceedings, as with many other benchmark episodes in English history, are silent on the subject. The situation of how William, the stadtholder of Holland, took the English throne is well summed up by Sir Simon Jenkins in *A Short History of England*: 'William's invitation from six peers was constitutionally irrelevant. England was attacked by a foreign ruler to usurp a legitimate monarch. The invitation was clearly treasonable, but as the saying goes, "If treason prosper none dare call it treason."'

If the Privy Council as a whole was not effective politically during
the Stuart period, it certainly carried out its role in the dignified part
of the constitution. William III died on 8 March 1702. The next day
was a Sunday but the Privy Council still called a meeting to proclaim
the accession of Queen Anne and heard her promise to maintain the
Protestant succession, now established in England, and also to continue to cut France down to size. Under Anne, the Privy Council also
lost its protection, which had been written into the 1701 Act of Settlement. This had decreed that when the House of Hanover succeeded
to the English throne, the Privy Council would regain its ancient right,
lost in Cromwell's time, of having to give consent to legislation passed
by Parliament. Her succession also marked a change in the relationship between a new monarch and Parliament. Previously, on the death
of a Sovereign, Parliament was automatically dissolved. Following an
attempt to assassinate William, the law was changed so that Parliament could sit for at least six months after a new king or queen came
to the throne. This, it was thought, would make a successful Jacobite
revolution unlikely. There was also another interesting, albeit informal,
constitutional benchmark at this time. In October 1710, the queen, having discussed the matter with members of the Privy Council, decided
to leave out of her address to the City of London the phrase originally
inserted by the Lord President that 'Her right to rule was divine'. This
theory of monarchy was never again discussed with any seriousness. By
now, Anne was appointing ministers in consultation with Whigs and
Tories in both Houses. They were still 'Her' ministers, but they were
not necessarily prominent Privy Counsellors. Parliament was controlling the purse strings, and that had an effect on who held high office.
It was beginning to be the case that it was possible to be a significant
and important person in the English establishment, and even perhaps
nominally a Privy Counsellor, but play no part at all in the activities of

the Privy Council. For instance, neither Professor Dicey in *The Privy Council* nor Sir Almeric Fitzroy in *The History of the Privy Council* gives even an index mention to one of the towering figures of Queen Anne's reign, the Duke of Marlborough.

It would be unfair to say that the Privy Council was moving towards its tipping point without some constitutional philosophers trying to check what seems in retrospect part of the inevitable march of history. One such person was the statesman and politician Sir William Temple. He had enjoyed a brilliant diplomatic career: in 1668 he had effected the alliance between England, Holland and Sweden, and more than anyone he had been responsible for arranging the marriage between Mary and William of Orange. Several times he turned down the offer of becoming Secretary of State, preferring to live quietly at his home in Moor Park, Surrey, writing essays and reports, helped by a friend and secretary who became one of our most famous satirists, Jonathan Swift. In Temple's memoirs, not published until 1720, some years after his death, he bemoaned the fact that Parliament had refused to take seriously his plan for the future of the Privy Council. He had proposed a Council of around thirty members, representing what he considered to be the three central components of the constitution: the Church, Parliament and the Judiciary. However, there was an unusual innovation suggested in his report as a way of raising money which might well give a clue as to why so many members of Parliament who were also Privy Counsellors found it unacceptable:

> One chief regard necessary to this constitution was that of the personal riches of this new Council, which in revenues of land and offices was found to amount to about £300,000 a year, whereas those of the House of Commons are seldom found to have exceeded £400,000. And authority is observed much to follow land, and at the worst, such

a Council might of their own stock, and at a pinch, furnish the King
so far as to relieve some great necessity by the Crown.

But, as Dicey writes in *The Privy Council*:

> The reason of Temple's failure lay much deeper than any causes which
> he assigns. His Council was too much or too little. It was too large for
> a Cabinet, too small for a parliament. It represented two inconsistent
> principles: appointment of Ministers for the sake of their Parliamentary
> influence and appointment of Ministers because they were accepta-
> ble to the king.

There was confusion. The monarch appointed ministers, but ministers
had to work in and with both Houses of Parliament in order to get their
work done. The correct status for the group of ministers that later evolved
into the Cabinet was regarded then and for many years to come as being
that of a committee of the Privy Council. In 1870, Dicey wrote that 'in
theory the Cabinet is nothing but a committee of the Privy Council, yet
with the Council it has in reality no dealings; and thus the extraordinary
result has taken place, that the government of England is in the hands of
men whose position is legally undefined'.

There were other attempts to use members of the Privy Council to
combat the growing power of Parliament. In the same years that Temple's *Memoirs* were published – perhaps inspired by them – Robert
Harley, then leader of the Tories but from a Whiggish family background, joined with the Duke of Shrewsbury and the queen herself to
investigate the possibility of establishing a 'Queen's Ministry Above
Party'. In *England Under Queen Anne: The Peace and the Protestant
Succession*, G. M. Trevelyan writes that 'they hoped to govern the land
by favour of the Queen and by the goodwill of the many moderate men

among her subjects'. But, like many others since, they found that political factions were now firmly entrenched in parliamentary life and their
efforts came to nothing.

It was towards the end of Anne's life that the Privy Council acted in
a way that secured not only the Act of Settlement and the Hanoverian
succession but also the future family line of monarchs for the foreseeable
future. And it seems in the twenty-first century that line is stretching to the
horizon and beyond. In doing so, the Council irrevocably lost its unique
and powerful status as the only body in the country with the authority
gained by 'ancient usage' to sort out problems of dynastic succession. It
came about in this way. In 1714, the queen fell ill, and by July it was obvious that this would be fatal. Early on the morning of 30 July, she called
together those members of the Privy Council who regularly attended her.
They met at Kensington Palace. The three members who were fervent
supporters of George of Hanover – the Bishop of London, the Duke of
Shrewsbury and Lord Dartmouth – were well prepared. They had been
talking with the seven doctors who had been treating the queen and
Shrewsbury's friend Jonathan Swift was in correspondence with one of
them, Dr Arbuthnot. They knew that the end was not far away. The Jaco-
bites, led by Bolingbroke, who always hoped the queen would finally turn
to appointing James and keeping the Stuart line, had no plan of action.
Shrewsbury had. He immediately sent two dukes, Somerset and Argyle,
to the house of George's agent in London to tell him to stand ready for
the news. The dukes then, though not summoned, exercised their right
as Privy Counsellors to see their monarch and entered the bedchamber.
As news spread that the queen was dying, there were real fears that the
Act of Settlement might not hold. Many politicians seemed to vacillate.
It was thought many might change their minds. Some did, several times
in a few hours. It was as though the Vicar of Bray had come among them
and they were seeking guidance from the comic opera refrain:

And this is law, I will maintain,
Until my dying day, Sir.
That whatsoever king may reign,
Still I'll be the Vicar of Bray, Sir.

The Stuart politicians were following the Stuart clergy. In this crisis what was needed was a firm and steady authority. These are the words of the historian G. M. Trevelyan:

> The instrument ready to hand was the Privy Council. The existing Cabinet had no dynastic policy which it cared to announce. Moreover the Cabinet was a meeting of the confidential servants of the Crown unknown to law, and drawing its authority from the presence of the Queen as its chairman. When therefore she was incapacitated by grave illness, the Cabinet lost much of its customary prestige. On this great occasion it made no attempt to assert itself. In normal times the Privy Council was gradually yielding power to the smaller and more partisan body but when sudden action of the highest importance had to be taken in the name of the laws and the safety of the Realm, the old constitutional power and authority of the Privy Council stood England in good stead.

Until this point, Privy Counsellors had been arguing among themselves. The queen had sacked Harley as Lord Treasurer on 27 July and for a few days the Secretary of State, Bolingbroke, had nobody above him. He had an opportunity to push the Jacobite cause and could not decide if it was worth taking. There was much speculation as to whether there was any real chance of a Stuart succession, and counsellors jostled for position, conscious that if they found themselves on the wrong side, their careers, status and finances would suffer. The final realisation that the queen only had a few days to live was the tipping point for the Privy Council and it concentrated their minds on the fact that the overwhelming odds were that George would very shortly become king. The Privy Council, realising the seriousness of the situation, convened a formal meeting of the Council later that same day, 30 July, in Kensington Court, under the President of the Council, the Duke of Buckinghamshire. As well as the chief officers of state, there were four dukes, five earls, one viscount, four lords and, from the House of Commons, the Chancellor of the Exchequer and the Vice-Chamberlain of the Household. They agreed urgently and unanimously that the queen be asked to appoint the Duke of Shrewsbury as Lord Treasurer. In a few years' time, this post, also known as the First Lord of the Treasury, would become better known under the incumbency of the Whig Robert Walpole as Prime Minister. Shrewsbury was trusted by both Whigs and Tories as a wise, kindly and decent man, popular in the country and liked by George of Hanover. Bolingbroke and his Tory friends realised that their best chance of advancement was to appear as supporters of Shrewsbury. To emphasise their unity in reaching this decision to Anne, Bolingbroke led the delegation, consisting of himself and Shrewsbury, the Lord Chancellor, the Lord Privy Seal and the Lord Steward. Although the queen was extremely ill, there is general agreement among historians that she knew what she was doing as she allowed the Lord Chancellor to guide her hand as she gave the staff of office to the Duke of Shrewsbury. He then set to work with the Council and its clerks to prepare for the queen's death and the ascension of King George I, and to issue the various proclamations that would be needed here and in the dominions. This was the last time that the Privy Council played a pivotal and decisive role in the appointment of a new monarch. But in no way was its work or influence over. There were new discoveries to be made.

CHAPTER FIFTEEN

THE PRIVY COUNCIL
AND THE NEW WORLD:
CORRUPTION AND
NAKED CELEBRATION

VEN THOUGH THE PRIVY Council had lost its commanding
position at the start of the Hanoverian period, it was still to play
a highly effective role in many of the offshoots of the old Council's work. To some extent, this was because George I had little
interest in the government of his new kingdom, did not understand the
customs of the country and could not speak the language. This left Parliament, and especially the man who was to be Prime Minister for over
forty years, Robert Walpole, free to develop a system of administration
in which the monarch and his Council had fewer and fewer opportunities to be involved – even if the king could understand how this might

be achieved, which he didn't. Though the Privy Council played less of
a central role, it maintained an important profile in many of the activities
of government, especially in foreign affairs and in particular with colonial development and the expansion of empire.

The history of the British Empire falls into several distinct periods.
The first dates from the sixteenth century to the Treaty of Versailles
in 1783, by which time Britain had built up a great overseas empire.
There are countless romantic tales of how Elizabethan sea dogs, spurred
on by their queen to break the Spanish monopoly on the New World,
embarked on maritime adventures. At one time, most schoolchildren in
England would be familiar with the exploits of Hawkins, Frobisher, Gilbert, Raleigh and Drake. Nevertheless, when Elizabeth died there was
no permanent English settlement overseas. The spirit of the sixteenth
century inspired adventure. It needed that of the seventeenth century
to encourage systematic colonisation. It is important to recognise that
when colonisation started, it was not considered piracy but carried on
with the authority of the British Crown. In 1609, Sir George Somers
annexed the Bermuda Islands. He raised the flag and did so in the name
of King James. He did not do it in the name of Parliament. Since anything to do with the monarch and the Crown involves the Privy Council,
there started a deviation in the administration of foreign affairs, which
continues in some measure into the twenty-first century. This area of
policy was first concerned with the colonies, then the British Empire,
the Dominions and the British Commonwealth, then the Commonwealth
of Nations. Of course, there have been ministers with specific responsibilities for these subjects. In the Conservative Cabinet of 1955, as well
as the Secretary of State for Foreign Affairs there was also a Secretary of
State for Commonwealth Relations in the House of Lords, with a junior
minister in the House of Commons and another full Secretary of State
for the Colonies in the Commons, supported by a Minister of State and

an Under-Secretary. The last government to have a Member with a title that mentioned the colonies was formed by Harold Wilson in 1964 and then the post was entitled Secretary of State for Colonial Affairs. But – and it is a very important but – the Head of the Commonwealth is always the British monarch.

All her prime ministers have found that Her Majesty Queen Elizabeth II takes this role extremely seriously, and there is a clear line in our unwritten constitution, from the geographical place of the old and current colonial overseas territories (whatever their status and name; and names frequently change) through the Privy Council to the Queen as Head of the Commonwealth. As Charles Moore wrote in the *Daily Telegraph* on 28 July 2014, at the time of the Commonwealth Games:

> It is a striking thought that our present Queen has probably held titular sway over more people than anyone else in our human history. This is partly because she has reigned so long, but mainly because she has been Head of the Commonwealth since 1952. The Commonwealth now has fifty-three members – having started with seven – and two billion citizens.

Once colonisation started, events happened quickly. North America serves as a good example. Early efforts to establish footholds in Newfoundland by Sir Humphry Gilbert and by Sir Walter Raleigh in Virginia had come to naught, apart from the legacy of their names for future generations. It wasn't until 1606 that the Privy Council granted a Royal Charter signed by James I to the Virginia Company to set up our first colony in America. This was entirely a 'plantation' settlement, developing for purely economic reasons. The impulse for many settlements was religion. In 1620, the *Mayflower* carried 143 Brownists to New England. The Pilgrim Fathers founded the colony of New Plymouth. The great Puritan exodus from Europe resulted in the establishment of Massachusetts in 1629. Maryland was founded in 1634 by Lord Baltimore as a refuge for Roman Catholics. Then colonies were established in Rhode Island, Connecticut and Maine, largely as a result of migration from Massachusetts. Settlements were taking place in the first fifty years of the seventeenth century in the West Indies, notably St Kitts, Barbados, Antigua, Montserrat, Anguilla and the Bahamas. Jamaica was a significant historical benchmark. It was the first British possession gained as a result of a war between countries of the Old World when, in 1655, Britain acquired the colony from Spain. Charles II and his Council, while weak at home, were especially diligent in following Oliver Cromwell's ambitions and encouraging overseas adventures. In *The History of the Privy Council*, Sir Almeric Fitzroy writes: 'The greatly increased interest in colonial affairs after the Restoration is very striking, as under Charles II it flowered into a definite colonial policy, the pursuance of which is regarded as an essential part of England's greatness.' The Carolinas were founded in 1663, New Jersey in 1665, and, in 1674, New Netherland, captured from the Dutch ten years previously, was finally confirmed in English hands and rechristened New York.

Eventually, of course, detailed policy relating to matters concerning the colonies and the Empire became the specific responsibilities of Parliament, but between 1613 and the Declaration of American Independence, the Register of the Privy Council shows that the Privy Council was heavily involved in events in America, Canada and the West Indies, and also especially with Newfoundland and Bermuda. The Council seemed particularly keen not just to pursue policy in the interests of the British Crown, but also to be conscious of local opinion and what they described as 'indigenous sentiment'. A precis of parts of this Register was published in 1905 at the instigation of Lord Elgin, a Privy Counsellor formerly holding the post of Treasurer of the royal household, who

was then Colonial Secretary in Campbell-Bannerman's Liberal government. Born in Montreal in 1849, when his father was governor-general
of Canada, he had served as Viceroy of India, and was committed to the
liberal advancement of overseas policy. Wearing another of his public hats
as Chairman of the Universities of Scotland, Elgin persuaded the Carn-
egie Trust to fund this project. The authors who worked on this project
came from the American Historical Society and the Canadian Archives
Department and co-operated with the Professor of Colonial History at
Oxford University, H. E. Egerton. The introduction to the first volume
comments that 'the present record of its activities gives a most favourable
impression of the Council as a governing body, anxious to help, willing
to take advice, free from preoccupations'.

    In *The History of the Privy Council*, Sir Almeric Fitzroy wrote: 'Ques-
tions came before the Council by way of petition either of individuals
or of corporate bodies and while matters of public importance were
not overlooked it was largely concerned with cases of private interest.'
Colonial development during the Stuart period was taking up so much
Council time that the same procedure was followed as in domestic matters of setting up separate sub-committees but gracing them with the
name of 'Council'. Thus, towards the end of the seventeenth century
there was a Council of Trade and also a Council of Plantations. After
twenty-five years of squabbling between the two, an entirely new committee was set up, the Right Honourable the Lords of the Committee
for Trade and Plantations, which became the real administrative centre
of the British colonies.

    One of the key figures in establishing British colonial policy on a broad
and comprehensive foundation was the philosopher and author John
Locke, the man who wrote in *An Essay Concerning Human Understanding*: 'New opinions are always suspected, and usually opposed, without
any other reason but because they are not already common.' Locke had

practical experience of this when he worked on the constitution of Carolina in 1669. It is true that Lord Shaftesbury, to whom Locke was secretary,
got much of the credit; even in the twentieth century, Professor C. M.
Andrews of Yale University said, 'Shaftesbury must be considered one of
the greatest of our colonial founders. To him more than anyone else do
North and South Carolina and the Bahamas owe their being.' But it was
Dr Williamson, in his book *Behind My Library Door*, who recognised
the part that Locke played in dealing with the Lord Keeper of the Privy
Council and the eight other counsellors who became the Governors of
Carolina. He writes of Locke's energy and experience:

> To Locke was entrusted the drafting of the scheme of government and
> constitution, and no colony was ever started with a more elaborate
> provision of social, political and religious organisation, the original
> text of which in a small vellum-covered volume of seventy-five pages
> is still preserved among the Shaftesbury muniments.

The essential factors, however, in the growing life of the colonies were
not to be found in the details of constitution but in the trading protocols and minutia of the Navigation Acts to protect the shipping of
products from the colonies to their protected market in Britain. The
colonies grew as plantations to further the commercial interests of the
mother country which guaranteed to safeguard their shipping lines and
provided restricted markets. An example of this was the Act of December 1660, which prohibited the planting, setting or sowing of tobacco
in England and Ireland. The colonists would have no competition in
English markets. For over two centuries this was the predominant trade
view not just for tobacco but also for sugar, ginger, rice and indigo. The
governors of all British colonies were continually urged by the Privy
Council to explore the possibilities of husbanding and exporting new

plants and, in 1668, the Lord Privy Seal especially asked the Governor of Jamaica to produce

> pepper, cloves, other spices and any new plants of that nature that come to be discovered and from time to time send some of the species to the Clerk of the Privy Council to be presented by him to the Board and that you make trials and take the best care you can by Cultivating and Transplanting them to Improve them to Public Benefit.

There was a real desire of the Council to break down the monopoly held by the Dutch Spice Islands on the production and growing trade of spices from the New World.

The Committee of Trade and Plantations eventually became known as a board, with the President of the Committee retaining the title of president in this new body. This title remained long after all authority for the board's activities had moved from the Privy Council to the government. For instance, in Sir Anthony Eden's Cabinet of 1955, along with the Lord President of the Privy Council, the Lord Privy Seal, the Chancellor of the Exchequer, the Lord Chancellor and the Chancellor of the Duchy of Lancaster, sandwiched below five Secretaries of State but above five departmental ministers, is Mr Peter Thornycroft, proudly bearing the title of President of the Board of Trade. In 1997, Tony Blair added the title of Secretary of State for Trade and Industry, and in 2001 this became the only name under which the department was known.

In the seventeen and eighteenth centuries, one growing aspect of this board's work was litigation. According to the report commissioned by Lord Elgin, 'With the increase of the Plantations in area and population, the appellate jurisdiction of the Council became more and more extensive as it penetrated every branch and touched every intimacy of colonial life.' Most of this work was concerned with appeals from individuals or

companies in the colonies against decisions by the governor of the colony concerned. Often the administrative body of the colony objected to
appeals going ahead to the Privy Council in London. (A state of affairs,
as shown in a later chapter, not unknown in the twenty-first century.)
Massachusetts in 1700 had actually decreed that allegiance to the colony
was 'of greater moment than allegiance to the Crown', and the government of Rhode Island had to be rebuked and reminded that 'it is the
inherent right of His Majesty to receive and determine Appeals from
all His Majesty's Colonies in America'. One problem with which the
Council had to deal was that the position and status of the 'governor'
varied from territory to territory, some being appointed by the Crown
and some chosen or elected by the people. The actual power of a governor depended on many things: the resources and commissions at his
disposal; his (nearly always a his!) personality and relationship with the
settlers as they established themselves and their families into permanent
residency; and the support from the Privy Council in London, in particular when military help was needed. The Elgin report found that one of
the standing abuses of the system was the corruption of governors. Illicit
trade was encouraged by making presents of money and contraband to
the governors. The haphazard arrangements that the Privy Council had
for paying governors' salaries provided a rich soil in which corruption
could flourish. This was exemplified by the way in which the Council
could not decide on a constant approach to changing conditions. They
were all in favour of expansion. But if the expansion resulted in valuable
gains, such as obtaining Nova Scotia after the Treaty of Utrecht, should
the governor be rewarded by more money for achievement or less because
of the opportunities now presented for personal advancement? In *The
History of the Privy Council*, Sir Almeric Fitzroy wrote that:

A valuable and exhaustive report was approved by the Council in 1709

and ordered to be communicated to the States concerned, review-
ing the salaries of governors payable in the West Indies, particular
mention being made of Barbados, Jamaica, the Bermudas, and the
'Governor-in-Chief' of the Leeward Islands. Augmentations on an
even more generous scale were approved for some of the American States, New York being dealt with liberally, and Massachusetts
rebuked for its habitual contumacy. In New Hampshire, 'where no
certain provision has yet been made', the Assembly is charged to
make a fitting salary. The arrangements in Virginia and Maryland
are approved, but 'as to the Proprietary and Chartered Colonies, viz,
Rhode Island, Connecticut, Pennsylvania, Carolina, and the Bahama
Islands, we cannot propose anything on this occasion, the governors
of those colonies not being appointed by Your Majesty and depending either on the Proprietors or the people from whom they have very
mean and uncertain salaries; which encourages them to connive at
unlawful trade and other Irregularities inconsistent with the Interest of this Kingdom, which great mischief can only be remedied as
we humbly conceive by reducing these Colonies to an immediate
dependence on the Crown'.

Of all the many examples of extreme corruption and criminality of and
by colonial governors, the activities of Captain Benjamin Bennett, twice
Governor of Bermuda, probably lead all the rest. In 1701, with the outbreak
of war between Britain and France anticipated by the Privy Council, they
sent Bennett with a party of fifty-five soldiers and two officers detached
from the 2nd Foot to safeguard the Islands. Though the Islands had their
own Assembly and in 1649 had even elected their own governor, Bennett
ran Bermuda as his own private empire. The only time the Council took
direct action from England was in 1704, when they insisted he immediately repeal a law introduced to use castration as a form of punishment.

Bennett infiltrated his own household servants and members of the 2nd
Foot into the myriad organisations of pirates that operated in the waters
around the islands. Piracy and wrecking were regarded as part of the normal commercial operations of the time. To celebrate a successful haul in
1717, one pirate, Benjamin Hornigood, openly presented in the harbour
a sloop, named *Bermuda*, to another pirate, Edward Teach. The pirate
who gratefully accepted this very fast, cedar-built, ten-gun sloop, later
became the well-known fictional character Blackbeard. Bennett thrived
in this atmosphere, illegally commissioning well over sixty ventures with
public money for his own private gain, cheerfully giving the public seal of
the Privy Council to pirate ships so that they could operate with impu-
nity. Stores and ammunition were embezzled and enormous amounts
of public money diverted for the governor's own use. Serving soldiers
were allowed to open public houses for the sale of smuggled rum and
brandy and to absent themselves from parade – with a commission to
the governor. The governor became more than reckless. He sacked the
Provost-Marshall, Edward Jones, who had arrested one of Bennett's
officers for smuggling and then appointed the officer, Colonel Anthony
White, as Chief Justice. There was a story that he organised a wedding
between his mistress and his son and then dispatched his son to England
to be kept in a lunatic asylum. Stories about his wild behaviour reached
London and the Tories made him step down as governor in 1713, only
for him to be returned to office a few months later by the Whigs after
the death of Queen Anne.

On taking up his post again, he found there were numerous complaints
from local sea captains about the increased ferocity of pirate attacks.
Nathaniel Catling reported that his sloop, *The Diamond*, was boarded
while sailing off Rum Key and that pirates led by Captain Vane, a well-
known villain, beat up the entire crew and looted the vessel of 300 pieces
of eight. Catling said that he was hanged until they thought him dead but

when cut down he was able to escape in spite of being hacked across the back of the neck with a cutlass. *The Diamond* was then destroyed by fire. Another Commander, Edward North, reported that his ship, the *William and Martha*, had also been attacked by Vane and one of his seaman had been bound hand and foot and had lighted matches put to his eyes until he revealed the whereabouts of all the money aboard the sloop. There is no record that Bennett took any action on these reports but there is an account of how he delighted the French at Martinique by giving in to their request that he return to them one of their ships and their seamen, captured by the Bermudan Navy. The governor agreed, but at the cost of a massive stock of wine and brandy for his own cellar, which he had enlarged for the purpose. The exchange took place in the dead of night on one of the smaller of the 300 or so Bermudan islands. What started as a quiet transaction did not stay that way. The French prisoners persuaded Bennett's deputation to sample some of the wine and no doubt it seemed only natural that the happiness of the released French and the gratitude of the receivers of the drink on that hot summer's night in an idyllic setting should express itself by all parties concerned stripping naked and dancing for joy.

CHAPTER SIXTEEN

THE AMERICAN PRINCESS
COOSAPONAKEESA AND
STAMP DUTY

T HE SEVEN YEARS WAR which ended in 1763 left Great
Britain with a load of debt. Parliament was dominated by
landowners who were increasingly fed up with the heavy
taxes they paid on their estates and thought that the American colonies should pay at least some of the cost of the army still kept
there. Also, there was resentment that from 1756 to 1761, when Great
Britain was paying out large sums to recompense the American colonies for their share in the attacks on Canada, the colonial merchants,
shipowners and captains were engaged in commerce with the French, to
England's injury and their own profit. Among the French West Indies,
on the Gulf of Mexico and along the northern Canadian frontier, colonial

provisions were carried to the enemy by means of every channel that the war provided.

It occurred to the British government that a considerable revenue was being raised in Britain by the sale of stamps made legally necessary to validate certain business papers. The government planned to introduce this in America. But the colonies, many of which were now more than a century old, resented this idea. They thought it was for them to decide what taxes they should pay and to which authority. The seeds of independence were flowering splendidly. This was readily apparent in New York. By 1754, the overthrow of the exercise of the royal prerogative was so complete that the *Proceedings of the Privy Council* could report:

> The Assembly (of New York) have taken to themselves not only the management and disposal of the public money, but have also wrested from Your Majesty's Governor the nomination of all officers of Government, the custody and direction of all military stores, the mustering and regulating of troops raised for Your Majesty's service, and in short almost every other executive part of the government.

The Council also rebuked Jamaica in strong language for saying that their assembly's contention that its powers did not flow from the grace of the king but from its own inherent rights was, 'heretical'. St Kitts was accused by the Council of 'corrupting its own constitution by affecting a power which they have not, analogous and co-equal to that of the House of Commons of Great Britain'.

With that climate of opinion it was not surprising that the Stamp Act was soon repealed. However, this repeal was accompanied by the Declaratory Act (1767), which asserted the full authority of the British Parliament over the colonies. It was easy to understand the objection of the colonies to taxation, such as Stamp Duty, which directly affected their internal affairs, but the British Parliament was lax in thinking that they could always continue controlling and putting duty on imports into the colonies. A new and inexperienced Chancellor of the Exchequer, Charles Townsend, led the House of Commons in imposing a duty on glass, lead, painters' colours, paper and tea. At once the colonies again raised vehement protests. It was unanimously resolved to use no English goods and to pay no debts in England until the tax was repealed. The chapter of accidents that followed has been well documented. Chatham's illness led to the Duke of Grafton being made responsible for the repeal of the Act. Grafton's inexperience in whipping legislation through Parliament meant that by one vote tea was omitted from the list of items to be included in the 'repeal' category. And then, whether through misplaced cunning, timidity or sheer inefficiency, the President of the Board of Trade, the Earl of Hillsborough, left out this vital piece of information in the official communication sent from the government to the colonial governors. This happened at a time when the East India Company had a problem of overproduction and thought it a good ploy to ship their extra stocks of tea to America to be sold in a protected market.

In retrospect, it is easy to say that something was bound to have happened for America to obtain independence, as there was no way that Britain could continuously put down revolt on the other side of the Atlantic. But, at the time, there were many who had no inkling of what the harvest would be. This was true of many of the Privy Counsellors closely involved in the development of the American colonies. It would be unfair to sound patronising but some were just too busy being 'paternal' to lift their eyes to the horizon. Just examine this paper commissioned by the Privy Council from a Doctor of Divinity and a Doctor of Physics, asked to provide a report on an 'imperial education' suitable for colonists:

Not so much to aim at any High Improvements of knowledge, as to guard against total Ignorance; to instil into the minds of Youth just Principles of Religion, Loyalty, and a love of our excellent Constitution, to instruction them in such branches of Knowledge and Useful Arts as are necessary to Trade, Agriculture, and a due Improvement of His Majesty's valuable Colonies, and to assist in raising up a Succession of faithful instructors to be sent forth not only among the Indians in alliance to His Majesty to teach both in the way of truth, to save them from corruption of the Enemy and to help remove the reproach of suffering the Emissaries of a false Religion to be more zealous in propagating their Slavish and destructive tenets in that part of the World, than Britons and protestants are in promoting the pure form of Godliness and the glorious plan of Public Liberty and happiness committed to them.

The paternal attitude of the Privy Council was also apparent in its desire to offer some protection to the rights and culture of Native Americans. They were particularly keen that the settlers should limit their demand for the westward expansion of their territory. The demand of the Ohio Company for large tracts west of the Alleghenies was met by instructions to the border states that no such grants were to be made, as settlements on Indian hunting ground had been the principal cause of the merciless devastations of the western frontier. The Council had some success but the tide of migration was by now impossible to stop, though one petitioner to the Council, who went under the name of Princess Coosaponakeesa and was the wife of a runaway missionary, gained protection for the land – Creek Nation – she claimed to rule by insisting that the Council follow up by actions the spirit of the words which it had issued in an Order in Council on 23 November 1761:

The granting Lands hitherto unsettled and establishing Colonies

upon the Frontiers before the claims of the Indians are ascertained
appears to be a measure of the most dangerous tendency and is more
particularly so in the present case, as these settlements now proposed
to be made especially those upon the Mohawk River are in that part
of the Country of the Possession of which the Indians are the most
jealous, having at different times expressed in the strongest possible
terms their Resolution to oppose all Settlements thereon as a manifest Violation of their Rights.

The Council saw the Princess as a trouble maker and thought the easiest
method of dealing with her was to help her protect her lands and subjects around Creek River, which they did; in the process they discovered
that her real name was Mary Musgrove Bosomworth.

In the long term, the Privy Council could no more protect the Native
Americans from the westward rush of the settlers than they could establish their right to rule the American colonies for much longer by imposing
legislation from London. However, they certainly tried, with new courts
being opened under the authority of the Admiralty to enforce the payment
of taxes at Boston, Charleston, Halifax and Philadelphia. The temper
of Lord North's administration, which was backed by British opinion,
was shown by the extreme seniority of the Committee of the Council for
Plantation Affairs set up in June 1770 to consider 'the disorders, confusion, and misgovernment which have lately prevailed in the Provence of
Massachusetts Bay'. This was really high-powered government activity,
aimed at putting the colonists in their place:

The First Lord of The Treasury (Lord North)
The Archbishop of Canterbury (The Rt. Rev. William Wake)
The Lord President of The Privy Council (Lord Gower)
The Lord Privy Seal (Earl of Halifax)

The Lord Justice General (Duke of Queensbury)

The Secretary of State (Earl of Rochford)

Groom of the Stole (Earl of Bristol)

President of The Board of Trade (Earl of Hillsborough)

Viscount Barrington (Secretary at War)

Treasurer of the Navy (Sir Gilbert Elliot)

Master of the Rolls (Sir Thomas Sewell)

Mr Speaker (Sir Fletcher Norton)

Take away Mr Speaker and the Archbishop of Canterbury and add the title Prime Minister to Lord North's name and it can be seen how at least one committee of the Privy Council is moving towards the composition of a present-day Cabinet. This constitutional development was taken a step further when it was decided by the Council that the amount and nature of the work undertaken by the Board of Trade was outgrowing its original remit. The extension of boundaries and the creation of new townships was a case in point. A new town was normally allowed a representative in the Colonial Assembly, so some rich political factions created settlements for that very purpose. This often caused trouble with the Native Americans. Officials concerned with the problems of trade were not equipped and did not possess the authority to deal with such matters. So, on the advice of the Privy Council, the king issued a proclamation for a new Royal Crown appointment, that of the Secretary of State for Colonial Affairs. This certainly seemed to streamline the transactions between London and the colonies, the number of judicial appeals dropping and complex technical and international problems being contained and eventually sorted out. An example was the comparatively smooth dealing with a petition from the Merchant Adventurers of Bristol for a separate Government and Legislature to be established at Dominica. This happened with a complicated rating system introduced to pay for it and was fully organised and set up in spite of the fact that for two years the island was in the hands of the French. Even with all this top-level diplomatic and political manoeuvring, the new Colonial Office was still handling enquiries that came firmly under the paternal label. In Canada, the Privy Council had made themselves extremely popular with the Iroquois and had given them much praise. In return, Sir Almeric Fitzroy wrote in *The History of the Privy Council*:

An embarrassing situation was caused by a number of squaws who petitioned thus:

'Hear the good words that you had to say which has afforded them great satisfaction; they now therefore hope that you will consider their fatigue in coming so far (to the Governor's office) and that His Present Majesty will follow the same good steps as his Royal Grandfather by considering their wants according to his example and afford them clothing and petticoats to cover them, as our warriors for want of ammunition cannot take care of them as formerly.'

The evidence shows that they did acquire the coveted petticoats.

One of the great areas of contention at this time was the question of 'prizes' won in battle. This was – as now – an area of legal complexity. There is an international convention that on the outbreak of war involving hostilities at sea, every country sets up a tribunal called a Prize Court, whose business is to examine the validity of the capture of ships and goods made at sea by their respective navies. In practice each country made its own rules of procedure. The first British Prize Court was commissioned in the seventeenth century by the Admiralty under the Great Seal and operated under the judicial authority of the Privy Council, as

it still does in the twenty-first century. In anticipation of the coming war
with the thirteen American colonies and questions as to what could be
considered 'prize' items, the Privy Council had prepared elaborate lists
of items to be prohibited from being exported to the eastern coast of
America. The customs officials of the Board of Trade started to apply
these somewhat early and with undue vigour, turning back ships laden
with flour and other foodstuffs. When a Memorial was presented to them
by the London Merchants they relented and the British garrison quartered in New York and preparing for battle was able to be fed. The Privy
Council records are full of such misunderstandings, especially concerning privateers which may, or may not, have been operating under the flag
of the Royal Navy, but were claiming prize money or goods.

What the records are not full of, the elephant in the room in modern
terms, is information about slavery. At a later date, William Pitt set up two
Privy Council Committees of Inquiry, but at this time there was almost
nothing; another example of how great events in our nation's story can
by-pass history according to the Privy Council. It can only be said in mit-
igation that the Privy Council was not trying to write history. However,
the official scriveners of the Council did have one element common to
many writers. When really angry, they used capitals. This is an opinion
– they were not able to send an instruction – the Council wrote to South
Carolina and Jamaica in an attempt to dissuade them from holding frequent elections to their assemblies:

> The Limiting of the Duration of the Assemblies to Short Periods
> and fixing their Determination by Law, Manifestly tends to the Dis-
> couragement of Industry and the Prejudice of Trade, Destroys Good
> Neighbourhood, keeps up ill Blood, nourishes a Spirit of Party Divi-
> sions, and gives Faction and Opportunity to Act with better Concert
> and to Greater Effect.

CHAPTER SEVENTEEN

'IT SHALL BE LAWFUL FOR
HIS MAJESTY BY ORDER'

WITH THE LINE OF succession to the throne settled for the foreseeable future, the functions and
duties of the Board of Trade firmly established
and a new appointment of Secretary of State for
Colonial Affairs to run a new government department answerable in
Parliament, much of the old, 'dramatic' work of the Privy Council was
being done elsewhere. Its judicial responsibilities were still in place,
though in many areas this was restricted in working terms to being the
final court of appeal, and the Council and its committees were continually used as a conduit for parliamentary and political inquiry. Most of
its day-to-day work was done by Orders in, or Orders of, Council. And
the difference? Well, here is the explanation given in 1928 by the former

Clerk (from 1898 to 1923) of the Council Sir Almeric Fitzroy in his book
The History of the Privy Council:

> The great mass of the Council's work is done through the medium of
> Orders in Council and to a less degree by Orders of Council, the dif-
> ference between which it is probably not going too far to say that not
> one man in a thousand could explain. Orders in Council are of the first
> rank in importance and in every case are approved by the Monarch
> in Council, while Orders of Council are of humbler administrative
> utility and may owe their sanction to two or three Counsellors or in
> some instances to the Lord President alone.

Immediately it is obvious what an extremely useful method this was –
and is – for a government to introduce legislation onto the Statute Book.
No debate in either of the Houses of Parliament! Perhaps a keenly eyed
Member of Parliament or peer might spot what is going on, but the whips
are on hand to deal with any possible trouble. Here is Sir Almeric Fitzroy describing the situation in his book, published over eighty years ago.
The first reaction of anyone who follows politics and parliament reading
this must be: this is true today:

> These Orders in English legislation have of late years come much into
> request, as with the growing difficulty in getting Bills through Par-
> liament they have appealed both to puzzled draftsmen and harassed
> Ministers as a convenient mode of forestalling or fending off obstruc-
> tion; so that the formula, 'It shall be lawful for His Majesty by Order',
> to do this or the other has become a very useful expedient, with the
> result of a large addition to the responsibilities of the Council.

For many periods when times were quiet during the end of the eighteenth

century the work of the Council attracted little attention, but this changed
with the outbreak of the Napoleonic Wars and the challenge this brought
to English commerce. Orders in Council concerning trade began to be
questioned; not just the substance of Orders but also their constitutional
validity. Both Britain and France adopted a tit-for-tat policy of trading
restrictions and the attempted blockade of each others' ports. A question was asked in the House of Commons, 'What power has the Privy
Council by an Order in Council to restrict commerce in an emergency
or otherwise?' The answer was,

> In these circumstances the power of the King in Council by Order to
> restrict commerce is exercised under statute, the goods prohibited
> being munitions of war, naval and military stores, and such things as
> may be converted into them including any sort of victual which may
> be used as food for man.

Britain (like France) issued licences of trade so that neutral countries
could still in certain circumstances trade with the enemy of the country
granting the licence – the ships would be let through a blockade. In the
case of Britain, an important constitutional development was evolving.
The King in Council was not issuing, or withholding, licences on their
own initiative but on the request, which was in fact an instruction, of the
executive government. The principle Orders with regard to the Napoleonic Wars were listed by the Privy Council in the *Annual Review* on
7 January 1807 and showed that their main aim was to pacify the trading
aspirations of neutral nations. When, five years later, these Orders were
attacked in the House of Commons, George Canning, who had been the
Tory Foreign Secretary when the Orders were issued, stressed that these
statuary instruments were not Orders of policy but of retaliation. It was
not the government initiating new measures, which would require an Act

of Parliament, but responding to events. A defence that has been used ever since, especially in wartime, when an Order has sometimes been attacked for not being based on a substantive Act. There is one other justification for issuing Orders in Council not based on a Parliamentary Act and that is 'ancient usage'. The very nature of this immemorial phrase means that explanations of case history are difficult. Illustration by example is much easier. The Royal Navy provided a case in point in the late eighteenth century. After Captain James Cook was murdered in the Sandwich Islands on 14 February 1779, an Order in Council was issued in the form of a prayer to the king asking for a pension to be granted to his widow and sons.

> This meritorious officer, after having received from your Majesty's gracious benevolence, as a reward for his services in two successful circumnavigations, a comfortable and honourable retreat, where he might have lived many years to benefit his family, he voluntarily relinquished that ease and emolument to undertake another of the voyages of discovery in which the life of a commander who does his duty must always be particularly exposed, and in which, in the execution of that duty, he fell; leaving his family, whom his public spirit had led him to abandon, as a legacy to his country.

This was the way the Royal Navy did – and to a limited extent still does – its business. Why did the Admiralty work this way? Here is the explanation offered by Sir Almeric Fitzroy:

> The practice is traditionally assumed to rest upon the close association of naval interests with the Crown, a theory which the investigation of past conciliar action affecting the functions and status of the Lord High Admiral goes far to confirm. This title goes back to the Plantagenets,

and the patronage of the Crown may perhaps be due to the lesser
risk of giving its fostering care to a fleet in preference to reliance on
feudal armies.

At that time much of work of the Admiralty came directly under the Privy
Council. This was mainly due to the tradition that had grown up of the
Lord High Admiral being one of the most senior posts on the Council,
much older than whatever formal title was held by whoever was in overall
command of the army. The War Office as an institution only dates back
to the Restoration. The Royal Navy dates back to the twelfth century.
No wonder it takes pride in being called the Senior Service. The Privy
Council has always taken a great detailed interest in the administration
of the Admiralty and by a series of Orders in Council have organised the
mix of sailors, politicians and civil servants who have had responsibility
for the fleet. The Board of the Admiralty, which consisted of the Lords
of the Admiralty under the Lord High Admiral, was formed from the old
Navy Board and was first put into commission in 1628. In 1831, it also took
over the Commissioners of Victualling, who were concerned with ship-
building, dockyards and naval stores. By 1914, the Board consisted of the
First Lord of the Admiralty as the government minister (sitting in either
House) and four Sea Lords concerned with preparations for war; personnel; ships and armaments; supply and transport. There was another
sailor as the Civil Lord with special duties. Two politicians from Parliament sat on the Board, a Financial Secretary and a Parliamentary Secretary
and three civil servants led by the Permanent Secretary. Over the last 100
years there have been many changes in the administrative structure of the
Admiralty, the most significant being when all three services lost their
separate voices in government. In the 1950s, though not in the Cabinet
but coming under the Ministry of Defence, there were three ministers of
Secretary of State rank, who served as:

The First Lord of the Admiralty (The Royal Navy)

The Secretary of State for War (The Army)

The Secretary of State for Air (The Royal Air Force)

The records show that, generally speaking, all who held these posts felt themselves on the side of their service battling for their respective interests in whatever administration – Liberal, Conservative or Labour – they served. The Prime Minister Margaret Thatcher changed that. In 1979, she had appointed the MP for Meriden, Keith Speed, as Parliamentary Under-Secretary of State for Defence for the Royal Navy. As the title could not at that stage be got rid of, Speed also became the First Lord of the Admiralty. (This is a common problem for prime ministers trying to manipulate our unwritten constitution to introduce what they consider will be improvements, as Tony Blair later found when he tried to get rid of the ancient office of the Lord Chancellor.) A former Royal Naval officer, educated at Dartmouth and a serving lieutenant commander in the Royal Naval Reserve, Speed was delighted to accept this appointment and redesigned and wore the uniform of the post made famous earlier in the twentieth century by the many pictures of Winston Churchill in that role. Fiercely loyal to the Senior Service, Speed protested privately and spoke publicly about the cuts the Prime Minister wanted to make to the navy. It was not in Mrs Thatcher's style to allow this and she asked Speed to resign. He refused and was therefore sacked. The Prime Minister then changed the structure of the Defence Department so that ministers were not able to identify with and speak for an individual service. This released pressure on all future prime ministers and they have been grateful for this. The structure of the ministerial team at the Department of Defence now, and for some time, has read, more boringly, along these lines:

Secretary of State for Defence

Minister of State for the Armed Forces

Parliamentary Under-Secretary of State (International Security
    Strategy)

Parliamentary Under-Secretary of State (Defence, Personnel,
    Welfare and Veterans)

Parliamentary Under-Secretary of State (spokesperson in House of
    Lords)

Parliamentary Under-Secretary of State (Defence Equipment,
    Support and Technology)

The name 'Admiralty' has not been entirely relegated to history. The judicial system still has Admiralty Courts. As for the triumphal Admiralty
Arch, with its commanding view from Trafalgar Square down the mall
to Buckingham Palace, there is talk of it being turned into private flats.

The nineteenth century was the period when the Privy Council started
to consolidate its role as the body that looked after the bits and pieces of
the constitution. Orders in Council were one of the bits which has grown
steadily over the years, often involving the Council in lengthy detailed
work with ministerial departments. In the nineteenth century, a typical
example of this was the commission of three civil servants set up by the
Privy Council to work with the Home Office and the Treasury looking
into the boundaries that would be needed to establish the electoral dis-
tricts for local government in the London area. Over the years when the
commission sat, 224 Orders in Council were signed by the monarch, the
result being the London Government Act, which passed through Parliament and received the Royal Assent in 1898.

An area of work that began to increase at this time was the awarding of
Royal Charters. This was due to the rise of the professions and the desire
by those working in them to achieve a royally recognised status. It was

especially true of all the branches of the medical and allied professions. As a result, as well as the corporate medical Charters, the following Acts of Parliament were also prepared and administrated by the Privy Council:

> The Pharmacy Acts
> The Dentists Acts
> The Veterinary Surgeons Acts
> The Medical Acts

The last of these was the most important, establishing in 1886 the General Medical Council and giving it the power to oversee qualifications and decide levels of reciprocity with medical practitioners from other countries. Perhaps of more interest and note was the Pharmacy Act, which gave the Privy Council the duty to study the recommendations of the Pharmaceutical Society and decide which substances should be added to the number of regulated poisons which often became an interesting footnote for the large numbers of readers of Victorian murder novels where the use of poison was a growing weapon of choice.

One of the most important functions of the Council was – and is – to issue public Proclamations. These are of two types. The first are purely formal and ceremonial, such as the death of the monarch, the dissolution of Parliament or the declaration of a bank holiday. The second is in response to events and, as Prime Minister Harold Macmillan famously replied when asked what was the most difficult thing to cope with as PM, 'Events, dear boy. Events.' It was at this time, between the Napoleonic Wars and the Great War, that the Privy Council had to get used to differences of opinion about this kind of Proclamation. The Privy Council had decided that after the disaster at the start of the Boer War there should be a Day of Humiliation. Queen Victoria objected. Sir Almeric Fitzroy described her attitude as 'being in substance that while prayer and humbleness before God was correct, humiliation suggested a craven spirit and a confession that her country was in the wrong, a position to which in no circumstances was she willing to accede'. The Privy Council backed down.

One of the Orders in Council affecting Proclamations which did, and still could, cause disagreement, is the monarch's obligation under the Royal Marriages Act to give consent in Council to all descendants of George II when they wish to wed. In 1905, Edward VII argued with the Council that as King of England he had no right to have any say over the marriage of the Duke of Coburg, as the duke was a reigning prince of another country. The Council insisted that if the duke was to retain his contingent rights the king's consent was essential, quoting as precedent Queen Victoria giving consent to the marriage of the Royal Prince of Hanover in 1842. Other cases examined by the Council were the marriages of Princess Alice of Albany, 1903, and the Duke of Cumberland in 1912.

One of the oldest duties of the Privy Council, the pricking of the sheriffs, almost resulted in the death of the entire Cabinet. This is another activity which takes its validity from ancient usage. The names of those about to become sheriffs are pricked by the monarch by thrusting a gold-headed bodkin through each selected name on a parchment roll. No one knows why. When King Edward VII asked, he was told by the Lord President, 'Sir, it goes back to a time when Your Majesty's ancestors were more expert with the sword than the pen.' The selection of sheriffs used to be done at dinner given by the Lord President of the Council to his colleagues. In 1820, this dinner was due to be held at 44 Grosvenor Square, London, the home of the President, Lord Harrowby. For the Lord President and the Cabinet, it could well have been their last meal.

CHAPTER EIGHTEEN

THE CATO STREET
CONSPIRACY

I T MAY SEEM STRANGE that an investigation into how correct pronunciation could be an aide for teaching children to improve their
reading and spelling was once the basis for a plot to murder the Prime
Minister and twenty-seven Privy Counsellors, including the entire
British Cabinet. But, in 1820, that was the case. This investigation, the
work of the self-taught, radical, educator Thomas Spence, had grabbed
the attention of Arthur Thistlewood, a fifty-year-old former army officer
from Lincolnshire whose whole life – apart from a year spent in jail for
challenging the Home Secretary Lord Sidmouth to a duel – had revolved
around intrigue and political plots. Travel in Europe and America had
put him in touch with revolutionary thought and practicing revolutionar-
ies. On his return to England in 1816, he joined the Society of Spencean

Philanthropists, committed to perpetuate the works of Thomas Spence, and soon became their leader. For Spence was more than an English teacher with new and, to many people, shockingly original ideas. He believed that if pronunciation was taught so that everybody spoke with the same accent, class distinctions established by language would disappear. According to his writings and speeches, he also believed that the goal of individual freedom could only be achieved by the collective and communal ownership of land and property.

Spence outlined his ideas in a pamphlet, *Property in Land, Every One's Right*, in 1795, which was later reissued under the title of *The Real Rights of Man*. For this to work fairly and effectively, everybody, men and women, had to have a vote. Spence was constantly in trouble with the authorities, spending long periods in prison on charges ranging from High Treason to seditious libel. He led a hand-to-mouth existence running a bookstall in London at High Holborn but he had a plan to change the world – or at least the way government worked in Britain. Given the first and most important aspiration of that plan, it is not surprising he attracted to his cause some of the most fiery and violent radicals in London. Spence's leading ambition as quoted from his plan was: '1. The end of aristocracy and landlords.' After he became their leader, his revolutionary supporters in the Society of Spencean Philanthropists were very happy to change their tactics and switch to more violent methods to achieve their political ends. They looked to encourage riots to entice the masses to bring down the upper classes and the government (though they made little distinction between the two) and more specifically and immediately to take control of both the Tower of London and the Bank of England.

The police by this time had managed to place a number of informers into the various radical groups operating in London and, through the activities of John Castle, who operated within the Spencean group, were well placed on 2 December 1816 to deal with a mass meeting called

outside the Dissenters' Chapel at Spa Fields in Clerkenwell for an upris-
ing to march on the Bank. Thistlewood and three others were arrested
and were due to be charged with High Treason but the police released
them, perhaps thinking it was easier to keep an eye on known leaders
rather than spend time establishing who had taken their place.

Like so many groups on the political left, the Spencean Philanthropists believed in organising themselves into various cells and meeting
in small groups. Then, if one group was discovered, others could carry
on. They met mostly in public houses, the Cock in Soho, the Mulberry
Tree in Moorfields and the White Lion in Camden being popular ven-
ues. Sometimes open meetings were held in pubs and audiences invited
to come and listen to readings from radical journals. One police spy
reported that 150 men attended a session at the Mulberry Tree to listen
to Robert Wedderburn read from the works of William Cobbett as well
as extracts from his own journal, *The Forlorn Hope*. In 1819, at a meeting
in Soho, Wedderburn charged people 6d a head to listen to what were
described as seditious and anti-Christian speeches. Wedderburn had an
interesting background: free born in Jamaica to an African house slave
and a Scottish doctor, he came to England and served in the navy and
then settled to a life of petty crime and radical politics, at some point
becoming a Unitarian Methodist preacher. He was heavily influenced
by William Cobbett's *Weekly Political Register* (later to become famous
as the author of the bestseller *Rural Rides*) and espoused the campaigns
against poverty and argued for land and property reforms. There is evidence that the police considered him a greater threat than Thistlewood
and, to get him off the streets and his sermons out of the chapels, tried
to fit him up as a brothel keeper. He was one of the leading exponents
of the Spencean group wanting to take direct action in the class war and
with Thistlewood managed to gather around them about thirty men
who talked longingly in pubs about their desire to murder the Prime

Minister Lord Liverpool, together with George Canning, Lord Sidmouth, Lord Harrowby, and all the other toffs who were the senior members of the Privy Council. Some were more vivacious than others, especially John Brunt, John Ings, Richard Tidd, William Davidson and George Edwards. Thistlewood found Davidson and Edwards particularly useful. Davidson had worked in Lord Harrowby's household as a servant and knew that as Lord President of the Council he would be holding the traditional Cabinet dinner to pick the country's new sheriffs on 24 February 1820 at his home in Grosvenor Square. Harrowby upset people. Not just servants like Davidson whom he had sacked a few months previously and who had found comfort and support among his new friends in the London pubs where they discussed and plotted rebellion and revolution. Harrowby also upset other politicians and statesmen, even the President of the United States James Monroe. When Harrowby was Foreign Secretary under Pitt's premiership in 1805, Monroe complained that every word the British Foreign Secretary addressed to him had been a calculated insult to both the office of President and to the American people. It was partly because of this tendency that the peer found himself demoted in Cabinet under Liverpool to serve as Lord President of the Privy Council, a post which had dropped a few notches in parliamentary ranking in the last fifty years.

This was not an attitude likely to deter those who saw blowing up his house as a method for showing their hatred of the governing class. The industrial revolution had created great social unrest. Population movements from country to town and the changing pattern and nature of jobs and working conditions had produced a climate of uncertainty, sometimes fear, and a deep distrust by many of both the Whigs and the Tories. At first, Lord Liverpool was not a leader inclined to look with any sympathy on those opposing him and instituted repressive measures after the riots of 1819. He later started to look for compromise in political action but, at the time Thistlewood and his friends were plotting, Liverpool was very unpopular. He had abolished Habeas Corpus in 1817, and passed a repressive Act of Parliament which limited both free speech and limited the right to meet in public places for the purpose of demonstrating against the government. The use of police informers was widespread. In this atmosphere, rumour and dissent flourished.

One who was adept at using these conditions to encourage the ambitions of the Spencean Philanthropists was George Edwards. Other members of the group found him a bit of a mystery man. They wondered how someone who had barely earned any money working as an assistant to a plasterer and statue maker could have afforded to open a shop near Windsor Castle and how he seemed both to have access to shady merchants who could supply gunpowder and weapons and also have friends who had secret information about Privy Council meetings. But as in those times conspirators operated under many different guises and in a variety of roles, the Spenceans accepted his enthusiasm and practical help. Indeed, Thistlewood appointed him his second-in-command. Edwards spurred them on with relish to launch an attack at the Privy Council dinner at the home of the Lord President. All the Cabinet could be killed in one night. Probably twenty-seven Privy Counsellors would be there, including eleven lords, plus the Duke of Wellington, who had entered the Cabinet the previous year in the post of Master-General of the Ordinance. Edwards also told them that the Master of the Mint, William Wellesley-Pole, would be present – what a great chance to get at the man who actually made the real money that the government then denied to ordinary people! The Cabinet also contained two members who had not exactly set a good example to the electorate in matters of decorum and high standards in public life. In his book *Pistols at Dawn*, John Campbell makes the point that the hostility between Tony Blair and Gordon Brown was both extreme and well known outside Westminster, but at least they didn't try to settle their differences as two previous Privy Counsellors did by fighting a duel on Putney Heath. Which is what Lord Castlereagh, who was Foreign Secretary in Liverpool's Cabinet, and George Canning (who was briefly – for five months – Prime Minister in 1827), then President of the Board of Control, had done on 21 September 1809. The actual confrontation was an anti-climax. Campbell writes that

> both missed with first shots; but Castlereagh, unusually, insisted on a second round, and this time hit his opponent as neatly as possible through the fleshy part of his thigh. Some reports claim that Canning shot a button off the lapel on Castlereagh's coat, if so, that sounds nearly more fatal than Canning's wound. As it was, however, neither man was seriously hurt.

How ironic it would have been if two leading political aristocratic Privy Counsellors, fellow ministers in the same Cabinet, having failed to kill each other were later killed together by radical political opponents at the house of the Lord President of their Council. There are traces of irony about the whole affair. The political fallout after the failed shots of the duel led to Spencer Perceval becoming Prime Minister. He was fatally shot in the lobby of the House of Commons on 11 May 1812 by John Bellingham and remains the only PM ever to have been assassinated. (The descendent of the murderer, Henry Bellingham, was elected Conservative MP for North West Norfolk in 2001.) And the sad irony continued. Two years after Thistlewood and Edwards had planned to murder the whole Cabinet, Castlereagh, who was now seriously ill with mental problems, cut his own throat at his home Loring Hall near Sidcup in Kent.

To plan their murders in detail, the conspirators had rented a small house, 6 Cato Street, on Lord Portman's estate in Marylebone, north London. In reality it was more of an attic above a stable. They decided that any attempt to destroy the whole of Lord Harrowby's mansion with bombs was unrealistic so they set their sights on obtaining enough guns, ammunition and daggers from Edwards's contacts to kill each Privy Counsellor individually. They would attack the Cabinet in the dining room and the heads of Lord Sidmouth, the Home Secretary, and his chief supporter, Lord Castlereagh, would be carried away in a bag to be displayed on spikes outside the Mansion House, to where they would march and set up the headquarters of a provisional government. There was apparently some dispute about the beheadings, one of the conspirators, a butcher, James Ings, insisted he would decapitate all the Cabinet and then display the heads on Westminster Bridge. There was certainly a dispute about the part played by George Edwards. A dispute which eventually led to a full-scale debate in the House of Commons about whether Edwards had been employed by the police as an agent provocateur. In fact, the Cato Street conspiracy was not much of a conspiracy. So many people seemed to have advanced knowledge about the plan that the operation could hardly be dignified with the title of a plot. On 23 February, the night that the murder of the Privy Counsellors was to take place, a London magistrate, Richard Birnie, was so confident that his services would be called upon before the day was out that in the afternoon he took up a position in a pub in Cato Street, supping his beer and waiting for a Bow Street runner to call him. He was later joined by a police spy, George Ruthven, who told him that the Home Secretary had arranged for a detachment from the Coldstream Guards, led by George III's grandson, Lieutenant FitzClarence, to raid the loft of No. 6 at around seven o'clock. The Bow Street runners, not wishing to be upstaged by the Coldstream, also launched an attack on No. 6 at seven. In the resulting brawl, Arthur Thistlewood killed a police officer, Richard Smithers, with a sword. Some conspirators fought; others climbed out of a back window. Eleven escaped completely but twelve others were caught in the next few days.

They came to court on 28 April charged with:

1. Conspiring to murder divers of the Privy Council.

2. Providing arms to murder divers of the Privy Council.

3. Conspiring to devise plans to subvert the Constitution.

4. Conspiring to levy war.

5. Conspiring to burn houses and barracks and to provide combustibles for that purpose.

6. Preparing an Address to the king's subjects, containing therein that their tyrants were destroyed and to incite them to assist in levying war and in subverting the Constitution.

7. Assembling themselves with arms, with intent to murder divers of the Privy Council.

Two of the captured conspirators, Robert Adams and John Monument, were given free pardons in return for providing king's evidence. The others were all sentenced to be hung, drawn and quartered. However, this was later commuted to transportation for five of them, while the ringleaders, Thistlewood, Davidson, Brunt, Ings and Richard Tidd, suffered the lesser punishment of being hanged and then beheaded. This took place at Newgate Prison on the morning of 1 May 1820 in front of a vast crowd whose sympathies were all with those being executed. Two troops of the Life Guards were on standby in case the Riot Act had to be read and the executioner and his assistants who did the beheadings were soundly booed.

By now it was generally believed that the whole episode had been set up by George Edwards, many believing at the instigation of the government. He was spirited away before the trial began and was the main subject of a debate in the Commons called by Matthew Wood MP, who accused the government of using Edwards for 'the purposeful entrapment of their opponents to smear their campaign for parliamentary reform'.

Wood maintained that it was all a set up and that no Privy Counsellor was ever in the slightest danger of losing his life. Nevertheless, the Cato Street story has been the subject of books, plays and radio drama. In 1827, the name of Cato Street was changed, but now that the little houses are smart town apartments, the original name has been restored and a blue plaque put in place as a reminder of what happened on the evening of 23 February 1820. Later on that night the Privy Counsellors sat down in the Lord President's house to enjoy their dinner and pick the sheriffs for 1821.

Nearly 200 years later, that tradition still continues. The duties and status of the post of High Sheriff used to be shrouded in mystery. Now at least the High Sheriffs' Association of England and Wales publishes a list of people who can't even be considered, such as postmen and tax collectors. This can't be a snobbery consideration because judges, MPs, officers in the armed services and Members of the Welsh Assembly are also excluded. Nominations for this most ancient of public positions are made to the Presiding Judge of the Circuit and the Privy Council and are then considered by the Queen in Council. After the monarch has pricked each successful name with the bodkin, the new sheriffs receive the following citation:

> WHEREAS HER MAJESTY was this day pleased, by and with the advice of HER PRIVY COUNCIL to nominate you for, and appoint you to be HIGH SHERIFF of the COUNTY of ... during HER MAJESTY'S PLEASURE; These are therefore to require you to take the Custody and Charge of the said COUNTY and duly to perform the duties of HIGH SHERIFF thereof during HER MAJESTY'S PLEASURE whereof you are duly to answer according to law.

The search for potential candidates has moved on from the old boys' network of past centuries, with consultative panels of independent members formed in every county, but there is one stipulation that hasn't changed and might well be as big a drawback for some candidates as it would have been in 1820. The High Sheriffs' Association makes this point very forcibly: 'The Office of High Sheriff is carried out on a wholly voluntary basis with no part of the expense incurred by the High Sheriff falling on the public purse.'

CHAPTER NINETEEN

'WHAT IS BAPTISM?'
THE PRIVY COUNCIL *V.*
THE BISHOP OF EXETER

WHILE THE CATO STREET conspirators were making their mark as a footnote in history, and would have made a much bigger one had they succeeded in their aims of murdering twenty-seven Privy Counsellors, the Reverend Henry Phillpotts, the 42-year-old vicar of the vastly rich living of Stanhope in Durham, was quietly moving towards his clash with the Privy Council. In the twenty-first century, for doctrinal matters of the Church of England to gain media attention, a large component of gender or sexual orientation has to be included. In the nineteenth century, a story concerning disputes in the higher ranks of the clergy about the meaning of baptism and the interpretation of the Gospels held the nation's attention. Henry Phillpotts relished controversy. The son of the land agent to the Dean and Chapter of Gloucester Cathedral, he had real ability as a public speaker. Having been elected a scholar at Corpus Christi, Oxford, at the age of thirteen, he graduated from Magdalen five years later and took Holy Orders in 1802. He became the University Preacher in 1804. He collected jobs and positions and hung on to them. Being a pluralist was not uncommon in the Church at that time. For two years he had held the Crown position of Vicar of Kilmersdon near Bath without actually living there but delegating all his duties to a curate, Daniel Drape. When he was appointed Bishop of Exeter in 1831 at a salary of £3,000, he retained a position in Durham as a canon of the cathedral for a fee of £4,000 per year. A high church Tory, he was forthright and dominant in his views and cared little about being an unpopular priest. In the same year that he became Bishop of Exeter, he saw himself being burnt in the Cathedral Yard as an effigy on Guy Fawkes night. He used his connections in high places to have a troop from the 7th Yeoman Cavalry stationed in the Bishop's Palace for his own protection. He later built another palace at Torquay (now the Palace Hotel) in Devon for the safety of his wife and eighteen children.

In *The Victorian Church*, Parts 1 and 2, Owen Chadwick describes the attitude towards him from the clergy of the Church of England:

> So long as Henry Phillpotts was Bishop of Exeter they avoided the Diocese of Exeter, for they knew that this doughty fighter would fight them to the end if he smelt something improper, whatever the cost to his pocket, however unfavourable the publicity, and whatever the inadequacy of his own legal standing.

He was the cleric who inspired the classic quotation from the Reverend Sydney Smith, the priest who famously believed that being in heaven would be like eating pate foie gras to the sound of trumpets. Smith said, 'I must believe in the Apostolic Succession, there being no other way of accounting for the descent of the Bishop of Exeter from Judas Iscariot.' Comments which can still be heard muttered in the comfort of the Athenaeum in Pall Mall – and not always about the old Bishop of Exeter.

If Phillpotts was looking for trouble, he found it in abundance in 1847 in his own diocese in the village of Brampford Speke in Devon, a few miles from Exeter. The spark that lit the conflagration which would eventually arrive at the upper reaches of the Privy Council was provided by an exceptionally bright Cambridge priest, George Cornelius Gorman, who had graduated with high honours but had his own views on the nature of baptism, which conflicted with the Established Church to such an extent that the Bishop of Ely expressed grave doubts when he ordained him in 1811. Sixteen years after Phillpotts took over the Diocese of Exeter, he had instituted Gorman as vicar of St Just in Cornwall. The diocese then stretched from the Dorset–Devon border to the Isles of Scilly and possibly it was the sheer size of the diocese and the many livings for which he was responsible that meant the bishop had not the time to engage with Gorman on his religious views. But in 1847 there was a vacancy for an incumbent at Brampford Speke and the bishop took it upon himself to conduct an examination with Gorman to judge his suitability for the post. And what an examination. It lasted five days. Unlike today's interviews with candidates seeking posts in the Church of England, there was no mention of outreach activities, media capability or skills with management and human resources. This was solid theology. In particular, the discussions centred on Gorman's views on baptism. To put it in the simplest possible terms – which it certainly wasn't at later stages in the Court of Arches and the Privy Council – Gorman did not believe that baptismal regeneration was absolute. He believed that the power of baptism was conditional on future promises being made when the infants could understand what they were doing. Actually, the bishop, in deciding that Gorman should not be appointed, did put it in simple terms. He called Gorman a Calvinist. The significance of that was that the 1689 London Baptist Declaration of Faith to which the Calvinists – more generally known as being part of the much wider United Reformed Church – regarded baptism not as a sacrament but as an ordinance. This was all very complex but one of the basic differences between a Calvinist priest and a vicar in the Church of England was that a Calvinist believed that only adults and the infants of believers could be baptised, whereas the Church of England believed that all infants could be baptised. If Gorman took the Calvinist view then, obviously, according to the Bishop of Exeter, he could not function as a Church of England priest.

Gorman followed the normal practice in his Church of appealing to the Court of Arches to overturn the Bishop's decision that he was not a fit person to become the vicar of Brampford Speke. The Court of Arches has been in existence since the thirteenth century. Its original home was – and still is – St Mary-le-Bow on Cheapside in the City of London, though it sometimes meets at St Paul's Cathedral. It is within the sound of the bells of St Mary-le-Bow that all true cockneys are born and the court takes its name from the arches in the crypt where the first sessions were held. It functions as the domestic court for the province of Canterbury (York has a similar Chancery Court). The presiding officer is called the Dean and must be a barrister or judge of some standing. The subject matter of its cases is widespread but many concern problems of the employment and morality of priests in the Church of England.

In 1847, the Dean of the Court was a Privy Counsellor, the Rt Hon. Sir Herbert Jenner-Fust, a King's Advocate-General who had been appointed as vicar-general to the Archbishop of Canterbury in 1834, becoming Dean and presiding judge of the Court of Arches two years later. On Gorman's appeal to the dean, the Bishop of Exeter, always willing to enter a fight, having refused him the living of Brampford Speke, also charged him with heresy. The trial lasted three years and aroused much interest, with over eighty different tracts and pamphlets being published expressing different points of view. Eventually the dean ruled in favour of the Bishop of Exeter and made Gorman liable for all costs. Gorman immediately appealed to the Privy Council, the parent body for the Court of Arches. The first duty that Lord Lansdowne, the Lord President of the Council, had was to form an appropriate court. For reasons not entirely clear, the body of the Privy Council to which appeals from the ecclesiastical courts were directed was the 3 and 4 Court established under William IV for the hearing of complaints from the colonies. According to Sir Almeric Fitzroy in *The History of the Privy Council*, 'This is because of the haphazard methods which were used in connection with appeals to the Crown in Council.' Under the terms of the Church Discipline Act, all prelates who were Privy Counsellors could sit in this court as Assessors. Fitzroy goes on to stress the haphazard nature of this procedure by writing that the court's jurisdiction 'embraces all concerns in Admiralty or Vice-Admiralty Courts in the domain of the Crown, and includes any other subject that may be referred by the Crown to the Judicial Committee for hearing and consideration'. The protocols of the work of this committee, sometimes described as a court, go back to an Order in Council of 1627, and are as follows:

1. The judgment of the Judicial Committee is made in the form of a statement of the reasons which determine them in advising the monarch to give effect to their decisions.

2. When the report is approved by the king meeting in Council an Order is made affirming that as the judgment of the king.

3. No record of dissentient opinion is permitted.

4. If voting takes place at any stage no publication is afterwards to be
    made of how the particular votes and opinions went.

5. It is the indefeasible right of the Privy Council to consult the Law
    Officers of the Crown should they feel the need arises.

The Lord President knew that the case of the Bishop of Exeter and
George Gorman would excite great public interest. Indeed, in Greville's
Memoirs, already referred to as the most celebrated record of social life
of that period, the Gorman case takes up more pages than any other episode outside of politics. Perhaps that is not surprising when one thinks
of the intense specialist and public debate that was to come only a few
years later following the publication of Charles Darwin's *The Origin of
The Species*. Rows concerning religion were hot topics in the middle of
the nineteenth century.

To select the most suitable committee, Lansdowne called a full meeting
of the entire Judicial Committee. It was decided that both Archbishops
and the Bishop of London were essential members of the court. Lord
Parke, who had been a most distinguished Lord of the Exchequer, was
appointed the senior judge, assisted by Sir Lewis Knight-Bruce, a Vice-
Chancellor of the Court of Chancery. Three lords, Langdale, who was
also Master of the Rolls, Kingsdowne and Campbell were also appointed
together with an experienced member of the Judicial Committee, Dr
Lushington. Having studied the papers for the case, the Lord President,
Lord Lansdowne, explained to the Court that he really felt out of his depth
in this argument but would always be available to offer any help that he
could. Both the Bishop of Exeter and George Gorman had learned counsel to represent them and, encouraged by the bishop, his lawyer, Edward
Badley, launched an attack on the Archbishop of Canterbury for allowing a man with such dreadful views as Gorman to become a priest in the
first place. The Archbishop agreed that he had given Gorman the living

but pleaded that he had no idea of Gorman's views at the time. As the argument raged back and forth, the point to be decided seemed to be focused on this: just because the Archbishops and senior bishops of the Church declared that 'something' was God's will – was that necessarily the case? Gorman's lawyer argued that if the bishop had said, 'This is God's will in relation to baptism,' and stopped, there would be no legal case for Gorman to bring forward because the Established Church was simply making an absolute declaration about God which it had a right, some might even say a duty, to do. It was because the bishop had got involved in theological discussion to try to prove his point that he had admitted that he had to accept that there were serious opinions – different to his – reasonably held by other members of the Church of England.

To the surprise of many following the case, which ran from the end of January to 9 March 1850, both the Archbishops agreed with Gorman, the Archbishop of Canterbury saying that 'opinions, if not identical, yet very like those of Gorman had been held by a host of great and good churchmen'. He was 'strongly of the opinion that the Bishop of Exeter was not justified in refusing to induct the Reverend George Gorman to the living of Brampford Speke'.

The Bishop of London disagreed. He thought that Gorman held and had expressed positions 'inconsistent with the efficacy of the Baptismal Sacrament'. All three prelates wrote papers giving their decisions, two for Gorman, one against. After hearing witnesses and involving themselves in much cross-examination, the members of the court then asked the Master of the Rolls to prepare an initial judgment, agreeing with a caveat from the Bishop of London that nothing should be written condemnatory of the Bishop of Exeter's substantive opinions on this matter. The Master of the Rolls declared that he thought the Court of Arches had made a mistake in supporting the Bishop of Exeter and also in awarding all the costs to be paid by Gorman. The presiding judge, Lord Parke, agreed

with the Master of the Rolls and Lord Campbell took a similar line. Dr
Luishington, who had spoken at length, reached a very firm conclusion
that the Bishop of Exeter was wrong not only in substance but in trying
to win such a case. If he won, it would mean that the King in Council
would have ruled that Gorman's opinions were heretical and that would
cause great ructions in the Established Church as evidence had shown
that many priests, admittedly to a lesser extent, shared Gorman's views
on baptism. The Vice-Chancellor, Sir Lewis Knight-Bruce, came out in
complete support of the Dean of the Court of Arches and the Bishop
of Exeter. Lord Kingsdowne was hesitant in expressing an opinion but
finally said that the decision of the lower court should be reversed. There
was criticism from the Privy Counsellors of both sides and the manner
in which they had conducted their cases. Dr Lushington said that at the
end of the proceedings he was still not exactly sure with what the Bishop
of Exeter had been charging Gorman, and he also had the greatest difficulty in working out what Gorman's doctrine really was.

So only two of the counsellors, the Bishop of London and Lord Kingsdowne, supported the Court of Arches, while the other seven, including
the two Archbishops, were in favour of Gorman. When this became
known, the Bishop of London, according to Sir Almeric Fitzroy in *The
History of the Privy Council*, 'gave a pitiable display of hesitancy and
vacillation, which brought home to his colleagues the earnestness of the
conviction that it would have better if his attendance had been dispensed
with'. On 8 March, the court was packed for the final judgment and the
building was surrounded with onlookers. Greville wrote in his *Memoirs*: 'The crowd was enormous, the crush and squeeze awful.' There
was jubilation at the outcome, especially in Exeter. Gorman was victo-
rious and no costs against him were awarded. The bishop was ordered
to offer the Reverend George Gorman the living of Brampford Speke in
Devon and Gorman accepted.

Henry Phillpotts did not take this decision by the Privy Council lightly. He considered it usurped his authority as bishop. He called upon the Archbishop of Canterbury to be excommunicated. Fourteen prominent Anglicans, including Phillpotts's lawyer, took matters further. They demanded the Church of England repudiate the views of the Privy Council and when the Church refused to respond they left and joined the Roman Catholic Church. Phillpotts lived out his life as the Bishop of Exeter. A complex character, he aroused strong opinions on all sides. When he died at the age of ninety-one, his obituary in *The Times* read: 'Fierce, fiery and intolerant of opposition to a fault, and sincere and earnest in an age which is not remarkable for earnestness in religion, he held the Anglican Church as the strongest safeguard against Romish and Calvinistic errors.'

Whether he ever came to any rapport with George Gorman is unrecorded, but he did actually give several thousand pounds of his own money to help repair the tower of Gorman's church at Brampford Speke. The bishop was certainly a rich man. In 1856, he founded the Bishop Phillpotts Library in Truro for the benefit of the clergy, which now flourishes with more than 10,000 theological volumes. Where his money came from has been much discussed and a possible answer was put forward in terms of an allegation at the General Synod meeting of the Church of England 137 years after his death when, in 2006, it was suggested that the bishop had based his fortune on the £13,000 (the equivalent of over £1 million today) he had received as compensation for his loss in a joint holding of 665 slaves when they had been emancipated under the Slavery Abolition Act of 1833. A claim which was repeated by the Member of Parliament for Rhondda, a former Labour minister, Chris Bryant, in the House of Commons. This brought an interesting act of serendipity to the nineteenth-century attack on the Bishop of Exeter by a fellow priest. Over 100 years later, the bishop was being attacked by another man who had taken holy orders. The difference between Bryant and Gorman was that Bryant was no longer a priest. He had been the first person to take advantage of the 2010 Removal of the Clergy Disqualification Act and stand for Parliament. During the twentieth century, clergy could only sit in Parliament in the House of Lords, either as prelates or as lesser clergy who had inherited family titles enabling them to be a member of the second chamber. And, for the record, Chris Bryant, whatever else he achieves, has one other historical footnote to his name. Not only is he the first former member of the clergy to sit as an MP but, on 27 March 2010, he became the first person to enter into a civil partnership in a ceremony in the Palace of Westminster when he was publicly united with his partner, Jared Cranney.

CHAPTER TWENTY

THE DOWNTON ERA – SIR ALMERIC FITZROY AS CLERK TO THE PRIVY COUNCIL

A FEW MONTHS AFTER THE Gorman case was concluded, a birth occurred which would have a significant impact on the future chronicling of the activities of the Privy Council. Let us record the event in the words of the new arrival himself, as written in his *Memoirs*:

I was born on 12 November 1851, of the marriage of Francis Horatio FitzRoy and Gertrude Duncombe, daughter of William, 2nd Lord Feversham, and Louisa his wife, daughter of the 8th Earl of Galloway and Lady Jane Paget, sister of the Marquess of Anglesey, of Peninsular and Waterloo fame. My father was the only son of Admiral Lord

William FitzRoy, KCB, sixth son of Augustus Henry, 3rd Duke of
Grafton, 1st Lord of the Treasury, 1766–1770, and his second wife, Elizabeth Wrottesley, a name which stands in the roll of the first Knights
of the Garter in the fourteenth century, and was borne by a President
of the Royal Society in the nineteenth.

Strewth! Note the capital R which appears in his surname. No wonder
Roy Jenkins described these *Memoirs* as outstanding. And the Rt Hon.
Roy Jenkins, one of the most perceptive politicians of the twentieth century was so right. The *Memoirs* are presented in diary form, the first
entry being dated 9 August 1898, and I can't help feeling that the date
is significant because it is six years after that brilliant book, recording
the suburban life of Mr Pooter, *The Diary of a Nobody* by George and
Weedon Grossmith was published. Not because Sir (as he later became)
Almeric FitzRoy was a nobody, far from it, but because I feel that perhaps
he may have been influenced by the style of the prose of the Grossmith
brothers. Here is an extract of Fitzroy's writing from 4 December 1898:

> We spent the Sunday at Stoke with the Allhusens. In the morning I
> took a long walk with Mr Astor, whose burden of £30 million seems
> to weigh heavily upon him. In the intervals, however, of chastened
> reflection, he was both genial and interesting. It is essential to the
> enjoyment of two people who are fond of walking, that they should
> respect each other's silences, and by such means we were soon estab-
> lished on a footing of mutual goodwill.

I would not wish to be unkind to Sir Almeric, but there are others with
some justification to do that. In Anthony Lentin's book *Banker, Traitor,
Scapegoat, Spy*, he describes Fitzroy's part in working towards the removal
of the sponsor of Captain Scott's Antarctic expeditions, the baronet Sir

Edgar Speyer from the Privy Council, as scuttling 'busily behind the scenes, malign and venomous, intent on assisting in his downfall'. Lentin also writes of the Clerk to the Privy Council, 'The social snobbery common in Edwardian society was personified in Sir Almeric Fitzroy.'

Certainly, when one reads the diary entries Fitzroy wrote about Speyer, that could be considered very fair comment. On 22 November 1909, he wrote: 'Sir E. Speyer, a most characteristic little Jew, was apparently quite ready to take the oath on the Testament, so long as he could do it with the rest; but I kept him to his Pentateuch and thus saved the Gospels from outrage.' Not wanting Speyer to become a Privy Counsellor in the first place, Fitzroy then carried on busily behind the scenes to try to obtain his removal, sending secret notes to the Home Office and encouraging judicial inquiry. Diary entry, 15 June 1915:

> The grant by a Divisional Court of a rule *nisi* calling upon Sir Ernest Cassel and Sir E. Speyer to show by what warrant they called themselves Privy Counsellors, raises some curious points. The reply of these gentlemen on the personal issue is direct enough: in presenting themselves to be sworn in they acted under proper authority exercised in obedience to the king's command; but the legal warrant covering the transaction, if it can be challenged, appears open to doubt should it be determined that the prohibition of the Act of Settlement (concerned with the rights of Naturalisation) is still operative.

In taking the view that he did, Sir Almeric Fitzroy was not alone. On the outbreak of the Great War, many people living in the UK but having German parents were ostracised and high society set an example which many followed. In his introduction to Professor Anthony Lentin's book on Speyer, *Banker, Traitor, Scapegoat, Spy*, Sir Louis Blom-Cooper QC writes, 'Sir Edgar Speyer (1862–1932) was a celebrated figure in the financial, cultural and political high life of Edwardian England, a friend of the Liberal Prime Minister, Asquith, he was a generous public benefactor.' But, because of the prevailing attitude in the country, Speyer's business dealings were closely examined and he was found guilty of disloyalty and of trading with Germany during a time of war. However, because there was great uncertainty as to how in the twentieth century Privy Counsellors could be removed from their positions, legal affairs rumbled on. Speyer's offer to resign was seen by some as a goodwill gesture to get the establishment out of a tricky situation and by others as a mark of disrespect to the monarch. It was no longer thought appropriate for the king to exercise royal powers and simply dismiss him. This 1915 state of affairs was described by Fitzroy in his *Memoirs*. It is worth quoting at length because, as well as the substance of the topic being described, it gives a fascinating glimpse of the political and social life of that time. And the way in which Fitzroy wrote of correcting the Lord Chief Justice on a point of law is pure Pooter:

19 December 1915:

I met Lord Reading (the Lord Chief Justice) at Hyde Park Corner, and in walking some way with him, had the opportunity of discussing the Privy Council judgment, on one point of which I had already written to him. He was very civil in promising to put right the error into which he had inadvertently fallen, and I finally put to him the question why he had differentiated in such a marked degree between the two parties to the case in the matter of costs. His answer entirely confirmed my own surmise. Cassel had, as we know, submitted to the Court an affidavit attesting in earnest language his loyalty to the king and to the country of his adoption, whereas Speyer, though formally represented, had in substance told the king and the Privy Council to go hang. His attitude had, in Lord Reading's opinion, been studiously

disrespectful, whereas the other had behaved with the utmost cor-
rectness. I then asked him what he thought of the Speyer firm in New
York becoming the depositary of the huge sum lodged by Germany
in America for furnishing supplies to vessels engaged in the destruction of British commerce. Did he not consider that as E. Speyer had
transferred his commercial activities to the America House, he ought
to be removed from the Privy Council, on either that account, or the
other. He replied, without hesitation, 'Yes.' I then asked him whether
he did not recognise the obligation to represent that view, as strongly
as possible, to the Prime Minister, and he again gave an unqualified
assent; indeed, he added, that unless some such step was taken, grave
trouble would ensure.

20 December 1915
The last meeting of the Royal Commission on Venereal Diseases took
place this afternoon...

Eventually the establishment found a way to get Sir Edgar Speyer removed
from the Privy Council. They revoked his citizenship and he therefore
became unable to serve on the King of the United Kingdom's Privy Council. There was no machinery available for stripping baronets of their titles,
even though there was and still is a permanent Privy Council Committee on the baronetage, so the establishment didn't even try. Not that the
word 'establishment' used in that sense would have been recognised
then. This definition was first coined by Henry Fairlie in *The Spectator*,
23 September 1955:

By 'The Establishment' I do not mean only the centres of official
power – though they are certainly part of it – but rather the whole
matrix of official and social relations within which power is exercised.

The exercise of power in Britain (more specifically in England) cannot be understood unless it is recognised that it is exercised socially.
Anyone who at any point has been close to the exercise of power will
know what I mean when I say that, 'the Establishment' can be seen at
work in the activities of not only the Prime Minister, the Archbishop
of Canterbury and the Earl Marshal, but as such lesser mortals as the
chairman of the Arts Council, the director-general of the BBC and
even the editor of the *Times Literary Supplement*.

That was over fifty years ago. How true is that today? Open to debate. You
might take one view from the City of London's wine bars, another from
the media and entertainment world, and yet a third from slipping into a
Pall Mall club – or one of around six Oxbridge colleges – at lunch time.

But certainly fifty years before Fairlie's piece appeared, 'the Establishment' – even if not called that – was a central part of what many considered
to be the natural order of things. A way of life now glimpsed at in *Downton Abbey*, but at the turn of the twentieth century a way of life which
those in it – for the most part – guarded jealously; and many wished to
enter its portals. Membership of the Privy Council was certainly on the
inside of those portals.

Sir Almeric Fitzroy's *Memoirs* satisfy all the requirements of the best
published reminiscences from Samuel Pepys, through Chips Channon
to Alan Clark. Perceptive and informed, his view of social and political
affairs was always presented through the prism of his own dispositions
and 'while he had a host of friends he also had a multitude of enemies
who eagerly reviewed his diaries with venom'. Words by Robert Rhodes James, a former Clerk of the Parliaments and later an MP – but not
words about Fitzroy. These were Rhodes James's comments in his introduction to the diaries of Sir Henry 'Chips' Channon, which he edited
in 1965. However – and this is the point – they could just as easily have

been applied to the *Memoirs* of Fitzroy. The comparison can be taken further. Rhodes James also wrote about Chips:

> So damning were the reviews that serious historians did not bother to read the diaries. One such was A. J. P. Taylor. Years later with nothing much else to do on a wet afternoon he began to read them and was so riveted that he finished them at one sitting. He then publicly applied the word 'classic' to them.

Substitute the name the Rt Hon. Lord Jenkins for A. J. P. Taylor and the word 'outstanding' for 'classic' and the comparison is complete.

Like Channon at a later date, Fitzroy is sometimes keen to hide his mistakes. Especially if they would be difficult to explain away in print. These episodes make interesting stories, asking but not answering fascinating questions. One such is the strange tale from the Privy Council of the Chancellor who wasn't a Privy Counsellor. There are normally three Chancellors in any UK government, though in the twenty-first century the old legal office of Lord Chancellor, who sat in splendid isolation on the woolsack in the House of Lords, has now been subsumed into the more prosaic Department of Justice. The other two Chancellors are that of the Exchequer, always ranked in the top five Cabinet posts, and that of the Duchy of Lancaster, which, although firmly fixed in the Order of Precedence as being between the Chancellor of the Exchequer and the Lord Chief Justice of England, is now a movable position in the government ranks. In 2014, it was held by the Rt Hon. Lord Hill, who was Leader of the House of Lords, and in a reshuffle it was switched to the Rt Hon. Oliver Letwin, a Privy Counsellor who occupied a curious and relatively new position in government: that of a minister who is not in the Cabinet – that is limited by statute to twenty-two members – but is able to attend their meetings. And there is a curious fact about the post itself.

Under a 1975 Act of Parliament, the salary paid to the Chancellor of the Duchy is reduced by the amount obtained from Lancaster in respect of his work for the Duchy. This tale from the Privy Council concerns the Chancellor of the Duchy of Lancaster.

The name comes from the lands which for several centuries belonged to the Sovereign as Duke of Lancaster. Not surrendered with the rest of the Crown lands by William IV, they still form a separate royal estate of over 18,000 hectares, from which the queen receives an income. They are mainly in the counties of Lancashire and Staffordshire and are managed by a council of which the Chancellor is head. The Duchy dates back to 1351 and all monarchs have taken a great interest in how it is run. That royal interest has inevitably been a factor in the minds of prime ministers when making the government appointment of the Chancellor of the Duchy, which is officially in the form of advice to the monarch, with the king or queen presiding at a ceremony held in accordance with the protocols of the Promissory Oaths Act of 1868.

On 5 May 1922, Sir William Sutherland was due to appear at an audience with George V to take the oath and receive the office of Chancellor of the Duchy of Lancaster. This was arranged to be held immediately after a meeting of the Privy Council held by the king at Windsor Castle shortly before he left on a visit to Belgium. Going through the papers beforehand, the king, who had a reputation among his ministers for sometimes being short tempered – he once told the Lord President that, 'This Privy Council meeting is quite unnecessary' – spotted that something was wrong. Trouble was brewing for the Clerk, Sir Almeric Fitzroy, and the trouble concerned Sir William Sutherland.

In Lance Price's book *Where Power Lies: Prime Ministers v. The Media*, Sir William Sutherland is described as 'the first of the modern spin doctors'. Sir William, born in 1880, was a colliery owner who had entered Parliament as a Scottish MP and become close friends with the Liberal

Prime Minister David Lloyd George, serving as his press officer and then as his parliamentary private secretary. It was generally accepted in London social circles that he was one of Lloyd George's go-betweens in the sale of honours for the Lloyd George Fund operated by Maundy Gregory. Gregory was the most prominent political fixer of the twentieth century. You wanted a knighthood for £10,000 (£300,000 in 2015 money)? No problem. £40,000 (£1.3 million) would get you a baronetcy. Some of the money, around £2 million, went to the Liberal Party, and sometimes to the Conservatives. Arthur Maundy Gregory pocketed the rest and became rich, buying houses, hotels and clubs in London and the Home Counties. His idea as to how to create his own fortune had been perfectly simple. He just approached the Liberal Party in 1918 and offered to sell peerages for payments that would go to party funds. Lloyd George employed him as a broker. Gregory was a bizarre fantasist in the same league as Titus Oates, who had clashed with the Privy Council in the 1670s (See Chapter Eleven). He had been at school in Southampton with another fantasist, the rector of Stiffkey, the Revd. Harold Davidson, who had preached against the Privy Council from a lion's cage in Skegness (See Chapter Twenty-One). Tales about Gregory abounded. Which were true; which false? Was he a spy? How much help did he get in his dubious activities from his closest friend, Sir Basil Thompson, the Assistant Commissioner of Scotland Yard's CID? What about the brothel he was alleged to own in Soho, which helped him in a career of blackmail? The left-wing MP Victor Grayson had disappeared in circumstances which are still unexplained. Was it because he had threatened to expose Gregory as the forger of Roger Casement's diaries – a British consul executed for treason in 1916?

For obvious reasons, Gregory was cultivated by social climbers and was able to hang on to the important political and society friendships he had made. But to many of the old British establishment he was *persona non grata.* That exclusion extended to Gregory's friends and working colleagues such as Sir William Sutherland. It is always possible for mavericks to thrive in politics if they are of use to party leaders. Both Gregory and Sutherland were more than useful to Lloyd George, but in terms of immediate post-Edwardian society, Lloyd George, the son of an elementary Welsh schoolteacher, was both a maverick and an outsider himself. Lord Grantham might well have invited him to Downton Abbey in the years when Lloyd George was Prime Minister, but not before or afterwards. It was certain that Gregory would never have been asked for the weekend, or 'Friday to Monday', as hostesses at that time would have put it, and neither would Sir William Sutherland.

But it was not so much Sir William's position in social society that worried King George V. It was his position in politics that perplexed the king. Why, George demanded, was someone about to be appointed as his Chancellor of the Duchy Lancaster not a member of the Privy Council? The king insisted to the Clerk of the Council, Sir Almeric Fitzroy, that every Chancellor of the Duchy since the fourteenth century had quite rightly been a Privy Counsellor, because they had one of the most important, and few, royal jobs in government. What was going on? In his normal manner, he asked the Clerk to give him a reason why he was shortly going to be asked to administer the Duchy oath to a man who had not been required to take the Privy Council oath.

There had been a slip-up. Someone had blundered. The Clerk should have foreseen this situation. The probable explanation was that Lloyd George thought he owed Sir William a more senior job in government. He had already been a Scottish whip, but the great joy of making him Chancellor of the Duchy of Lancaster was that it had no specific departmental duties and Sir William could carry on his spin-doctoring role as an adviser, fixer and dealer with the press. In all the troubles Lloyd George was experiencing in 1922 – he later lost the premiership to the

Conservative Andrew Bonar Law – it could be reasonable to accept that he had forgotten about the Privy Council problem. Whatever the situation today, eyebrows would have certainly been raised if a political press officer had been put forward to be considered by the monarch as a member of the Privy Council. It could also have easily slipped his mind that, in spite of all the demands of politics, the Chancellor of the Duchy of Lancaster does actually in fact have (a very few) royal duties to perform. George V was not amused. Here is how Sir Almeric explained the situation to the king:

> 5 May 1922
>
> Sir W. Sutherland came in after the Privy Council meeting to take the oath and receive the seals of the Duchy of Lancaster. The king evinced some surprise that he was not sworn of the Privy Council, and sent for me before the Council to enlighten him on the subject. I had to admit that for at least sixty years the holder of the office had been a member of the Privy Council but we had no instruction that Sutherland was to be admitted. I pointed out that he had only been three years in Parliament and that the Prime Minister was understood to think that his introduction might be postponed for a time, and I further explained that as he was not to enter the Cabinet there was nothing in his position which required the protection of the Privy Council oath; a point which appeared to remove the last scruple from His Majesty's mind. Sutherland presented a very subdued appearance.

Note the masterly civil servant's phrase, 'the Prime Minister was understood to think'. Only somebody well versed in the jargon of the civil service (which the king wasn't) would have picked up on that point and asked, 'Really? Understood by whom? How did the PM actually convey this understanding?' Note, also, the quite unconstitutional way in which the Clerk anticipates the thinking of the Prime Minister that Sir William Sutherland will not need the protection of the oath. Many might feel that with the job which Sutherland was brought in to do as Chancellor of the Duchy of Lancaster, to be the eyes and ears of Lloyd George, he would know so many government secrets that the protection of the oath was exactly what he would need. Anyway, this story showed that Sir Almeric Fitzroy was able to cope with George V as he had done with Queen Victoria and Edward VII and it had a fitting ending in that, a few weeks after being sworn in as Chancellor of the Duchy of Lancaster, Sir William Sutherland was also, with little fuss, sworn to the Privy Council.

We owe Sir Almeric a lot. Not only do his *History of the Privy Council* and his *Memoirs* contain a great deal of substantial history and background about the Privy Council, the *Memoirs* especially provide a marvellous flavour of the times in which he worked. And they both provide valuable starting-off points for other tales from the Privy Council.

Unfortunately, his public career finished under something of a cloud when, in October 1922, he was found guilty of trying to molest a woman in Hyde Park. Although he was cleared on appeal and all costs awarded to him, the new Lord President of the Council, the 4th Marquess of Salisbury, thought that at the very least Fitzroy had been indiscreet and that it would be better for all concerned if he quietly resigned his post which, being the good public servant that he was, he duly did in May 1923.

CHAPTER TWENTY-ONE

THE RECTOR OF STIFFKEY ASKS: 'WHAT ARE BUTTOCKS?', AND OTHER QUESTIONS LINKING THE PRIVY COUNCIL AND THE CHURCH OF ENGLAND

A T AROUND THE SAME time that Sir Almeric Fitzroy was asked to step down as the Clerk of the Privy Council following a possible indiscretion with a young lady in Hyde Park, the Revd Harold Davidson, the rector of the parish of Stiffkey in Norfolk, was engaged in his own series of indiscretions in the West End of London, which would eventually bring him to the attention of the disciplinary courts of the Church of England and their final court of appeal, the Privy Council. Davidson's problem, according to Ronald

Blythe in *The Rector of Stiffkey*, was that he loved girls: 'Not *a* girl, not five or six girls even, not a hundred, but the entire tremulous universe of girlhood ... firm breasts and good strong teeth besotted him.' He was especially fond of waitresses and managed to get himself banned from many of the cafés and teashops of Mayfair, much to the bemusement of his bishop, who commented that he knew it was not unknown for members of the clergy to be barred from public houses, 'but teashops!' There was one important constant factor in the rector's behaviour. As Matthew Parris stresses in his book on errant clergy, *The Great Unfrocked*, 'They were always pretty. Ugly girls, he thought, were in no moral danger.'

Harold Davidson came from a strongly religious family. Over twenty members of them had been, or were, priests. His father was vicar of St Mary's, Sholing, near Southampton, and his mother was the great-niece of the famous headmaster of Rugby School Thomas Arnold. At school, Harold showed much talent as an actor. A fellow pupil was Leon Quartermaine, who was to win fame on stage and screen. He encouraged Harold to neglect his studies and try to find a career as a professional comedian. While performing in London, Davidson was walking home late one night along the Thames Embankment when he encountered a young girl about to throw herself into the river. Having saved her from suicide, Davidson maintained that it was a turning point in his life and he then told his father he wished to enter Holy Orders. The problem was that having concentrated on drama at school, he had no scholastic qualifications; but his family could help. A firm friend of his father was the slave trade reformer William Wilberforce, and he managed to get Davidson into Exeter College, Oxford. Here, he constantly failed his exams, and got secretly engaged to a visiting actress at the Playhouse Theatre, but by charm of manner persuaded the Bishop of Oxford to ordain him in 1901, at the age of twenty-eight. Davidson certainly had charm in large measures. In 1905, as a curate at St Martin-in-the-Fields, he helped a friend of his, another actress, Gladys Sutherst, to succeed in her attempt to marry the 6th Marquess Townshend. This was some achievement, as Gladys's determination to marry into the aristocracy was hampered by the facts that her father was a bankrupt businessman from Yorkshire and members of Townshend's family had clubbed together to try to have the marquess certified.

Townshend showed his gratitude by appointing Davidson the rector of one of the parishes to which he was a patron, Stiffkey, in Norfolk. In 1906, the year Davidson was appointed, this was a village of around 300 people, very near the sea and lying on either side of the River Stiffkey. Davidson had done well. He had a stipend of £500, a huge Georgian rectory and the income from 24 acres of glebe land. Although Davidson quickly became popular with the villagers, he got involved in an immediate row with the largest local landowner, Colonel Groom, on account of the colonel openly parading his mistress in the village. It was another retired soldier, Major Philip Hammond, who first publicly objected to the new rector's ministry. It wasn't Davidson's preaching or his views on the scriptures that upset the major; it was his habit of sometimes filling the very large rectory with actresses, waitresses and chorus girls from London. To the consternation of the rector's wife, Molly, he once had twenty girls to stay on the same weekend. Then another soldier came onto the scene. While Davidson was serving as a Royal Navy padre in the Great War, Molly sought consolation in the arms of a Canadian colonel, and had a child in 1919. After returning from the war, the rector, a bit miffed at finding an unexpected new baby, settled into a routine of staying in London during the week and carrying out an independent ministry among young women whom he considered were in danger of entering a life of prostitution. With some, he had long-lasting friendships. Some who knew him believed that this work was Christian-inspired and genuine. Others were doubtful – extremely doubtful. It is certainly true that he proudly flaunted his work and described himself as the 'prostitutes' padre', telling his bishop that there was no finer work a priest could do. The doubtful included Major Hammond, who was enraged by Davidson's failure to return from London in time to conduct the 1930 Armistice Day service around the Stiffkey village war memorial. Hammond complained to the Bishop of Norwich, the Rt Revd Bertram Pollock, and the bishop's legal adviser, Henry Dashwood, suggested that because of his activities in the London Diocese, Davidson be brought before the Court of Arches and charged under the 1892 Clergy Discipline Act for immoral behaviour. Though he was reluctant, fearing the ensuing publicity, the bishop accepted that this would have to be the case.

As was inevitable, the story appeared in the local press and was immediately picked up by the national newspapers. Thirty years later, Bernard Levin on the BBC's *Any Questions?* programme said the Davidson case was a classic example of the bedevilled Church of England's key media problem: the fact that the word 'vicars' rhymed with 'knickers'. The Norwich Diocese recognised that there would be intense public interest in the trial and arranged for a special consistory court to be held not in Norwich but in the Church of England's headquarters at Church House, Dean's Yard, Westminster. The full details of the trial are brilliantly recorded in Matthew Parris's book *The Great Unfrocked*. He writes: 'Probably not until Mandy Rice-Davies appeared in the trial of Stephen Ward during the Profumo affair was an English court of law to see a beautiful female witness as cool as Barbara Harris, or have so much fun.' Miss Harris was the first witness and not only charmed F. Keppel North, the presiding Chancellor, but held the whole court in thrall as she described how she and her Indian lover entertained Davidson to tea in their bed. Fresh stories were continually emerging, which the papers joyously passed on to their readers. They had a field day when the rector of Stiffkey was asked about the time a prostitute treated a boil on his buttocks. He responded, 'I do not know what the buttock is.' The rector was then shown a photograph of himself in clerical dog collar examining the back of a naked young lady. As Parris comments, 'The rector could now be in no doubt what the buttock was.' Among the team of lawyers the Church had briefed to present its case was the future Cabinet minister Walter Monckton, then Attorney General to the Prince of Wales. He later said that it gave him a fascinating insight into the complexities of the relationship between Church and state. A steady procession of actresses, waitresses, shop assistants and actual or potential prostitutes appeared as witnesses for the prosecution. Davidson did not help himself by reverting to the kind of banter he had once used as a late-night cabaret comic. After six weeks he was found guilty on five counts of immoral behaviour and ordered to be defrocked as a priest. Knowing there would be a delay in his bishop carrying out this sentence, the rector dashed backed to Stiffkey, where he sought out Major Hammond, who had instigated the proceedings. Having given him a good kicking (for which he was later fined £2; the major kicked back but wasn't fined) Davidson then went to his church, where a congregation of over 1,000 had gathered. They heard Davidson preach that Christ had lived among the poor and despised and would have supported his work with young women. He made bitter attacks on the Court of Arches, the Archbishop of Canterbury and the Privy Council, a body to which he announced he intended to appeal as soon as he could raise the money to pay the costs awarded against him and afford to start a new campaign.

He appealed twice to the Privy Council, first on the grounds of false evidence given in court and secondly on various points of law. Both appeals were rejected.

During this time he lived in a style of great publicity, disturbing church services, insisting on still preaching in his own church – on one occasion, the poor curate in charge handed the Bible to Davidson and let him carry on in order to avoid a riot – and using every opportunity to gain both

public support and funds for his protests. This included interrupting
the actual ceremony at Norwich Cathedral on 22 October 1932, when he
was stripped of his ecclesiastical appointments and deposed from holding Holy Orders. Despite the rector of Stiffkey's appeals, the Bishop of
Norwich and his judicial party publicly proclaimed him defrocked and
processed out of the cathedral, leaving the (no longer Reverend) Harold
Davidson ranting of the injustices to the empty pews. On another occasion, he was forcibly ejected from a meeting at Church House when he
tried to shout down the Archbishop of Canterbury.

    To raise money for his appeals, he let his imagination for exhibitionism
have free rein. He preached on Hampstead Heath next to an enormous
dead whale; he sat in a fairground booth being probed by a robotic devil
with a pitchfork; he appeared in a song-and-dance act on stage at Wim-
bledon; his antics in Harrogate got him banned from their Nudist Sun
Bathing Society; and, almost most famously of all, he took up residence
in a barrel on the promenade at Blackpool and charged the public 2d to
see him. When the crowds reached over 6,000, the local authority fined
him for obstruction. He moved on to his last and most famous arena of
protest. This was another seaside venue, on the east rather than the west
coast: the famously bracing Skegness. Not so bracing for Harold Davidson, though. For his attacks on the Church of England, the Archbishop
of Canterbury, the Bishop of Norwich and the Privy Council, the former rector of Stiffkey had chosen to address anyone who would listen
from the lions' cage in the Skegness Amusement Park. He shared the
cage with a normally docile lion called Freddie. Matthew Parris tells the
story in *The Great Unfrocked*: 'One hungry evening, Freddie, perhaps
in despair at Davidson's loquacity, or perhaps unable to resist precedent
from the ancient world, turned on the deposed priest.' On the back cover
of his book, under a photograph of the former rector of Stiffkey, Parris
summarises the story in just seventeen words: 'Harold Davidson, the

self-styled "Prostitutes' Padre", unfrocked in 1932 and eaten by a lion in 1937.' Davidson is believed to be the last Christian to have met that end.

Sir (as he later became) Walter Monckton had commented that the relationship between Church and state was complex, an observation made, perhaps unsurprisingly, when dealing with the Norwich Diocese. It was the Norwich Diocese that, just over sixty years later, illustrated just how complex that relationship could be. In 1999, the church wardens of five parishes in the diocese declared themselves independent in protest at the sacking of their vicar. To deal with this, the General Synod proposed legislation to allow a bishop to remove a church warden for 'good or reasonable cause'. As it had to, by an Order in Council of the Privy Council, the General Synod Legislative Committee took this proposal to the all-party Ecclesiastical Committee of Parliament, which includes members of both Houses. The procedure is that this committee can either accept a proposal from the Synod and present it for a vote at Westminster or it can reject the proposal. It cannot amend it. The committee rejected the legislation. John Gummer MP, a former Cabinet minister and very active Christian declared, 'The Church has not needed legislation to suspend church wardens for over 700 years and it does not need it now. They have invented a solution for a problem that does not exist.' The Archbishop of York Dr David Hope countered with the argument that as well as having a duty to their parish church, wardens also had a duty to their bishop and therefore the bishop should have some say in how the wardens worked and have the legal right to suspend them if he (this was long before the days of women bishops) thought fit.

This outraged the Church Commissioner Stuart Bell MP, who answered questions concerning the 'Established' Church of England from the back benches of the House of Commons. He said: 'This had no chance. I am amazed they even tried to put it forward. The idea that church wardens could be suspended because "it seemed right to the

bishop" is the language of the abuse of power.' This led to more complicated discussion about whom bishops were accountable to, having been
appointed by the monarch on the advice of the Prime Minister of the
day. Some clergy looked enviously towards Wales, where the Church had
become disestablished in 1920, and which had six bishops, who elected
their own leader. Some took a more informed look at the fifty years of
wrangling in Wales about who the actual land, buildings and artefacts
belonged to and who would get compensation, and reached the decision
that in England disestablishment could never happen.

This was the same conclusion reached by two old friends, both very
senior Privy Counsellors, sitting having a drink one evening in July 1984
in the Lord President of the Privy Council's room in the House of Lords.
The Lord President, Willie Whitelaw, was entertaining his lifelong friend
and former fellow soldier of the 3rd Battalion Scots Guards (they both
won the MC in WWII) Robert Runcie, who for four years had been the
Archbishop of Canterbury, and who in 1988 was to preach at Viscount
Whitelaw's memorial service in the Guards' Chapel in Wellington Barracks. The Archbishop had maintained that the Church of England would
only become disestablished if the country became a republic. That, they
both agreed, was not going to happen, because on the basis of the evidence it was extremely difficult to come to any other conclusion. When
asked what evidence, Lord Whitelaw replied, 'The evidence of observ-
ing and examining the evolution of our unwritten constitution.'

Church and state are bound together by almost intangible threads. One
of these is the continuing existence of the oldest body of government in the
world, the Privy Council. This body is the nuts and bolts of a system by
which an elected democratic government can have a hereditary monarch
as head of state. An Established Church helps oil those nuts and bolts.
Consider: the monarch, as head of the Church of England (the official
title is Supreme Governor) on the advice of the Prime Minister, appoints

the Archbishop who sits in the House of Lords unchallenged under the umbrella of 'ancient usage'. The Archbishop crowns the monarch. The monarch – and Queen Elizabeth II is the great example of this – sees prime ministers and archbishops come and go, but only has the power of influence to warn and advise. All Acts of Parliament can only become lawful when signed by the monarch in the presence of Privy Counsellors. The Privy Council always includes the Archbishops of Canterbury and York and the Church Commissioners always include the Prime Minister, the Speaker and the Lord President, who, until a Church of England Measure in 1974, had the special role under the Act of Uniformity 1662 of being responsible for the protection of the *Book of Common Prayer*, and for any changes made in it. These normally concern the changing of titles affecting members of the royal family, and the Lord President was always grateful for a vigilant Clerk to spot when these alterations were coming up.

Such a Clerk was Sir Almeric Fitzroy, who recounts one of these occasions in his *Memoirs*:

> 23 June 1910
>
> The Duke of Cornwall to-day, being his birthday, received the title of Prince of Wales. Accordingly a meeting of the Privy Council had to take place, in order to makes the requisite changes in the Prayer Book. The Lord President, The Archbishop of Canterbury, Pentland, and Winston Churchill met in the room of the last named at the House of Commons for the purpose. The Archbishop of Canterbury was inclined to carp at the Recital in the Order of the names of the other members of the Royal Family who are mentioned in the Liturgy, but it was in fact the only way of doing it without clumsiness. I told him that it was the usual and ordered way of procedure, adding that antiquity was a better judge of ceremonial than this slipshod age, after which he had nothing further to say.

The Lord President's responsibility for the *Book of Common Prayer* goes back to the days when the Crown held the copyright of all printing and publishing carried out in the UK. The last remnant of this copyright was vested in the authorised version of the Bible, and in the *Book of Common Prayer*. This was the case until after the Second World War, and was illustrated by a parliamentary question put down in 1947 by the Labour MP for Bedford Thomas Skeffington-Lodge, who was also chairman of the Socialist Christian League. He was conducting his own campaign on government waste, a popular topic in those post-war days, and wanted to know why seven identical copies of an amendment to the *Book of Common Prayer* concerning the naming of the Duke of Edinburgh had been sent to the Archdeacon of Bedford. The Table Office of the House of Commons established that this was the responsibility of the Queen's printers, Cambridge University Press. The actual publishers were Eyre & Spottiswoode, but they had been taken over by CUP in 1901. However, the publishers didn't own the actual copyright, only a letter patent issued by the Crown. Anything to do with the Crown that it was allowable to raise in Parliament (and a lot wasn't) came under the remit of the Privy Council. So the Lord President Herbert Morrison, the grandfather of a later Lord President, Peter Mandelson, answered the question. Actually, he kicked it into the long grass, but after all, that is what the long grass is there for. In the 1970s, the responsibility for the *Book of Common Prayer* was handed over to the Church of England by royal warrant, probably much to the relief of all concerned.

The Second Church Commissioner is always appointed by the monarch and has to be a sitting backbench member of the House of Commons. Time must be provided for him or her to be questioned by other MPs. There is also the all-party Ecclesiastical Committee referred to above.

This is all part of an unwritten constitution. From time to time, small

changes are made. Some survive, some don't. At the moment, the Secretary of State responsible for sport is a Church Commissioner though
not the minister in charge of education, even though there is a formal
requirement for each school to hold a religious ceremony every day. When
Gordon Brown was PM, he came to an arrangement with the Church of
England that they would set up a committee to advise him on the appointment of bishops. They would offer him two names in the expectation that
he would advise the Queen to pick the first. That might last; it might not.
Not surprisingly, perhaps, for someone who lived in the Cathedral Close
at Salisbury and had been editor of, the *Church Times*, Ted Heath had
thought it was a good idea that constitutionally he had a say in picking
bishops. In his biography, *Edward Heath*, Philip Ziegler writes:

> While Prime Minister he recommended forty-five men to the Queen
> to be diocesan or suffragan bishops and believed that they were bet-
> ter appointments than they would have been if the choice had been
> left entirely to the Church. Sometimes he overruled the Church's
> own recommendation. In 1973, the London-Vacancy-in-See Commit-
> tee had shortlisted Graham Leonard to be Bishop of London. Heath
> preferred Gerald Ellison.

Ellison got the job. Leonard had to wait a few years.

Because the history of the Church and its relationship with the Privy
Council is well documented, it is easy to see patterns of behaviour
repeated. Some say that this is because the Church of England, whatever left-wing and trendy vicars it may produce from time to time, is by
its nature conservative at the top – the Established Church for the establishment – and reluctant to embrace social change. This was seen in the
twentieth century with its attitudes to equal opportunities and the rights
of women – as it was in earlier centuries with the position the Church

took on slavery. In the twenty-first century, we are seeing this behaviour pattern repeated in the official policy of the C. of E. towards gay priests. It can be argued that the Established Church takes these positions because it wants so much to try to be fair to everybody and, even if it leads to charges of indecisiveness, it does not want to exclude anybody from its mission of bringing God's love to the world.

Sometimes, what may appear to be reluctance by the Church to act is simply a desire to allow everybody to have their say in an open marketplace. This was seen in 2011 when large numbers of protesters, demonstrating against many ills they saw in society, gathered in tents outside St Paul's and for a few weeks turned that part of London into a campsite for multi-purpose campaigning. This gathering included Christians who believed that what they were saying outside the cathedral should be being said by the clergy inside. The problem was that the clergy could not agree what line to take. History was being repeated. Up until the sixteenth century, the ground around St Paul's was the site for some of the most controversial religious and political debating. The crowds were massive. The area became so congested that in order to speak publicly you needed a written licence, granted by the Privy Council. The speakers to whom the Council gave permission suggested that either the Council, including the Archbishop of Canterbury, could not make up their mind on an 'established' opinion or they were testing the crowds to see what views emerged as most popular. For instance, in March 1540, the Bishop of Winchester, Stephen Gardiner, argued to a crowd of several thousand people that the king should suppress many Protestant doctrines. A fortnight later, Robert Barnes, the Prior of Barnwell Priory in Cambridge, opposed Gardiner with a vicious attack on his interpretation of the will of God. Barnes was later burnt at the stake as a heretic. After a few weeks which included invitations to enter St Paul's, the protesters of the winter of 2011 eventually returned to their homes.

For most people, the relationship between the Church of England and the Privy Council only becomes of any interest when the Judicial Committee of the Privy Council is acting as the final court of appeal for sacked clergy, and then – as in the case of the rector of Stiffkey – the interest is sometimes sensational. There may be another sensational piece of tabloid journalism waiting to be written. In the twenty years that the Church has had woman priests, not one has been sacked. The official term for this, as we saw with Harold Davidson, is that the priest is 'defrocked'. Hardly a suitable expression to use when a woman priest is removed from Holy Orders. I am told the Privy Council is working on a new description – and hoping that it is accepted by the Westminster Ecclesiastical Committee.

CHAPTER TWENTY-TWO

THE HIGH COURT
OF CHIVALRY ASKS ITSELF:
'DO WE STILL EXIST?'

ITIES AND TOWNS ARE very proud of their coats of arms and
they safeguard and protect them. In 2012, Aberystwyth con-
fidently threatened legal proceedings against a Facebook
user for the unauthorised use of their coat of arms. They
were confident because, half a century earlier, Manchester Corporation
had successfully used the same legal route to prevent their coat of arms
being misused by the Manchester Palace of Varieties. The route was to
go to the Privy Council – more specifically, the Judicial Committee of the
Privy Council – and to absolutely exact the sub-court of the Council, the
High Court of Chivalry. When the court convened itself in 1954 to discuss the Manchester case, it was the first time it had sat for some centuries

and, according to G. D. Squibb in *The High Court of Chivalry: A Study of Civil Law in England*, it had to first satisfy itself that it was still in existence. That done, it soon found in favour of the Manchester Corporation.

The Judicial Committee of the Privy Council is the final court of appeal in certain areas of jurisdiction. These can be divided into: A) domestic; and B) overseas. It was also for a time the court of last resort for matters of devolution in the United Kingdom, but this responsibility was passed to the newly created Supreme Court of the United Kingdom in October 2009. In Group A there are seven domestic sub-courts that hear appeals to the Privy Council:

> Appeals from the High Court of Chivalry
>
> Appeals from the ecclesiastical courts (the Court of Arches for the
>   Canterbury Province and the Court of Chancery for York)
>
> Appeals against schemes of the Church Commissioners, who
>   control the estate of the Church of England
>
> Appeals from the Court of Admiralty of the Cinque Ports
>
> Appeals from Prize Courts
>
> Appeals from the Disciplinary Committee of the Royal College of
>   Veterinary Surgeons
>
> Disputes under the House of Commons Disqualification Act 1975

The first one of these, the High Court of Chivalry, was established in the fourteenth century to deal with the misuse of heraldic arms. It thus had a close working relationship with the College of Arms, incorporated and endowed by Richard III in 1483 to attend the Earl Marshal and Lord High Constable (see Chapter Four) and determine on descents, pedigrees, escutcheons and the like. The college is composed of three Kings of Arms (Garter, Clarenceux, and Norry); six Heralds (Windsor, Chester, Lancaster, York, Richmond and Somerset) and four Pursuivants (Rouge Croix, Bluemantle, Rouge Dragon and Portcullis) and two extra Heralds.

They make an impressive display at public processions and can be seen escorting the Sovereign at the State Opening of Parliament.

Even if the High Court of Chivalry is not called upon to sit all that often, it demonstrates very clearly that the tentacles of the Privy Council are deeply embedded in the evolution of our history. It depends upon the College of Arms for advice and indeed meets on its premises, which since 1669 have been in a splendid mansion in Queen Victoria Street, London, built by Sir Christopher Wren. The members of the college are nominated by the Earl Marshal. The Earl Marshal, who, of course, among his many titles, also has the position of Chief Butler of England, is one of the most senior members of the Privy Council. Since the office of Lord High Constable of England was downgraded in 1521, the hereditary Earl Marshal of England, the Duke of Norfolk, is now the only permanent judge of the High Court of Chivalry. It goes round in circles.

The High Court of Chivalry is also involved in a historic footnote concerning the growing recognition, over the centuries, of the role of different civil courts. In the fourteenth century there was sometimes confusion as to which was the correct civil court for a particular case. This was at a time when courts were competing for business and plaintiffs were realising that, with knowledge, resources and contacts, they could search for the courts most suitable for their pleas. In his book *The King's Council in England during the Middle Ages*, Professor J. F. Baldwin quotes from L. W. V. Harcourt's *His Grace the Steward and Trial by Peers*:

> According to the statute, 13 Ric. II, c. 2. if anyone complain that plead pending in the Court of Chivalry might be tried by common law, the plaintiff shall without difficulty have a writ of the Privy Seal directed to the Lord High Constable and Lord Earl Marshal to surcease in that plea, until it be discussed by the King's Privy Council whether that matter ought to be tried in that court or otherwise by common law.

Most of the domestic courts that come under the jurisdiction of the Judicial Committee of the Privy Council, founded in 1882 by the Privy Council Appeals Act, are, like the High Court of Chivalry, much older than their parent body and have names which convey a certain romantic and historic past. Take, for instance, the Court of Admiralty of the Cinque Ports. There were once nineteen different coastal courts of the Admiralty, each one presided over by a Vice-Admiral of the Coast. In 1875, together with the High Court of the Admiralty, these were absorbed into the new Probate, Divorce and Admiralty Division of the High Court (a strange combination) – except for the ancient courts of the Cinque Ports. This was a group of towns in Sussex and Kent originally consisting of Hastings, Romney, Hythe, Dover and Sandwich, Winchelsea and Rye being added afterwards. When England was being constantly threatened by invasion from the Continent, as seaboard towns they were relied on to provide help to beat back the enemy, and in return enjoyed certain privileges. As time went on, the Cinque Ports continued to be regarded as the first line of defence against a foreign foe, and their obligations and privileges were definitively set forth in a Charter granted by Edward I. This Charter provided that, in return for a contribution of fifty-seven ships for fifteen days in the year, they were to have exemption from all taxes, and a criminal and civil jurisdiction of their own, under the authority of a Warden who would act as a Vice-Admiral.

The contribution of the Cinque Ports was the backbone of the navy until the time of Henry VII, after which their influence declined. Their Charter was surrendered to the Privy Council in 1688 and most of their administration was brought into line with the rest of England by the Municipal Corporations Act of 1835. The ancient office of Warden, a post held for a long time by the late Queen Mother, and a residence at Walmer Castle still survives, and the Cinque Ports still come under the authority of the Admiralty Court for certain matters to do with the sea and coast. The jurisdiction of the court spreads from Shore Beacon in Essex to Seaford in Sussex. The last full sitting of the court was in 1914, but it meets to solve problems of salvage and in 2002 it had to decide what to do with the body of a dead whale. More serious matters are passed upwards to the Privy Council.

Of all the domestic courts of the Privy Council, the Prize Court is perhaps the most complex and most liable to be affected by factors outside of the control of the Privy Council – specifically, war. On the outbreak of hostilities between countries at sea, all involved set up a Prize Court, whether or not they have a standing court already. Each country makes its own rules of procedure to examine the validity of capture of ships and goods at sea. This is complicated by piracy, by the traditional 'laws of the sea' and by changing international law. The British court is a standing court dating back to the seventeenth century which was much in evidence during the development of our colonial empire, but is now likely to be subsumed by international agreements and obligations.

Of the other domestic courts, the tales of vets seeking to explain why they should not be struck off occasionally make stories in the newspapers, as do appeals about the Church Commissioners, especially if the subject is money or land. And, as we have seen from the cases of Titus Oates, the Bishop of Exeter and the rector of Stiffkey, appeals from the Court of Arches to the Privy Council can generate great public interest. However, probably the most significant changes in the domestic courts of the Privy Council that have come about in recent years concern the Court of Disputes under the House of Commons Disqualification Act 1975. This Act itself was an update of the 1957 Act and is from time to time amended by Privy Council Orders. The two recent changes that stand as benchmarks in our constitution are: 1) that ordained priests of the Church of England can stand for election to the House of Commons; 2) that hereditary peers who no longer sit in the House of Lords can become MPs. Two men have successfully done so: the former priest Chris Bryant sits for a Welsh constituency as a Labour MP, and Viscount Thurso has become a backbench Liberal Democrat.

The main disqualification for sitting in the Commons used to be having an office of profit under the Crown. But as a principle, this became something of a nonsense when ministers of the Crown received payment to sit in the Cabinet. Indeed, up until 1919, if an MP was offered a government post, they had to resign their seat and win a by-election before taking up their position. Disqualification still applies for some jobs, such as judges and serving officers in the armed forces and, most specifically, anyone appointed to be the Steward of the Chiltern Hundreds or the Steward of the Manor of Northstead. Bizarrely in the twenty-first century, under the rules of our constitution this is the way in which a Member of Parliament resigns their seat. The Chiltern Hundreds consist of the three Hundreds of Burnham, Desborough and Stoke in the Chiltern Hills of Buckinghamshire. A nominal salary of a £1 a year goes with this stewardship for the duties of keeping the Hundreds free from robbers. These Hills are Crown property and get their name from the responsibility, dating back to the thirteenth century, for the Steward to raise 100 fighting men when required to do so by the Privy Council. Since 1841, a similar situation has related to the Manor of Northstead in Yorkshire. Technically, once MPs have been elected and have taken the oath of office they are forbidden from resigning, so the legal fiction has been created that they apply for one of these two posts, which, since the 1701 Act of Settlement, have been in the gift of the Chancellor of the Exchequer. Taking an office of profit under the Crown, they thus automatically disqualify themselves from the House of Commons. They hold the post until the next MP wants to leave Parliament. Sometimes that tenure can be extremely short, as in 1985 when several Ulster Unionist MPs walked out on the same day.

Privy Council domestic activities were not confined to the domestic

sub-courts of their Judicial Committee. One of the reasons for the survival of the Council is that, operating within an unwritten constitution,
there has never been a definition of its powers. It has taken on duties
and responsibilities as the need arose and not attempted to hang on to
them when times and the public mood changed. The classic example of
that is the abolition of the Star Chamber. When, in 1641, its harsh and
often unjustified behaviour was challenged by Parliament, the Council
did not resist its closure. The Council has always shown a flexible attitude, holding sway with both vested interests and public opinion. This
was seen in the 1590s when the organisers of the highly profitable bear-
baiting competitions complained that the number of new stage plays
being performed in London was taking away their audiences. The Privy
Council banned all theatre performances, both indoors and outdoors,
on Thursdays so that the bear-baiters could have a clear run for at least
one day of the week. They held that view until 1835, when, under pressure from the public mood, they banned bear-baiting entirely.

The Council were very keen to have control over theatres, recognising the power that drama could have. To try to influence productions,
they granted licences to companies that wished to produce plays and, in
1603, with the blessing of James I and under the leadership of William
Shakespeare, they established the King's Men in a Royal Charter granted
under the Great Seal of England. But, as Sir Almeric Fitzroy points out
in *The History of The Privy Council*, what they really wanted was the
power of censorship, to control the content of productions. In the nineteenth century they waged an unsuccessful campaign against the royal
household for censorship to pass from just one Privy Counsellor, the
Lord Chamberlain, to the Council as a whole. Supported by the various
monarchs, the Lord Chamberlain hung onto this most influential and
high-profile of jobs. By the middle of the twentieth century, the position
of the Lord Chamberlain and his staff as they ran their blue pencils over

scripts and deleted rude words made this great office a laughing stock and also produced very real anger. Peter Hall, writing in *The Guardian* on 2 October 2002, asked:

> How many plays were never written because of the presence of the Lord Chamberlain? For 200 years the Lord Chamberlain removed the adult, the accurate and the outspoken from the British stage, as well as the lewd, the raucous and the plain dirty. This meant the banning not only of Aristophanes or Henry Fielding, but of moralists such as Shaw and the great Ibsen himself.

And of course, as was often pointed out, the amazing thing was that the Lord Chamberlain himself, although being subjected to this filth on an almost daily basis, remained completely uncorrupted and unaffected by it.

Peter Hall complained that the Lord Chamberlain's Office was largely staffed by retired naval officers with extraordinarily filthy minds. One day he went to ask that some lines the censor had cut from one of his plays be restored. The request was refused. When he asked why, he got this reply from a retired naval officer: 'We all know what's going on here, Hall, don't we? Look at it. Look at it. "Up periscopes." We all know what that means.' Hall looked baffled, 'No, what does it mean?' and got the answer, 'Buggery, Hall, buggery.'

'Actually,' returned Hall, 'it doesn't.'

So perhaps the Privy Council was quite glad that they didn't have to deal with all the fallout from the negative publicity that accompanies censorship. In fact, they had a much more discreet way of dealing with matters of which they disapproved. In 1760, they offered a pension to John Cleland, the author of the pornographic novel *Fanny Hill*, on the condition that he went to live quietly in the country and didn't write any more. He accepted.

By the late 1960s, the whole concept of stage censorship by a member of the royal household was recognised as being utterly absurd, and anyway, playwrights and producers who wanted to make serious points that might have upset the Lord Chamberlain, or who just wanted to put on sexy plays, could operate from private clubs outside the jurisdiction of the law. So, by common consent the Theatres Act of 1968 abolished the censorship of stage productions. Unlike the question that the High Court of Chivalry asked itself in the 1950s, 'Do we still exist?', the question the Censorship Department of the Lord Chamberlain's Office asked themselves in the 1960s was, 'How on earth did we last so long?'

CHAPTER TWENTY-THREE

SENTENCED TO DEATH IN JAMAICA – REPRIEVED BY THE PRIVY COUNCIL IN LONDON

N 1993, AS LORD Pannick QC points out in his book *I Have to Move My Car: Tales of Unpersuasive Advocates and Injudicious Judges*, the Judicial Committee of the Privy Council ruled that 'it was unlawful for Jamaica to execute offenders after a "shocking" delay of twenty-four years since the sentence of death was imposed'. This made newspaper headlines, which brought to public attention the overseas work of the Privy Council, now done almost entirely through their Judicial Committee sitting in London, though on rare occasions judges have made visits to countries concerned. One of the greatest legacies of the British Empire has been that as the dominions and colonies have merged into the Commonwealth, so many countries have built into their constitutions their retention of the Privy Council as their final court of appeal. Acting as an international court of appeal in a changing world is complicated, and decisions concerning the death penalty offer a fine example of the complexities involved. There has been a worldwide movement against using the death penalty as a judicial punishment, but not everywhere, and those countries that have abolished capital punishment have not moved at the same pace. So we have the bizarre situation that a country such as the United Kingdom, which has abolished execution, is home to a court that has to make judgments on whether or not to kill people.

The last person hanged in Australia was Ronald Ryan in February 1967. His appeal to the Privy Council failed. Shortly afterwards, Australia abolished the death penalty. The Bahamas still has mandatory capital punishment for murder but many of the appeals to the Privy Council focus on the fact that this punishment conflicts with the written constitution, which states that all prisoners must be treated humanely. In the eastern Caribbean and Belize, the death sentence is no longer mandatory and the Privy Council has accepted all appeals on the grounds that capital punishment is in breach of their respective constitutions.

The twentieth century saw many heartbreaking stories arriving at the Privy Council, as the court of last resort, that not only had happy endings but, through the publicity engendered, allowed badly needed law reforms to be introduced in some countries. In the 2014 exhibition of its work held at the Supreme Court under the title *A Court at the Crossroads of Empire*, the Judicial Committee of the Privy Council highlighted many such stories. One involved a British doctor working in Ghana in the 1920s who was found guilty of the murder of his wife after being tried under Ashanti regulations without defence counsel, without a jury and, under local Ghanaian procedure, with no right of appeal. The outcry in Britain meant that grounds were found for him to appeal to the Privy Council, where his death sentence was commuted,

and the publicity resulted in 'due processes' of legal appeal being introduced in British West Africa.

Not all significant appeals were, or are, to do with the death penalty. In the 1930s, the Privy Council upheld the appeal of five Canadian
women against Canada's Supreme Court ruling that they were ineligible
to hold seats in the Senate under the British North America Act 1867. A
landmark decision. But of course the majority of cases hold little interest to anybody except those taking part and their families and friends.
Recent cases such as the owners of a property that disappeared in a land-
slip arguing that the First Caribbean International Bank had a duty to
ensure that their (the couple's) insurance was in order probably didn't
even make the pages of the *Trinidad and Tobago News*. And the result of
the appeal by a police constable in Trinidad presenting a case to show
that he didn't have to actually sit an exam to be promoted to sergeant
might have created interest if he had won and created a precedent. But
he failed, so it didn't.

What is of interest is the bigger picture. Why, in 2015, does the Privy
Council in the UK, through its Judicial Committee, hold jurisdiction in
appeals from thirty-one countries? Most of these appeal to 'Her Majesty
in Council', but four of these nations are actually republics, so Dominica, Mauritius, Trinidad and Tobago and Kiribati appeal directly to the
Judicial Committee. Even more peculiar is the situation with Brunei, an
independent member nation of the Commonwealth which has a 'legal
agreement' with the Privy Council that their Judicial Committee hears
any appeals to the Sultan of Brunei and reports back to him. With so
many diverse territories coming under the legal umbrella of the Privy
Council, there are myriad fascinating stories, often giving point and coun-
terpoint to their historical development. One of the pictures belonging
to the British Library Board provides an admirable illustration of this.
It is a painting of Shah Alam, the Mughal Emperor from 1759 to 1806,

conveying the grant of the Diwani to Lord Clive in August 1765. This document gave the East India Company the power to collect taxes on behalf of the Emperor from the eastern province of Bengal, Bihar and Orissa. The agreement included the legal ruling that any dispute in these matters would be settled by the Privy Council in London. This was, in practice, the beginning of British rule in India.

Some stories are still developing, especially in Hong Kong, where their court system has been changed since the handover of sovereignty from the United Kingdom to China in 1997. The position was summarised by Lord Millet, a retired law lord sitting as a non-permanent judge in the (Chinese) Court of Final Appeal, in *China Field Limited v. Appeal Tribunal (Buildings)* in 2009:

> Decisions of the Privy Council on Hong Kong appeals before 1 July 1997 remain binding on the courts of Hong Kong. This accords with the principle of continuity of the legal system enshrined in Article 8 of the Basic Law (of China). Decisions of the Privy Council on non-Hong Kong appeals are of persuasive authority only. Such decisions were not binding on the courts in Hong Kong under the doctrine of precedent before 1 July 1997 and are not binding today. Decisions of the House of Lords before 1 July stand in a similar position. It is of the greatest importance that the courts of Hong Kong should derive assistance from overseas jurisprudence, particularly from the final appellate courts of other common law jurisdictions. This is recognised by Article 84 of the Basic Law (of China).

There are stories of revolution, such as in Grenada from 1979 until 1991, when appeals to the Privy Council were abolished. There are stories of fights for independence. The Anglo-Irish Treaty of 1921, which created the Irish Free State, gave Ireland the right of appeal to the Privy Council.

Ireland tried to abolish this right in 1931 but was warned by the Attorney General of England and Wales that it had no power to do so. Sensing a great deal of trouble, the Privy Council itself issued a statement saying that legally, under the Statute of Westminster 1931, Ireland's action was valid, and they accepted it.

Several countries just 'grew out' of needing to have appeals to the Privy Council as their international position and status increased, though in Canada's case this took some time, the Canadian provinces being loath to give up the right of direct appeal against decisions taken by the federal government; they argued that their treaties with England pre-dated the formation of a national government. The Second World War delayed a conclusion to this matter, and it was not until 1959 that the case of Ponoka-Calmar Oils *v.* Wakefield became the last appeal from Canada to be heard by the Privy Council. Canada, in fact, now has its own Privy Council, with Queen Elizabeth II as its head. It is chaired by a President and meets in full only for ceremonial affairs of state.

In contrast to Canada, Ceylon moved extremely quickly. As soon as the country achieved independent status as Sri Lanka in 1972, it abolished all appeals to the Privy Council. New Zealand kept the right of appeal to the Privy Council until the twenty-first century, but in the Commonwealth as a whole there has been a growth – often a slow growth – of a desire to be entirely independent from the UK in judicial arrangements. And the UK has maintained a completely supportive attitude to that position since the Balfour Declaration of 1926: 'It was no part of His Majesty's Government in Great Britain that questions affecting judicial appeals should be determined otherwise than in accordance with the wishes of the part of the Empire primarily affected.'

There has been a steady decline in appeals to the Judicial Committee of the Privy Council since the Second World War, with perhaps around 100 cases being heard each year. Recently, Jamaica and Trinidad and

Tobago topped the appeals list, with an average of eight or nine appeals each. The system has its critics. In June 1999, the lawyer and author Lord Pannick QC wrote a piece in *The Times*: 'End This Nonsense of Our Hanging Judges', and a past President of the Supreme Court of the United Kingdom, Lord Phillips of Worth Matravers, is quoted as saying in an interview with the *Financial Times*: 'In an ideal world, Commonwealth countries, including those in the Caribbean, would stop using the Privy Council and set up their own final courts of appeal instead.' Of course, for some overseas territories, current status, historical relationships, size and cost are all factors to be considered. Nevertheless, while it may seem entirely appropriate that citizens of Gibraltar, Jersey or the Isle of Man can appeal to the Privy Council, it still must seem odd to that famous 'man on the Clapham omnibus' that someone living in St Lucia, where they still have the death penalty, has as their final court of appeal the Privy Council in London, but he hasn't.

The truth is that each of the overseas territories presents widely different factors to be considered in their relationship with the Privy Council, and this is well illustrated by the case of the Channel Islands and the Isle of Man. Constitutionally, these islands come under the jurisdiction of the Privy Council, but the day-to-day work with them is carried out under the auspices of the Home Office. The sovereignty of the English over the Isle of Man goes back to the fourteenth century. The connection with the Channel Islands is much older. The Dukes of Normandy had annexed the islands in 933, over 100 years before William the Conqueror, Duke of Normandy, became King of England. This long history can produce problems under the concept of 'ancient usage' that are rarely, if ever, tested by law. Such a situation occurred in 1967 when the UK applied to join the European Economic Community. This had lawyers referring back to the name that appears so often in the context of the Privy Council, Professor Albert Dicey, and quoting the difference Dicey marked between the law of the constitution and the established conventions that in practice govern how we live. With regard to the Channel Islands, a former deputy bailiff of Jersey, F. de L. Bois, wrote in his pamphlet 'Parliamentary Supremacy in the Channel Islands (1983)': 'The relationship between the governments of the United Kingdom and the Islands should continue to be regulated by common sense rather than the law.' It may be that the same cannot be said about all the territories with such confident optimism. For a list of all such territories, see Appendix A at the end of this book. But for all the variations between the different overseas territories that come under the jurisdiction of the Privy Council as their final court of appeal, there does seem to be a spirit of 'togetherness'. It is difficult to define but, according to many lawyers, possible to both recognise and experience. This spirit is well shown by another story from Lord Pannick's book *I Have to Move My Car*:

> In his study of the British Empire, *Pax Britannica*, James Morris recorded that the elders of an Indian hill tribe involved in a legal dispute sacrificed an animal 'to propitiate a distant but omnipotent deity'. The elders explained that they knew nothing of him but that he is a good God and his name is the Judicial Committee of the Privy Council.

CHAPTER TWENTY-FOUR

WHERE IS THE UNIVERSITY
OF BASILDON?

A MAN SET OUT TO visit a sick friend in Basildon University Hospital. Never having been in the town before and having some time to kill before catching a bus home, he thought he would take a look at Basildon University. He hadn't heard of it before; hadn't even realised that Basildon had a university. He couldn't find it. Not surprising, really, as there is no university at Basildon. After making further enquiries, he discovered that the hospital tagged the word 'university' onto its name because it came under the umbrella of a teaching hospital in the region that was part of a university. A similar situation exists in south London, where a sign on a station platform invites people to 'alight here for Lewisham University Hospital'. Leaving aside the fact that Network Rail must be the last organisation to use the word 'alight', this wording does cause confusion. There is no Lewisham University, though there is a Lewisham College. But there is a fully-fledged proper university in the Borough of Lewisham, Goldsmiths University of London, situated in Lewisham Way. Many at Goldsmiths think that this is a bit of a con, on a par with the old *Goon Show* joke:

> 'Isn't that a Cambridge tie you're wearing, Eccles?'
> 'Oh, yes. That's a Cambridge tie.'
> 'I didn't know that you went to Cambridge.'
> 'Oh, yes. I went to Cambridge.'
> 'Well, what did you do at Cambridge?'
> 'I bought a tie.'

So, if Basildon University doesn't exist and there is no University of Lewisham, how is it that these descriptions are allowed? The answer is that the situation satisfies the official requirements. Whether or not it applies to the self-styled University of the Third Age is yet to be decided. They haven't made a formal request to use the word 'university' in their name and as yet no one has complained about that. Until comparatively recently, the responsibility for deciding if the word 'university' could be used in a title rested with the Privy Council. This duty has now passed to the Department for Business, Innovation and Skills, and they have decided that in the cases of Basildon and Lewisham, because the hospitals concerned come under the authority of a teaching hospital in the region, it is OK to use the title 'University'. Ho. Hmm.

The actual title of 'University' can still only be officially conferred at a meeting of the Privy Council. Of course, some outfits use the word without government permission, and civil servants haven't the time, money or staff to chase up every café or shop that includes it in their title just because it happens to be near one of the 120 or so institutions in the

UK that can now award degrees. It can also be argued that, before the switch from the PCO to BIS, when the Further and Higher Education Act 1992 stated that 'the Privy Council is responsible for the use of the word university in titles' there was a different consensus as to the concept of a university. Consider this paper written by Andrew McGettigan and posted by the Council for the Defence of British Universities on 15 August 2013:

> Last week, it was announced the government had conferred the university title on BPP, formerly a university college specialising in professional courses in law, accountancy and business. Although presented in the mainstream press as the second UK for-profit university, BPP University is a not-for-profit subsidiary of BPP Holdings, which in turn is owned by Apollo Global. It is not a charity but is barred from distributing profits to its parent company.

The first university to be recognised in this way was the College of Law, before it was sold to Montagu Private Equity.

The difficulty of tracking down the University of Basildon is symptomatic of the difficulties in understanding the position of all English universities in the overall scheme of education in this country. This is true of the relationship between education and government generally. Yet it all started off so clearly and simply. The social reforming zeal of the early and mid-nineteenth century encompassed schooling as one of its main activities. Where parts of the country were not provided for by church or charitable schools, state boards were set up to fill the gaps. This all needed money, so in 1839 the Lord President and the Chancellor of the Exchequer set up a committee to award grants and supervise their distribution. Naturally, this resulted in a certain amount of discussion about the criteria on which the money was to be given, and in 1857

a Board of Education was established, which was eventually to become
ministry and later a department. In the second half of the twentieth century, big changes were afoot in the organisation of government. While
Leader of the Opposition, Harold Wilson had made a famous speech at
Swansea talking of the coming 'white heat' of the scientific revolution.
On winning the 1964 general election, he immediately created a new
department, Education and Science. This caused problems, as there
were other departments with a vested interest in science, such as Avia-
tion, Health, Defence and Power. Departmental feuds were a feature of
Harold Wilson's first administration. In an attempt to satisfy the aspirations of George Brown, the Prime Minister had created an entirely
new department called Economic Affairs. The Treasury saw that off.
Then there was Fred Willey, given so little money at Land and Natural
Resources, that he was known in the Commons as 'the Minister landed
without any Natural Resources'.

   'Science' as a departmental title lasted twenty-eight years and then in
1992 it was shifted to the Cabinet Office, which caused more problems,
especially for those wishing access to it. Five years later, the Department
of Education had 'Employment' added to its title, which presumably
meant preparing young people for the world of work. That was never
quite clear. Then in Tony Blair's administration of 1997, all kinds of new
positions appeared in the Department of Education and Employment.
(Note the second word is now 'of', not 'for'.) The use of these two words
seems to be interchangeable throughout the long history of this department without any thought having been given to the most appropriate
meanings. This department now had various different ministers such as:

   Minister for Employment and Disability Rights
   Minister for School Standards (in fact, there were two ministers
      here)

Minister for Lifelong Learning

Minister for Employment and Equal Opportunities.

So very different from 1955, when a department was called a ministry and normally had a one-word title such as 'War', 'Fuel', 'Supply' or 'Air'.

There was one significant new addition in Tony Blair's published list of ministers: for the first time, a junior minister for universities was named. Baroness Blackstone became Minister for Higher Education.

In 2001, the name was changed again – to the Department for Education and Skills, Employment being hived off to a newly created Department for Work and Pensions. There were also new specific jobs for ministers, for example 'Young People' and 'Adult Skills and Workforce Development'. There was still a Minister for Higher Education, Stephen Timms, but he had to double up his duties with looking after lifelong learning. In 2007, Prime Minister, Gordon Brown, split the Department for Education and Skills into two, creating the Department for Children, Schools and Families and the Department for Innovation, Universities and Skills. In David Cameron's first administration in 2010, this became the Department for Business, Innovations and Skills, the word 'Universities' being dropped from the title but the responsibilities being covered in that ministry by a Minister of State, who was also a Privy Counsellor. Thus, one factor has remained constant in the position of universities in relation to government in the UK. Since universities were first conceived in the twelfth century (some say a lot earlier), the link that universities had, often tenuous and sometimes rowdy though it was, with whatever form of government was being practised at the time was through the Privy Council. In 1997, the government established the Quality Assurance Agency to monitor and advise on the suitability of institutions to award degrees, but the Privy Council is the only body that can formally award the title of University on behalf of other government departments. If, as some think, consumer rights legislation will mean that different means of assessment will be used in the future, there is no likelihood that the formal position of the Privy Council in relation to our universities will be changed. That will be true no matter what government department uses the word 'universities' in a description of its work. If asked why that is the case, the answer is 'ancient usage'.

Long before there were government departments, long before there was argument about whether the most appropriate government base for universities was 'Education' or 'Business' – or indeed, as some radicals thought, 'Culture' – the *Proceedings of the Privy Council* carried reports showing the Council's concerns with our universities, or, to be specific, with the only two that existed in the sixteenth century, Oxford and Cambridge.

Oxford troubled them more than Cambridge and the disputes were nearly always on two levels: fighting between students and townsfolk, and power struggles between the university, in the person of the Vice-Chancellor, and the city, in the person of the Mayor. Or, as it became known, Town and Gown. One persistent source of discontent was a ruling from King Edward III that the University of Oxford be granted under '*Ahauncient Priveleges*' profits from the sale of bread, wine and ale. The Mayor of Oxford was reluctant to allow this, and put every impediment in the way. The university appealed to the Privy Council. This was not the first (nor indeed the last) time that this matter came before the Council. Apart from the question of status, a considerable amount of money was involved. As a note from the *Proceedings of the Privy Council* shows, at its meeting in Westminster on 19 April 1546, the Lord Chancellor and the Lord Privy Seal took a very strong line on this and instructed a letter to be written to the Mayor stressing the displeasure of Henry VIII:

To the Mayour and his Bretherne of Oxford, that whereas the Kings

Majestie was advertised that contrary to a certain Ordre by the Counsell
taken concerning thassie of bred, wyne and ale, with all the amercia-
mentes and other proffites thereunto belonging which by the thauncient
privileges of the Universitie of the same being of late restored and confirmed by His Highness rightfully appertained unto them of the same
Universitie, the same Mayor and his Bretherne had hitherto neglected
and withstood that Ordre, expressly denying their right thereby to levy
the said proffites and americamentes, albeit the evident approbacion
thereof by the said Decree, with the annuall allowuance towards the
Baylives there of vth of the Exchequer at the rendie of their accomptes
therin in recompense of thither; His highness marvelled not a little
at such of their wilfulness in so plain a matter and therefore straytley
charged them no longer to persist in any further empeachment in that
behalf, upon pain of His Majesties high displeasor.

That was not the end of the matter. At a meeting of the Council in August
of that year, the Mayor, Richard Gunter, and the inhabitants of Oxford
were ordered to pay compensation to the university. To make completely
clear their contempt for the Mayor, the Privy Council took away his
responsibility for arranging masses in the town for the memory of Edward
III and passed that duty to the Vice-Chancellor. They also ordered that
the Common Seal of the Town be handed to the university for safe keeping. Not really surprising that periodic fights broke out between the
members of the university and the citizens. The background of 'Town
and Gown' is not a mythical one. Thirty years later, the arguments in
Oxford between rights and privileges had reached a point where, at a
Privy Council meeting at Hampton Court, Mr Secretary Walsingham was
instructed to send letters to Queen Elizabeth I's Attorney, the Solicitor-
General and two other justices asking them to meet and report upon
the situation. The Mayor objected to this and was ordered not to leave

Oxford unless he was called to appear before the lawyers elsewhere. The lawyers reported back the following year and, at a Privy Council meeting in Greenwich, both the Mayor of Oxford, Roger Tailour, and the Vice-Chancellor of the University, Doctor Humfrey, were called before the Council to have the report read to them. This takes up ten pages in the record and basically sets out the separation in terms of powers and controls of Town and Gown, distinctions which, with one or two hiccups, were still a tangible presence in Oxford – Bulldogs, Proctors, the wearing of gowns etc. – until the start of the 1960s.

Cambridge, in contrast, gave the Privy Council a much quieter time during this period. The Council agreed that its scholars should be excused paying taxes and would not be called to the muster, and there was a slight squabble in 1589 with the Lord-Lieutenant when he was told he did not have authority over the Vice-Chancellor to ensure that students ate no meat during Lent. Oxford also had trouble with a Lord-Lieutenant that year when the Privy Council told him that he had no right to shoot at scholars (as opposed to other residents of Oxfordshire) trespassing in his private woods.

The position of higher education in the seventeenth century is well summarised in Professor John Guy's book *Tudor England*:

> Higher Education was largely restricted to persons entering the two universities and four inns of court … known as the third university, since increasing numbers of the young gentry finished their education there. Charles I's Privy Council described them as Seminaries and Nurseries wherein the Gentry of the Kingdom and such as serve His Majesty in the Common Wealth are bred and trained up.

Unlike Scotland and, to some extent Wales, the growth of universities in England was slow. Durham, whose roots go back to the thirteenth century, was granted a charter in the 1830s and it wasn't until 24 April 1831 that the Privy Council met to, as Fitzroy describes it in *The History of the Privy Council*, 'hear the Petition of London University praying for a Charter ... and the counter-petitions of Oxford and Cambridge and the medical bodies'. The diarist and sometime Clerk to the Privy Council Charles Greville had great fun in recording in his *Memoirs* what sounded very knockabout proceedings:

> The Assemblage was rather curious, considering the relative polit-
> ical position of some of the parties. All the Cabinet ministers were
> summoned: Lords Grey and Holland were there, the Chancellor,
> Denham, Lyndhurst, Eldon, the two Archbishops and the Bishop
> of London. Old Eldon, now eighty-two years of age, got a fall as he
> came into the House of Lords and hurt his head. The Lord Chancel-
> lor, Lord Brougham, and the rest were full of civilities and tenderness
> but Eldon said, '*It's of no consequence for the brains have been knocked
> out long ago.*' Wetherell made an amusing speech but did not con-
> clude. It is seldom that the sounds of merriment are heard in these
> walls but he made the lords laugh and the gallery too. The extreme
> gravity of old Eldon struck me forcibly as contrasted with the air of
> ennui, the frequent and audible yawns and the flippant and sarcastic
> interruptions of Brougham, the Lord Chancellor. The most striking
> incident occurred in the answer of Bickersteth (the lawyer appearing
> for London University who later became a Privy Counsellor, Master of
> The Rolls, and the 1st Baron Langdale) to one of the Lord Chancel-
> lor's interruptions. He said, talking of degrees, '*Pray, Mr Bickersteth,
> what is to prevent the London University granting degrees now?*' To
> which Henry Bickersteth replied, '*The Universal scorn and contempt
> of mankind.*'
>
> The Lord Chancellor said no more; the effect was really fine.

London duly got its Charter in 1836. The capital was followed by some of the major industrial towns of northern and central England, Manchester in 1851, Birmingham in 1900 and Leeds in 1904. There was a steady growth of universities during the first half of the twentieth century, often typecast as civic or red-brick. These were followed by the expansion spurt in the 1960s of Essex, York, Sussex etc. and by the evolution into universities of combinations of polytechnics, schools of art, teacher training colleges and other institutions in higher education, which took place during the end of the twentieth century and the start of the twenty-first.

As the Privy Council had and still has overall responsibility for universities, this considerably increased the workload of the Clerk to the Council, responsible for monitoring the Charters, protocols and statutes of the new institutions. And in the 1980s there was still more work heaped on the Clerk when the Conservative government led by Margaret Thatcher, with Sir Keith Joseph as Secretary of State for Education and Science, decided to tackle what they saw as a problem in universities: that of staff tenure. As Julian Critchley, the writer and Tory MP, put it, 'Margaret couldn't see an institution without trying to hit it with her handbag.' In the *Times Higher Education Supplement* of 30 December 1983, David Jobbins wrote: 'Ministers are determined to break university teachers' tenure and have advised the Privy Council to take every opportunity to include dismissal on grounds of redundancy in Charters submitted whenever institutions petition for a new or supplementary Charter.' This provoked a big parliamentary row. Dr John Mark, the Labour MP for Wrexham, said,

> The question is whether the Privy Council's arm is being twisted. I think it is. The Privy Council is an independent body and while there is nothing to stop Sir Keith Joseph giving his views, it should tell us whether it is taking his views into account and if so why.

The deputy general-secretary of the Association of University Teachers, John Acker, accused the government of wishing 'to use the Privy Council for political purposes which have nothing to do with the proper running of the universities'.

Briefly, this topic provided the starting point for a debate on the role of the Privy Council in general. Because it is such an eccentric part of the English constitution and because it deals with such a range of disparate subjects, the belief of many, especially academics, was that it was impartial and above politics. As the education commentator Ngaio Crequer wrote in *The Times* on 4 March 1984:

> There was much concern when the Privy Council started to implement government policy on tenure, refusing new statutes or changes to them, if they did not include redundancy as grounds for dismissal. But the concern was misplaced. As Sir Neville Leigh, the Clerk to the Council, said: 'The Privy Council in this field is part of the machinery of government and Privy Counsellors who take part are ministerial councillors.' Sir Neville insists that the Privy Council does not act in a party political way but only implements ministerial policy.

Nowadays, when so many statements by civil servants are almost automatically subjected to the 'Sir Humphrey Approval Test' by their listeners, I feel that Sir Neville would score high marks for that last comment. Of course, there is another question that remains to be decided: is the Clerk to the Privy Council a civil servant? Sir Neville also made the point that although this aspect of the Council's work had received much publicity, especially in relation to the Universities of Sussex and Hull, the Council had a long tradition of working quietly with institutions to arrive at results by agreement and compromise without having to resort to official Orders. He mentioned the clause-by-clause work being done with

the London Institute of Education to convert their status to that of a full
school of London University, and with Aberystwyth over the academic
representation and role of the Welsh language in its Charter. However,
the government felt that this public discussion of the status of the Privy
Council was not in the best interests of the Council, and acted, as they
saw it, in the traditional and sensible way: by setting up another body
to deal with the problem. Almost before the universities realised what
was happening, it tucked away into the Conservatives' 1988 Education
Reform Act, under 'Miscellaneous and General', a few clauses about
staff tenure now becoming the responsibility of a new outfit, the University Commissioners. Over the next twenty years, they were able to
make sure that the tag 'Jobs for Life' could no longer be applied to new
lecturers taking up posts in English and Welsh universities. The debate
about whether or not the Privy Council was a 'political' body again faded
into the background.

But the Council did not give up either its overall responsibilities for
universities or indeed one specific duty which is still so much in the
background that the vast majority of staff and students have no concept
that it exists at all. That is the position of the Official Visitor. Type in an
enquiry about the Visitor in any university or college website and you
will get a whole lot of guff about open days and parking arrangements.
Yet the Visitor was once a key element in university life. He or – only
very recently – she was the representative of the founder to see that the
founder's wishes were being carried out under the terms of the Charter
establishing the institution. Often, because so many colleges were eccle-
siastically based, the Visitor was the local bishop. This custom continues
today. The Bishop of Durham is Visitor of Durham University, and the
Archbishop of Canterbury is Visitor of the much newer University of
Kent. The Visitor was an extremely powerful person. He was able to rule
on disputes inside institutions and also make judgments on whether or

not the university had acted fairly in not accepting a student who then appealed to him. In a test case in 1694, it was established that a decision by the Visitor could not be overturned by any other court. This arose from a quarrel at Exeter College, Oxford, where the Visitor, the Bishop of Exeter, ruled that the rector had been wrong to deprive a member of the college of his fellowship. Events became extremely heated. The rector shut the bishop out of the college. The bishop sacked the rector and appointed a successor. Both sides appealed to the Privy Council, which found in favour of the Bishop of Exeter.

The role of the Visitor in this respect was a useful, contained and cheap way of making decisions which, if allowed to go to outside courts, could be expensive and take up a great deal of time that could be used in teaching and research. Where the Visitor was a member of the royal family, the Privy Council, in the person of the Lord President of the Council, became involved at a much earlier stage. The Lord President actually acted as Visitor throughout the whole process. In the twentieth century, much of this work (and there was a great deal of it) was to do with students appealing against their exam marks and grades. But changes to the Visitor's jurisdiction were made by the Higher Education Act of 2004. No longer can the Visitor consider any complaints from students, potential, present, or past. Nor can staff disputes on matters or terms of employment be brought before the Visitor. What the Visitor does have the unchallenged right to do is now limited but very clear. The Visitor is the ultimate authority on the interpretation and application of the institution's Charter, statutes, ordinances and protocols, and can accept petitions from academic staff to make a judgment where there is uncertainty and conflict. Where an institution has no Visitor, the Lord President will act in that capacity if required.

These changes were not made so much as a result of serious philosophical studies to do with the role of government but rather because of the horror with which it was realised that if disputes among staff and students continued to rise at the same rate throughout the growing number of institutions (125 and climbing) able to confer degrees, all other work by the Privy Council would grind to a halt. So there was a regrouping. There was a concentration on essentials. 'Ancient usage' prevailed and the Privy Council, and not the Department of Education, nor the Department of Business, nor any other government department, can award the title of 'University' to an institution, and that is the main role of the Privy Council in regard to higher education.

CHAPTER TWENTY-FIVE

SPYING, PRIVY COUNCIL CONFIDENTIALITY, D-NOTICES AND THE BAKER STREET ROBBERY

I F THIS SEEMS A long catch-all title, the events to which it refers in the 1960s and 1970s certainly catch two fine illustrations of different facets of the Privy Council: the way in which the Privy Council oath binds members together at the expense of their party allegiances and the way in which counsellors will work together in what they perceive is the national good in spite of their political instincts.

On 15 July 1963, responding to a point made by the Prime Minister, the Rt Hon. Harold Macmillan, the Labour front-bench spokesman the Rt Hon. Harold Wilson said:

I can confirm what he has just said. In the two meetings which we
have had, he has given my Rt Hon. friends and me a very full and
frank account of this case, which raises a number of issues which,
frankly, cannot be discussed across the Floor of the House. While
we still have some grave anxieties about the way in which it has been
handled, which I think it best we should pursue in further confiden-
tial discussions with the Rt Hon. gentleman, we feel that in the public
interest this is a matter which should now be left where it is and not
made the subject of further public discussion or inquiry.

The subject under scrutiny – but not by the members in the Chamber
of the House of Commons, only by Rt Hon. MPs (i.e. Privy Counsellors) – was the work of the security services. The Prime Minister had
earlier pleaded with the House 'to trust the relations between the two
parties to discussions between the Leader of the Opposition and the
Prime Minister'. So Conservative and Labour Privy Counsellors could
come together and be briefed on matters concerning national intelligence
under the Privy Council oath but could not break that oath and use the
information they had learnt in public debate either inside or outside the
House. The specific matter, of great speculation in Parliament and the
media, was that a few days earlier a government minister, Ted Heath, had
announced that the Foreign Office was satisfied that it was the traitor Kim
Philby who was the so-called Third Man – the man who had tipped off
the spies Burgess and Maclean and allowed them to get out of the UK.

Macmillan was only too grateful that the Labour Party had offered
him a degree of protection on the floor of the House of Commons. Stories of spying had become legion. Dealing with them was taking much
time away from government business. Since Burgess and Maclean had
defected to Russia in 1955 there had been growing public alarm over
spying. Spies had been caught having infiltrated the secret Underwater

Weapons Establishment at Portland Bill. Then a British agent of the security services, George Blake, was found guilty of treachery and sentenced to forty-two years' imprisonment. At that point, Macmillan had called a meeting of the senior Privy Counsellors from both sides of the House. Hugh Gaitskell, the Leader of the Opposition, brought with him George Brown, Emmanuel Shinwell and Lord Alexander. The PM had with him the Home Secretary, the Lord Privy Seal and the Cabinet Secretary. They agreed to proceed on Privy Council terms. The Prime Minister would set up a review of security procedures and practices and, where appropriate D-notices, would be issued to the press.

D-notices (Defence Advisory Notices) were first introduced in 1912 and are still officially classified as 'advisory requests'. It is a voluntary system affecting journalists and broadcasters, with subtle – or sometimes not very subtle – pressures being applied by civil servants, normally retired service officers. Editors are encouraged to use the system by seeking advice from the secretary of a committee entitled DPBAC (Defence, Press and Broadcasting Advisory Committee). The expectation is that everybody works together in the national interest and follows the guidance of the secretary on what to publish and what to leave well alone. The review Macmillan set up was chaired by Lord Radcliffe. He was ideal: a member of the Privy Council and Fellow of All Souls who had served as Director-General of the Ministry of Information during the Second World War. He won plaudits from all sides as chairman of boundaries committees working in Pakistan following the Indian Independence Act. Although not a rich man, he refused any salary for this. A Lord of Appeal, he achieved distinction with his reports on monetary policy, his BBC Reith Lectures and the many public inquiries he chaired. This was a typical illustration of the Privy Council being able to find from within its ranks someone who would have the trust of the political parties, the media and the public.

At this point, Macmillan must have thought that he had done as well as he could in the circumstances and that the Privy Council had helped him cope both with Parliament and with keeping the trust of the public. But worse was to come. As he wrote in his *Diary* on 28 September 1962, 'There has been another espionage case … in the Admiralty … an executive officer giving away material … for five or six years … There will be another big row.' Later he recorded in his autobiography, *At the End of the Day*: 'The attacks now became even more fantastic. The First Lord of The Admiralty, Lord Carrington, was accused of sheltering traitors in the Admiralty and almost of treachery itself.' The executive officer was John Vassall. At that time, homosexual activity was illegal. Vassall was caught in a honeytrap situation while serving in Moscow and subsequently blackmailed by the KGB into spying for Russia. Although only a relatively lowly figure in naval intelligence, on his return to London he was able to supply the KGB with such a constant stream of information that it enabled the Russians to build up a pretty complete picture of what the UK was working on, especially in the fields of radar, torpedoes and anti-submarine equipment. Vassall was exposed by a senior Russian agent, Anatoliy Golitsyn, who defected from the KGB to the United States in 1961. Rumours abounded, in particular one that suggested Vassall had been sacrificed by the Russians to protect a much more highly placed spy in the Admiralty.

In his *Diaries*, Harold Macmillan complained that he was having sleepless nights. Not only were there real fears at this time that America and Russia might be drifting into a Third World War, he resented issues such as spying disturbing his concentrating on what he saw as one of Britain's key problems of the early 1960s: getting the Commonwealth to understand the reasons for the UK's application to join the EEC. He felt that he wasn't always getting the right support from his colleagues. Here is a *Diary* entry for 5 November 1962: 'The Vassall case is getting more embarrassing. I'm afraid the Minister of Defence took the debate last Friday with too Palmerstonian a touch – in a word, *flippantly*. When it was said that Vassall lived *above* his income in Dolphin Square, he said, 'We are all living above our incomes in all the London squares.'

Contributing to the idea that the government was in a real mess concerning matters of national security, Vassall was arrested on 12 September 1962, shortly after the Radcliffe Report had been published on 5 April 1962. There had not been time to act on Radcliffe's recommendations or indeed for the politicians and media to absorb them properly – and of course it hadn't even mentioned John Vassall, who by then had been sentenced to eighteen years in jail. Radcliffe had started his work by studying the 1956 Conference of Privy Counsellors Report into the perceived dangers of communists in British life, and how they should be identified. The Radcliffe Committee thought that this was inadequate and that it was also necessary to guard against those who, thanks to defects of character such as the lack of ability to refrain from drinking, or to relatives living behind the Iron Curtain, were vulnerable to pressure from the KGB. There were also somewhat patronising proposals made as to how to help the trade unions and the civil service staff associations protect themselves from communist infiltration. If this seems over-paternal, it must be remembered that the situation of a possible Russian/American armed conflict in the Bay of Pigs in Cuban waters had raised genuine alarm among serious commentators that the Cold War against Communist Russia was about to escalate into a hot war. There were also solid recommendations in the report on how to improve vetting. But real examination of the Radcliffe Report was swamped by the consistent attention given to (or perhaps it would be more accurate to use the phrase 'commanded by') scandals involving spying. Look at the timeline:

1961: January–March: The Portland Bill case

1961: May: George Blake sentenced to forty-two years

1961: May: Radcliffe Committee set up

1962: April: Radcliffe Report published

1962: September: Vassall arrested

1963: February: Philby umasked as 'Third Man'

1963: March: Profumo case raised in House of Commons

The publicity given to the Profumo affair eclipsed everything else. It was not just the sex. In Andrew Marr's *A History of Modern Britain*, the author writes that the affair John Profumo, Privy Counsellor and Cabinet minister, started with Christine Keeler would probably have remained unknown, 'except for a rotund, cheerful Russian military attaché, and spy, called Yevgeny Ivanov'. Ivanov was also sleeping with Keeler. And the fact that the Cabinet post Profumo held was that of Minister of War enabled Leader of the Opposition Harold Wilson's security adviser, Colonel George Wigg MP, to raise the matter on the floor of the House of Commons on the grounds that national security was endangered. (There is an interesting footnote here for the annals of the Privy Council. Chapter Seven describes the pawning of the Sancy Diamond, one of the most precious stones in the Crown Jewels. The stone changed hands several times, ending up in the hands of the Astor family. It was at the Astors' family home, Cliveden, in Berkshire, that Bill Astor, Profumo's friend, introduced the Minister of War to Christine Keeler. Whether they were both shown the Sancy Diamond is not recorded. It was Bill Astor who finally sold this relic of the Crown Jewels to France.)

The following year, the Labour Party won the general election in October 1964 and a new set of Privy Counsellors found themselves in the Cabinet, with more worries about security and D-notices waiting for them just around the corner. In fact, the worries waited like birds out of

sight over the horizon until the Labour Party had won a decisive majority nearly twenty months later in the general election of March 1966.
The first bird to appear was a jailbird, George Blake. Or rather, he disappeared. He climbed over the wall of Wormwood Scrubs and made his
escape having served only five years of his long sentence.

Members of the government reacted to this news in different ways.
Some Cabinet ministers were having talks with Prime Minister, Harold
Wilson, at Chequers. It was late on the night of Saturday 22 October
when, as Richard Crossman, the Lord President of the Privy Council,
wrote in *The Crossman Diaries* (edited by Anthony Howard),

> Someone rushed in to say that George Blake had just climbed over
> the wall of Wormwood Scrubs and made his escape. George Brown
> woke up and said that we should alert all the ports. The PM asked
> what statement we should give to the press. I asked why we should
> make any statement at all … we're not much good, as Ministers, in
> trying to catch a prisoner who has run away.

Later, Crossman recorded the reaction of Harold Wilson to the escape of
the famous spy: 'That will do our Home Secretary a great deal of good.
He was getting too complacent and he needs taking down a peg.'

Actually, a year later it was the subject of spies and spying that brought
Harold Wilson down a peg or two, by the Privy Council, in what has
become known as the D-notices affair. This centred, as so much comment about the UK security services did at that time, on articles in the
Daily Express by Chapman Pincher. Pincher had enraged the former
prime minister, Harold Macmillan by his writing. 'Where does he get
his information from?' Macmillan used to ask his intelligence experts. If
the experts knew, they kept quiet. Wilson had inherited this … paranoia
might be too strong a word, so let's say 'focus of feeling' from Macmillan.

In response to a piece by Pincher in the *Daily Express* on 21 February 1967 which said that 'thousands of private cables and telegrams sent out from Britain by the Post Office or from commercial cable companies are regularly being made available to the security authorities for scrutiny', the Prime Minister lost the plot. It just so happened that later that day the Conservative MP Sir John Langford-Holt, Member for Shrewsbury and a retired Royal Navy officer, was due to ask a question in the House of Commons to Harold Wilson about D-notices. There is no evidence to suggest that Pincher placed his article to coincide with this question. However, the Prime Minister used the opportunity to attack the *Daily Express*, and added, 'What I am concerned with today is a clear breach of two D-notices in spite of the fact that the newspaper concerned was repeatedly warned that they would be contravening the notices.'

There was no need for Wilson to add that. Langford-Holt's question was about keeping the number of D-notices to the minimum and had been tabled many days before. By enlarging on the subject, the Prime Minister had given Chapman Pincher scope to expand his attack on the government, and Pincher made good use of it. The next day, Pincher wrote in the *Daily Express* that he had discussed the story with the secretary of the D-notice committee, Colonel Sam Lohan, who was known to be a friend of his. Lohan had urged him not to write it but had assured him that there was no D-notice about the story. Wilson again repeated in the House of Commons that a D-notice had been issued to the *Daily Express* to prevent Pincher from writing about telegram and cable intercepts. At that time, in order for the security authorities to take such action they needed a warrant issued under the 1920 Official Secrets Act.

The Leader of the Opposition, Ted Heath, asked that the Prime Minister set up a Privy Council inquiry into the direct contradiction between what the PM had said in the Commons and what Pincher said Lohan had told him. Wilson wanted the members of the D-notice committee to decide whether or not the story should have been published. The press members of the committee refused to sit in judgment on another newspaper, and the editor of the *Daily Mirror*, Lee Howard, resigned. At that point, Wilson bowed to Heath's request and set up a committee of three Privy Counsellors to report on the situation. And who should be appointed as chair? Step forward once again, Lord Radcliffe. The other two members were the Labour MP Emmanuel Shinwell, and former Tory Chancellor of the Exchequer, later to be Speaker of the Commons, Selwyn Lloyd. All three were very experienced Privy Counsellors. It took the three of them four months to produce their report. When Dick Crossman read his advance copy, he wrote in his *Diaries*, 'I found the Radcliffe Report a fascinating exposition of civil service stooges and idiocy. Evelyn Waugh at his most fantastic could not have invented it. It will do Harold untold harm.'

The report had found against the Prime Minister, who then insisted on issuing a White Paper giving his side of the story. Several of his Cabinet colleagues, led by Dick Marsh, warned him not to do this as it would seem as if he was setting up Colonel Lohan as a fall guy, but the general view was that if this was the way the PM wished to protect his honour, so be it. Then the whispering campaign began. It was rumoured and later confirmed that Colonel Lohan had never been positively vetted and didn't have full security clearance for his post. Blame was then attached to senior civil servants, and the press were encouraged to attack them. The bad feeling between the Prime Minister and the secretary of the D-notice committee was an open secret in the Westminster village. Wilson accused Lohan of being a womaniser who couldn't hold his drink. He wanted to get rid of him. Wilson's views were confirmed in 1999 when the official secret state papers for the 1960s were released. Writing in *The Guardian* on 13 April 1999, Alan Travis explained how, a month after the Radcliffe Report had been published, Wilson 'was told that Lohan had spoken

disparagingly of the PM and his colleagues at a drinks party ... He held
a series of secret Privy Council meetings with the Conservatives Edward
Heath and Alec Douglas-Home and the then Liberal Leader Jeremy
Thorpe to discuss what to do with Lohan.' According to another Cabinet minister, Barbara Castle, 'Harold Wilson went off his rocker.' But he
managed to drive the colonel out of office and Lohan resigned in July of
1967 with muted thanks from the establishment.

When the Conservatives were returned to power in 1970, Margaret
Thatcher's administration also had an early problem with a D-notices
– or did they? That is the difficulty with D-notices. Because they are
advisory and concerned with secrecy, no one can be quite sure whether
or not they have been issued. Often it is a good workable policy to start
and then perpetuate a rumour that a D-notice has been sent to various
journalists and commentators. This might silence other media outlets, or,
depending how the policy is operated, it can create interest in a subject
which might otherwise be ignored. And, on the other side of the coin,
if editors want to offer an explanation to writers (or the proprietor) as
to why they are not touching a certain story, they only have to murmur,
'D-notices. You know how it is.'

One such incident occurred in the second year of Thatcher's government, and in the forty-three years since, various claims have been made
as to whether or not there was an attempt to silence the press. Writing
in the *Daily Mirror* in 2008, Tom Pettifer said that it had often been
reported that after four days of news coverage the authorities issued a
D-notice requesting that such reporting be discontinued for reasons of
national security. Certainly, the man who broke the story, Robert Rowlands, believed that D-notices were involved. He told the press that the
police had attempted to prevent him from talking to them by means of
a D-notice. The incident is still being researched by those who love
exploring (and sometimes exploding) conspiracy theories. A broadcast

on BBC's Radio 4 in the summer of 2014 was pretty definite that no D-notice had been asked for by any government department so none had been issued. What was all this about?

Shortly before midnight on 11 September 1971, Robert Rowlands found that he was eavesdropping on robbers preparing to steal cash and safe deposit boxes from a branch of Lloyds Bank on Baker Street. He was a radio ham and had picked up the conversations from their two-way radios as they tunnelled beneath a restaurant to gain access to the bank's basement. Rowlands phoned Scotland Yard, who sent policemen to his flat in Wimpole Street. They were unable to pinpoint the actual bank – there were over 700 banks within 10 miles of Mr Rowlands's receiver. These took some time to check, and by the time they arrived at Baker Street the robbery was complete. The total amount stolen in cash and in safe deposit boxes was in the region of £3 million. For a few days the newspapers marvelled at the magnitude and audacity of the crime and then they turned their attention to the details of the possible contents of safe deposit boxes. Rumour and speculation abounded. Some of it reached the press. Other stories were confined to whispers in high places and public houses with criminal connections – this is why there was conjecture whether D-notices were used. Were there some things about which the public should not know? The former Conservative MP and author of *The Power of the Prime Minister* Humphry Berkeley said that Margaret Thatcher should follow the example of Harold Wilson and set up a cabinet of senior Privy Counsellors to investigate. He said, 'Half the stories one hears are obviously arrant nonsense; the difficulty is to decide which half.' A lot of the speculation was based on the secret Cabinet discussions – revealed to be correct by publication of official state papers in 1994 – about the Denning Report. Lord Denning had carried out an inquiry on behalf of the government into the sexual scandals (real and imagined) in public life in the 1960s and the role of the security services.

Many of the Cabinet thought that he had got his critique of the security services wrong; he was too soft. On the basis of that, there were rumours that one safe deposit box belonged to the Labour MP and former minister John Stonehouse, whom some thought to be a Czech secret agent. This was later confirmed to be true by Christopher Andrew in *The Defence of The Realm: The Official History of MI5*, but for diplomatic reasons was hushed up by the then Prime Minister, Margaret Thatcher. In 1974, wanted by the authorities for financial offences, Stonehouse faked his own death by pretending he had drowned in Miami. By an odd quirk of fate, he was discovered by police in Australia who were actually looking for Lord Lucan and had made Stonehouse pull down his trousers to see if they could identify him by the 6-inch scar Lucan had on right thigh. Taken back to England, he remained an MP while awaiting trial in Brixton Prison but resigned from the Labour Party, thus making them a minority government. Another whisper was that the Duchess of Argyll had photographs relating to her divorce in 1963 in a safe box at the Baker Street Bank. The most popular urban myth of the time was that there was a box that contained papers and photographs belonging to Princess Margaret, which would be damaging 'to the national interest' if made public. This last idea supplanted the view that the robbers had taken the boxes with a view to blackmail by one which suggested the whole operation was organised by MI5 'in the national interest' and that was why the government refused to set up a committee of Privy Counsellors to look into it.

The robbers were arrested, convicted and imprisoned in 1974. There was speculation that a 'Mr Big' who has never been caught was the mastermind behind it all. So far, no details of the contents of over 100 safe deposit boxes have come to light. There was a film made about the incident, *The Bank Job*, in 2008. This was written by Dick Clement and Ian Francis, scriptwriters of *The Two Ronnies* and *The Likely Lads*, and starred David Suchet and Peter Bowles, with a cameo role from Mick

Jagger. It perpetuated the idea of MI5's involvement and maintained that D-notices had been issued. No doubt from time to time other urban myths will reappear about this escapade in the media. It is unlikely that any D-notices will be issued in an attempt to stop them.

CHAPTER TWENTY-SIX

THE HOUSE NEXT DOOR

THE PRIVY COUNCIL OFFICE is currently housed at 2 Carlton Gardens, London SW1. This has not always been the case. Some Lord Presidents of the Council, for instance, Richard Crossman MP, the Labour Leader of the House of Commons in the 1960s, and later William Whitelaw MP, the Conservative Leader of the House of Commons in the 1970s (and, as Viscount Whitelaw, Leader of the House of Lords in the 1980s), preferred to be in Downing Street. It was impressive to watch as each day, obeying the demands of Willie Whitelaw's duties, his private office switched seamlessly from Downing Street to the Lords. But a John Nash house in Carlton Gardens is a very suitable headquarters for the Privy Council. In the twenty-first century, this is often described as just another department of government, albeit one which brings other ministries together.

However, when you consider the Cabinet itself is only a committee of
the Privy Council, this is being cavalier with our unwritten constitution. With its elegant, early nineteenth-century façade, the house, on the
south-west side of a small square with a well-tendered lawn in the middle, still gives the appearance of what it once was: a hub of aristocratic
residences in the Victorian period. Field Marshal Earl Kitchener lived
at No. 2 in 1914–15. The Gardens, and Carlton House Terrace, of which
it is an extension, have been the home for many prominent politicians.
Both Palmerston and Balfour – at different times – lived at 4 Carlton Gardens and two other prime ministers, William Gladstone and Earl Grey,
owned houses in Carlton House Terrace. And it wasn't only politicians
who were attracted to the style and grandeur of the houses. The famous
gaming-club owner William Crockford, lived at 11 Carlton House Terrace. Another resident had been the high-profile Lord Curzon, much
talked about as a Foreign Secretary, and equally well known as a Fellow
of All Souls and Chancellor of the University of Oxford. As an anony-
mous poet in the 1870s put it:

> My name is George Nathaniel Curzon,
> I am a most superior person.
> My face is pink, my hair is sleek,
> I dine at Blenheim, once a week.
> I know all there is to know and as I dine in college,
> I can say with truth, if I don't know it – it isn't knowledge.

This setting seems absolutely right for what is probably the world's most
ancient surviving body of government. It is serene. Unlike other organisations of government, it doesn't bustle, it doesn't rush and it doesn't
panic. No visible armed guards; no disturbing sense of high security. The
Privy Council fits in with its 21st-century neighbours, the Royal College

of Pathologists (well, the Privy Council did give the college its royal title), the Royal Society of Portrait Painters (ditto), and the Turf Club. But probably the neighbour with which the Privy Council has most in common is the one immediately behind it, Marlborough House. Both architecturally and historically, it is an extremely grand residence, built for Sarah, Duchess of Marlborough, who obtained a fifty-year lease of land adjoining St James's Palace from her friend Queen Anne. It has many royal connections. The future George V was born there and later lived there as Prince of Wales. His widow Queen Mary moved to Marlborough House in 1936. A few years after her death, the house was given to the Commonwealth and is now the home of the Commonwealth Secretariat. If the Privy Council is the nuts and bolts that link the monarchy to the government, then it is certainly in the right place, sandwiched between the Mall and Pall Mall and in an almost direct line through Marlborough House, St James's Palace, Clarence House, Lancaster House, to Buckingham Palace. Assuming that the Privy Council will be staying where it is for some centuries, every so often – but not too often, we hope – the physical link of the private driveway from Carlton Gardens to St James's Palace will be useful.

For, after the demise of the Crown (the correct etiquette for describing the death of a monarch), St James's Palace is where the accession of a new Sovereign is proclaimed, and it is one of only two occasions – the other being the announcement of the engagement of a reigning monarch – when all Privy Counsellors are summoned to attend, and they are reminded every year to keep the Privy Council Office updated with their contact details. This ancient ceremony is presided over by Garter King at Arms, who stands on the balcony of Friary Court, one of the four courts of St James's Palace (the others being Ambassadors', Engine and Colour) accompanied by the Kings of Arms, the Heralds and the Pursuivants, each one in a splendid uniform. After a fanfare from the State

Trumpeters, the official proclamation will be read; the mostly old words
from a new parchment scroll. The last time this proclamation was read, the
new monarch, Queen Elizabeth II, with her husband the Duke of Edinburgh, had just returned home from east Africa. Their royal Argonaut
airliner *Atalanta*, escorted by an RAF Lancaster, had been delayed by a
storm in Uganda, and the Queen had missed the first Accession Council meeting. This meeting had been held on the day of King George VI's
death, Wednesday 6 February 1952, when key decisions were made concerning the Accession Proclamation to be read on 8 February, firstly at
St James's Palace and then at Temple Bar and on the steps of the Royal
Exchange in the City. On that Friday morning, before the Proclamations,
the Queen held her first Privy Council. It was to them that she gave the
first of the many thousands of speeches she would deliver in her reign.
Nearly 200 Privy Counsellors were assembled in the Entre Room at St
James's Palace. Unlike previous occasions, most wore morning dress
and not Privy Council uniform. These are the words of her Accession
Declaration:

Your Royal Highnesses, My Lords, Ladies and Gentlemen,

By the sudden death of my dear Father I am called to assume the
duties and responsibility of sovereignty. At this time of deep sorrow
it is a profound consolation to me to be assured of your sympathy
which you and all my peoples feel towards me, to my Mother and my
Sister, and to all the other members of my family. My Father was our
revered and beloved head as he was of the wider family of his subjects.
The grief which his loss brings is shared among us all.

My heart is too full to say more to you to-day than that I shall always
work, as my Father did throughout his reign, to uphold constitutional government and to advance the happiness and prosperity of

my peoples, spread as they are all the world over. I know that in my resolve to follow his shining example of service and devotion I shall be inspired by the loyalty and affection of those whose Queen I have been called to be and by the counsel of their elected Parliaments. I pray that God will help me to discharge worthily this heavy task that has been laid upon me so early in my life.

At the end of the Privy Council meeting, the Garter King at Arms, Sir George Bellow, stepped out onto the balcony and made the first public Proclamation of the Accession:

Whereas it has pleased Almighty God to call to His Mercy our late Sovereign King George the Sixth of blessed and glorious memory, by whose decease the Crown is solely and rightfully come to the high and mighty Princess Elizabeth Alexandra Mary:

We, therefore, the Lords Spiritual and Temporal of this Realm, being here assisted with these of his late Majesty's Privy Council with representatives of other members of the Commonwealth, with other principal gentlemen of quality, with the Lord Mayor, Aldermen and citizens of London, do now hereby with one voice and consent of tongue and heart publish and proclaim that the high and mighty Princess Elizabeth Alexandra Mary is now by the death of our late Sovereign of happy memory become Queen Elizabeth the Second by the grace of God, Queen of this Realm, and of Her other Realms and territories, Head of the Commonwealth, Defender of the Faith.

To whom her lieges do acknowledge all faith and constant obedience with hearty and humble affection, beseeching by God, by Whom Kings and Queens do reign, to bless the Royal Princess Elizabeth the Second with long and happy years to reign over us. God Save the Queen.

There will be particular interest in Marlborough House, the house next door to the Privy Council offices, in the proclamation, not least because from his or her desk, whoever is the Secretary-General of the Commonwealth will get a perfect view of the ceremony through their window overlooking Friary Court in St James's Palace. But there will be two more substantial reasons for the interest of the Commonwealth. In 1952, there were only eight countries in the Commonwealth. Now there are fifty-three. If they all want to send representatives, where do they stand? The Privy Council itself has a similar problem. All 600-plus members must be summoned; suppose they all come – and, even now official Court Dress has been abolished, suppose they all want to borrow uniforms? The other substantial and great point of significance for the Commonwealth is that in 1952, Queen Elizabeth II inherited the title Head of the Commonwealth from her father, George VI. Times have changed and it has been agreed that on the demise of the Crown it will be for all the countries of the Commonwealth to decide on their new head. This could mean hasty telephone calls over a short period to get the right wording into the proclamation.

It is amazing how much confusion there is even at the highest level about the matter of the Commonwealth and titles. In his book *In the Ring: a Commonwealth Memoir*, Don McKinnon, the Secretary-General of the Commonwealth from 2000 to 2008, describes his first meeting with Gordon Brown, at a dinner in 10 Downing Street. The Prime Minister introduced him to another guest: 'Do you know Don McKinnon? He's Head of the British Commonwealth.' McKinnon laughed and said, 'Sorry, Gordon. You are wrong on two counts. The Queen is the Head and the British Commonwealth died in 1949, before you were born.'

Apart from the physical proximity of their headquarters, the Privy Council and the Commonwealth are close in a number of other ways. As Chapter Twenty-Three shows, there is almost daily interaction between many Commonwealth countries and the Judicial Committee of the Privy Council. Then so many prominent figures from the Commonwealth are members of the Privy Council. Probably over 10 per cent at any one time. Indeed, a quarter of the 2006 committee on Commonwealth membership – P. J. Patterson from Jamaica and Baroness Amos from the UK – were Privy Counsellors. It is interesting to look at one of the recommendations of that committee: if 'new' members wished to join the Commonwealth, then 'as a general rule' they should have historical constitutional connections with an existing member or a 'substantial' relationship with the Commonwealth as an institution.

The other recommendations were much as could be expected. English should be used as the official language of the Commonwealth and all countries must recognise Queen Elizabeth II as Head of the Commonwealth. The comments on the rule of law, equal opportunity and human rights were couched in terms of demonstrating commitment, rather than having arrived at a universally accepted panacea.

The whole tone of the committee's report was open ended. They were not trying to tie up the loose ends of different countries' understandings of government and democracy so that they could perfectly fit into an international organisation. Much of this attitude towards world affairs flows from the outstanding leadership of Sir Shridath 'Sonny' Ramphal, who was Secretary-General of the Commonwealth from 1975 to 1990. Richard Bourne, in his book *Shridath Ramphal: The Commonwealth and the World*, quotes Nelson Mandela's tribute: 'Shridath Ramphal is one of those men who have become famous because in their fight for human justice, they have chosen the entire world as their theatre.' Working with an enlarging group of so many different and differing countries, one of Ramphal's guidelines was that discussion towards agreement was far more effective than voting for decisions. That was a lesson many thought useful for the Commonwealth to pass on to other international organisations. Monti Malhoutra, a former Assistant General-Secretary to the Commonwealth Secretariat, said of Shridath Ramphal:

> One of the things we all admired and stood the Commonwealth in good stead was his ability as a draftsman. His political skills and legal background made him a superb bridge-builder between different points of view. 'You must always be ahead of the game by having a draft ready in your pocket to table at the right moment,' he said. It was this tactic which contributed greatly to the resolution of divisive issues at successive Heads of Government meetings.

By these methods, Ramphal played a key role in joining together the overlapping interests of the Commonwealth, the Crown and the Privy Council in the Lusaka Accord on Rhodesia, where, according to Malhoutra, 'he cobbled together common elements from the positions of Julius Nyere, Kenneth Kaunda, and Margaret Thatcher'.

Both the Commonwealth and the British Privy Council, through their counsellors working together, have been able to offer the world tried-and-tested skills in reaching consensus on some of the most difficult problems. One of the best examples of this was in 1980, when former Prime Minister Edward Heath worked with Shridath Ramphal and the former German Chancellor Willy Brandt on the final report of the Brandt Commission on international development, 'North-South: A Programme for Survival'. In Richard Bourne's book *Shidrath Ramphal: The Commonwealth and the World*, in the chapter entitled 'A Global Citizen', Kaye Whiteman from the European Commission in Brussels writes: 'What is probably not known outside the narrow circle of the commission's operation was the difficulty faced by the commission in concluding a consensus report. The commission was divided between those who wanted to hold rigidly to a radical programme of change ... and others who had a more liberal stance.' The sticking point was the detail over recommendations for finance and commodities. To break this deadlock, Willy Brandt got Heath and Ramphal to produce a working draft. They worked away from the tensions in Brandt's headquarters in Geneva. They settled down to write in the Commonwealth Secretariat headquarters at Marlborough House, then moving with Willy Brandt and other members of the commission to – as described by Kaye Whiteman – 'the amenable, elegant and art-rich atmosphere of Leeds Castle in Kent in England'. They succeeded in producing a report admired both by campaigners and by the international community. He goes to say, 'Perhaps no other international development report had such salience when it was launched. At the Hague over 4,000 people turned up to welcome it. In London there was a mass lobby of 10,000 supporters.'

Although at the moment it is reasonable to say that the work of the Commonwealth on the world stage does not gain the publicity it merits, that may change on the occasion of the sad demise of the Crown – if the title of Head of the Commonwealth does not pass to Prince Charles. Then, merited or not, there will be publicity. Charles Moore, writing in the *Daily Telegraph* on 28 July 2014, notes that:

> My impression is that a large part of the decision will rest with who-
> ever is secretary-general of the Commonwealth when the Queen dies.
> If they decide to make heavy weather of the Commonwealth succes-
> sion, doubts could appear in some member states, and Prince Charles
> might not become Head. But if that happens a workable alternative
> will be impossible to find. The Commonwealth will discover too late
> the strange fact that its only focus of unity comes from the House of
> Windsor.

If the headship of the Commonwealth did pass from Britain to another country, whether or not the grand setting of Marlborough House would remain as headquarters of the Commonwealth Secretariat would become an open question. The Privy Council Office might have new neighbours. This would be a pity as both institutions have much in common and, as they continually develop, can learn from each other. Unlike any other world bodies, they both operate (at the moment) under a non-elected head. It is the same head and she carries with her a respect and prestige which is unique and is loved and applauded around the world. Both the Privy Council and the Commonwealth are still evolving and adapting to changing conditions internally and externally. This makes them different from most other international organisations such as the United Nations, or NATO, or the Council of Europe, which were planned and codified from their very beginnings. Both the Privy Council and the Common-wealth bring an experience of how to live with loose ends. There are wide differences between various Commonwealth countries, but the Commonwealth copes. Questions are always being asked about the role of the Privy Council. There is a desire by some to try to pin down exact answers to their enquiries. This even comes from Privy Counsellors them-selves. For example, Lord Rodgers of Quarry Bank asked in a debate in the House of Lords on 12 May 2009, 'I want to know what Privy Coun-sellors are for.' A few seconds later he asked, 'Is membership of the Privy Council a titular honour?' Then he enquired, 'Does the Privy Council have a significant function within the processes of government? I have wondered about this since I became a Privy Counsellor more than thirty years ago.' But this is not the right approach for trying to understand the ancient institution of the Privy Council.

It is refreshing in an age when so many people, organisations and institutions are concerned with getting matters regulated, buttoned-up and with fixed boundaries around their activities that the Privy Council and its next-door neighbour, the headquarters of the Commonwealth of

Nations, are able to continue to evolve, asking questions about themselves as they do so, and always being open to new ways of working.

CHAPTER TWENTY-SEVEN

FROM REMOTE ANTIQUITY TO PCOSECRETARIAT@ PCO.X.GSI.GOV.UK

N HIS AWARD-WINNING ESSAY on the Privy Council, Professor Albert Dicey, Fellow of All Souls and one of the most distinguished lawyers of his time, wrote of the Privy Council:

> It seems to have a life, an individuality, a destiny of its own. It is the creation of man, but it is greater than its creators, for it lives on while they perish. Yet, the work of man, it too is mortal; and meets with disease, decline and death. If any institution can claim a sympathy, generally accorded rather to human beings than to their works, the Council of the English monarchy may demand our especial interest. It boasts a history stretching back to remote antiquity.

That was written in 1860 and published in 1887. It is the template on which Sir Almeric Fitzroy based his book *The History of The Privy Council*, written in 1928. Nearly ninety years on, the Privy Council has succumbed to neither disease or death. It has embraced the digital age, with one of the most impressive websites any arm of government has put into the public domain. And while Professor Dicey and Sir Almeric would find today's technology difficult to cope with at first, they would certainly have recognised some of the topics being dealt with by the Privy Council in the twenty-first century.

Take these two items from the agenda of a meeting of the Council held at Buckingham Palace on 5 November 2014:

> Item: Saint Helena Act 1833; The Russia, Crimea and Sevastopol
> (Sanctions) (Overseas Territories) Amendment Order 2014 (SI)
> Item: Order granting a Supplementary Charter to the Royal
> College of Veterinary Surgeons.

This illustrates the almost complete remit the Privy Council has as the authorising body for both government action and legislation. In home affairs, it has an ordinary piece of business to do with a body holding a Royal Charter, probably of little interest to anybody outside the veterinary profession. In foreign affairs, the meticulous use of the Saint Helena Act 1833 'in response to the continuing illegal annexation of Crimea and Sevastopol and the unprovoked violation of Ukrainian sovereignty and territorial integrity by the Russian Federation' is explained by a memorandum prepared by the Foreign and Commonwealth Office. The FCO declared that 'this Order is made in exercise of statutory powers under the Saint Helena Act 1833, the British Settlements Act 1887 and 1945 and the legislative power of the royal prerogative'. The Order, applied to the UK's overseas territories, covered all the sanctions imposed on Russia by the European Union and specifically highlighted a ban on the supply of assistance related to the transfer of oil exploration technologies. In a note attached to this Order, the Privy Council Office ruled that 'as this Order is not subject to parliamentary procedure and does not amend primary legislation, no statement is required'.

The constitutional expertise of the Privy Council Office is impressive. But, as one former Clerk said to me, 'We have been doing it for some centuries.' Sometimes they have to deal with what many would regard as smallish matters, such as changing the text in notes concerning the Chartered Institute of Loss Adjusters so that 'he' becomes 'they' to recognise that there are now many woman in the profession. Sometimes their Orders can be of international importance, such as the following Order in Council issued from Windsor Castle on 4 April 1982, at the time of the Falklands War: 'A Secretary of State or the Minister of Transport or the Lords Commissioners of the Admiralty may requisition for Her Majesty's Service any British ship and anything on board such ship wherever it may be.'

The Privy Council meets about once a month. Normally three members make up a quorum but sometimes as many as six can be summoned. Occasionally, counsellors request a summons to attend, if, for example, a relative or close friend is being sworn to the Council. Sometimes it is asked what would happen if a counsellor just turned up and insisted on being ushered into the meeting. Probably the most satisfactory answer to this was given in the last century by the Clerk Sir Almeric Fitzroy, when he replied, 'They would be snubbed.'

Nearly all the counsellors I talked with and all but one of the memoirs I have read give the impression that Privy Council meetings are filled with a tangible sense of responsibility. One counsellor said to me, 'To pinch a quote from Tony Blair, when I stand there I do feel the hand of history on my shoulder.' Lord Kingsland, the Conservative shadow Lord Chancellor, said in 2009, 'The Privy Council oath – we have been told that its origin goes back to the thirteenth century – certainly makes the taker

wonder whether he can live up to the very high duty that he owes to Her
Majesty.' The Labour Lord President of the Council Robin Cook was
worried that he sometimes might have made others think that he didn't
take it seriously enough, but another Labour Cabinet minister, Richard
Crossman, was the only Lord President to express scorn at the proceedings. However, he made it clear that this was directed not at the monarch
but at those who made the arrangements for the meetings. In *The Crossman Diaries*, he complains of having to travel to Aberdeen by sleeper for
a Privy Council meeting the next day at Balmoral, only to find that when
he arrived in Scotland no hotel room had been booked for him where he
could bath and change. He wrote on Tuesday 20 September 1966:

> The Privy Council is the best example of pure mumbo-jumbo you
> can find. It is interesting to reflect that four Ministers, busy men, all
> had to take a night and a day off to go up there with Godfrey Agnew
> to stand for two and a half minutes while the list of titles was read out.
> It would be far simpler for the Queen to come down to Buckingham
> Palace but its *lèse-majesté* to suggest it.

A study of the agenda of any regular meeting of the Privy Council gives
a fair picture of the range of subjects covered. Here is an example which
it is worth reading in full because it illustrates the variety and scope of
the matters that come under the remit of the Privy Council, from sanctions against Syria and housing on the Island of Sark to burial grounds
in Yorkshire and double taxation in Barbados – not to mention approving of the marriage of one of the Queen's cousins.

ORDERS APPROVED AT THE PRIVY COUNCIL HELD
BY THE QUEEN AT BUCKINGHAM PALACE ON 12
DECEMBER 2012

COUNSELLORS PRESENT:

The Rt Hon. Nick Clegg (Lord President)

The Rt Hon. Michael Gove

The Rt Hon. Chris Grayling

The Rt Hon. Philip Hammond

The Rt Hon. Theresa May

The Rt Hon. Patrick McLoughlin

ROYAL MARRIAGES ACT 1772: Declaration of Consent to
the marriage of Louise Alexandra Patricia Nicolson and Charles
Christopher Thomas Morshead.

PRIVY COUNSELLORS: An Order appointing Sir Richard
McCombe as a Member of Her Majesty's Most Honourable
Privy Council.

PROCLAMATIONS: Two Proclamations:

Determining the specifications and design for fifty-pence coins
commemorating the hundredth anniversary of the birth of
Benjamin Britten.

Determining the specifications and design for fifty-pence coins
commemorating the hundredth anniversary of the birth of
Christopher Ironside.

And two Orders directing the Lord Chancellor to affix the Great
Seal to the Proclamations.

CHARTERS: Order granting a Charter to Marylebone Cricket Club.

CHARTER SURRENDER: Order accepting the surrender of
the Charter of the Salvage Association.

SAINT HELENA ACT 1833: 1. The Guinea-Bissau (Sanctions) (Overseas Territories) Order 2012 (SI);

2. The Syria (Restrictive Measures) (Overseas Territories) (Amendment) Order 2012 (SI).

UNIVERSITIES OF OXFORD AND CAMBRIDGE ACT 1923

Order approving amendments to the Statutes of Churchill College Cambridge.

UNITED NATIONS ACT 1946

The Al-Qaida (United Nations Measures) (Overseas Territories) (Amendment) Order 2012 (SI) and three other measures involving the Cote d'Ivoire (Sanctions), the Democratic People's Public of Korea (Sanctions) and Somalia (Sanctions).

FINANCE ACT 1960

Concerning NATO, Visiting Forces and International Military Headquarters (Tax Designation).

HEALTH SERVICE COMMISSIONERS ACT 1993

Concerning Special Health Services.

NORTHERN IRELAND ACT 1998

District Electoral Areas Commissioner.

SCOTLAND ACT 1998

The Scottish Administration Offices Order.

INCOME TAX EARNINGS AND PENSIONS ACT 2003
Concerning Visiting Forces.

CIVIL PARTNERSHIP ACT 2004
Registration abroad amendment.

TAXATION (INTERNATIONAL AND OTHER PROVISIONS)
Double Taxation Relief: Affecting Enforcement: Bahrain,
Barbados, Liechenstein, Singapore and Switzerland.

JERSEY
Concerning the Royal Court Law; Banking Business and
Bankruptcy.

GUERNSEY
Concerning the Financial Services Commission, the Foundation
Law and the Sewerage system.

SARK
An Order dismissing a Petition and approving the Housing
(Control of Occupation) (Sark) Law 2011.

BURIALS ACT 1853
Order prohibiting further burials in the churchyards of:
St Katherine's, Rowsley, Matlock, Derbyshire;
St Bartholomew's, Marsden, Huddersfield, West Yorkshire;
St Michael and All Angels, Tenterden, Kent.

PETITIONS

Order concerning a Petition of the Worshipful Company of
  Chartered Surveyors Praying for a grant of a Charter of
  incorporation to be referred to a committee of the Privy Council.
Order concerning a Petition of the Worshipful Company of
  Hackney Carriage Drivers Praying for the grant of a Charter of
  incorporation to be referred to a committee of the Privy Council.

Many of the items, such as the coins commemorating the composer
Benjamin Britten and the coin designer Christopher Ironside, are self-
explanatory. For other items, notes are provided. For instance, this report
from the Committee of the Council for the Affairs of Jersey and Guernsey:

> In accordance with Your Majesty's General Order of Reference of the
> 22nd day of February 1952 the Committee have considered the Peti-
> tion of Sir David Barclay and Sir Frederick Barclay dated 5 August
> 2011 objecting to the Housing (Control of Occupation) (Sark) Law,
> 2011. The Committee have considered the Petition and have agreed to
> report that it may be advisable for Your Majesty to dismiss the Petition.

Her Majesty, of course, as she has to, took the advice of the committee and
later in the meeting agreed to a Petition of the Chief Pleas of the Island of
Sark that humbly prayed 'that Your Majesty might be graciously pleased
to sanction the Housing (Control of Occupation) (Sark) Law 2011, and to
order that it shall have the force of law in the Island of Sark'. No doubt all
the meeting was aware that the two knights who had petitioned against
this measure getting Royal Assent, the Barclay brothers, were in fact the
owners of the Island of Sark.

The Privy Council has a number of standing committees. The committee referred to above concerned with the affairs of the Channel Islands

dates back to the Poynings' Act of 1495. These committees are the *modus operandi* for the discharge of a significant part of the work of the Privy Council. Some of these, such as the one dealing with housing on Sark, act under statutory sanction. Another one is the committee concerned with the Universities of Oxford and Cambridge. (There is a separate one dealing with Scottish universities, which may have to be amended in terms of future devolution.) This committee considered the changes in statutes wanted by Churchill College, Cambridge – mostly to do with regulations affecting retirements and resignations – and, as they had received no petitions against the proposals, advised Her Majesty to allow them to go ahead, which she duly did.

It must be stressed that these meetings are not about debate or discussion. There is no voting. The Lord President reads through the measures the Privy Council are presenting either on their own behalf or for the government as a whole or for individual (sometimes multi) government departments. Every so often the Lord President pauses and the Queen says, 'Approved', unless the subject is a petition for a new Charter, in which case she says, 'Referred'. This is a prime working example of how an elected government and an inherited head of state operate seamlessly to ensure the smooth running of the country. That is (one of) the things the Privy Council does. And it is of vital importance. Get the timing wrong and whole areas of legislation could be in danger or indeed lost – not just in the UK but also in our overseas territories. The legislation of the Seychelles Islands, which had been a Crown colony since 1903 and had held elections in 1966, needed Privy Council authorisation, for vital domestic reasons, to prolong its government in 1967. This had to be done by 11 October, which in the UK clashed with the Labour Party – then the governing party – conference. After some heated discussion with the then Lord President, the Clerk, Sir Godfrey Agnew, managed to get four Privy Counsellors from the Labour Party to Balmoral in time for a meeting a few hours before the Seychelles legislature would have collapsed.

Some committees which at first sight may seem to have been set up by the Privy Council for specific inquiries do not in fact report to the Lord President of the Council, nor are they serviced by the Privy Council Office. But they are made up of Privy Counsellors appointed by the Prime Minister. These are non-statutory committees composed entirely of Privy Counsellors, established to look into events which have been of great public interest, such as Lord Franks's review into the Falkland Islands in 1982, and the examination of intelligence of weapons of mass destruction in Iraq in 2004, chaired by Lord Butler of Brockwell. These are often far more appropriate than judicial inquiries, as the problem of judges getting drawn into questions of politics is avoided. The Butler Inquiry was also an interesting exercise because some members of the committee whose expertise was thought essential to have on board but who weren't members of the Privy Council were quickly sworn so that they could operate under the Privy Council oath and have the same access to intelligence information as all members of the committee.

As will be seen from the agenda of the Privy Council on 12 December 2012, not all committees have such exciting remits. The Order referring a petition of the Worshipful Company of Chartered Surveyors for a grant of incorporation to a committee of the Privy Council may not be everybody's idea of public service. But somebody has to do it. That somebody is the Privy Council.

The exercise of the Privy Council's rights to grant Royal Charters and to deal with charities and learned societies means that there are many thousands of people going about their daily lives unaware that they have been affected by the Council's work. A friend of mine has given me permission to quote from this letter he sent me:

I didn't quite realise quite how right you were about the Privy Council being involved in all sorts of unexpected aspects of our lives. I happened to glance at the wall of my study earlier today and the words *PRIVY COUNCIL* suddenly jumped out at me to catch my eye. It was on the scroll of my Chartered Mathematician certificate. When the Duke of Edinburgh, a past President of the Institute of Mathematics, obtained the Royal Charter for the Institute, all elected Fellows of the Institute were automatically designated Chartered Mathematicians. The scroll reads, 'This is to certify that in accordance with the byelaws of the Institute as confirmed by the Order of Her Majesty's *PRIVY COUNCIL* David Armstrong being a Fellow of the Institute is thereby designated a Chartered Mathematician.' The significance or even the presence of the words *PRIVY COUNCIL* had never struck me before. These blighters really do get in everywhere.

Much of the work of the Privy Council Office is done in areas of constitutional and legislative uncertainty. This is bound to be the case in a country with an unwritten constitution. A clear case of this is seen in that last item on the Privy Council's agenda: that about the closure of burial grounds. It is a brave committee that ventures into those grounds, especially that of ownership and responsibility for upkeep once a closure has taken place. But, again, somebody has to deal with the mix of Church, local authority, private companies, bankrupt firms, developers and individual petitioners. Again, that somebody is the Privy Council.

The decisions of government that are formalised at Privy Council meetings are recorded in Orders which have the force of law. Previous chapters have dealt with the basic difference between Orders in Council which have to be approved personally by the Queen and Orders of Council which can be made by ministers acting as the Lords of the Privy Council. Orders of Council, although they are expressed as having been

made in the Privy Council Chamber, are normally done by correspondence and no actual meeting takes place. Since 1946, all Orders are statutory
instruments and have to be numbered and published by the Stationary
Office. They are now available online at www.legislation.gov.uk. One of
the problems the Privy Council sometimes faces is with Orders issued
before 1946, especially to do with the pay of the navy, which relates to
the Naval and Marine Pay and Pensions Act 1865, and with the closure
of churchyards, which comes under the 1853 Burial Act.

The times when the work of the Privy Council comes to the attention
of the public are mostly to do with the exercise of the royal prerogative.
How can that be defined in a country without a written constitution?
Like many other lecturers, Patrick McAuslan, former Professor of Public Law at the London School of Economics, used to refer his students
to Professor Albert Dicey's explanation that 'the royal prerogative is the
residue of discretionary power left at any moment in the hands of the
Crown, whether such power be exercised by the Queen herself or by her
ministers'. As an example of this, McAuslan would give the declaration
of war and the making of peace. This is a discussion taking place today,
in 2015, and as yet no constitutional answer has been reached. Times
change, but certainly when there was last a realistic threat of a land invasion of the UK in the late 1930s and early 1940s, the idea that Parliament
should vote beforehand on whether the country should or should not
declare war had little support. Ministers reacted with horror to the idea
that the enemy should not only see the numbers of MPs and lords who
didn't want to fight but also be able to identify them.

Public and media debate also flourishes when the topic is national
security. In the 1980s, there was much unease when the Prime Minister, Margaret Thatcher, said in the House of Commons that the Master
of the Rolls, Lord Donaldson, was correct in saying that that 'where
members of the security services do commit illegal acts, there is always

the prerogative power not to pursue criminal proceedings'. Again, that debate is still continuing.

The constitutional worry is that when ministers discover that they can't proceed with a certain course of action because there is no statutory instrument giving them authority to do so, they turn to the royal prerogative. That normally happens in a situation no one had imagined would occur, or which simply hadn't been planned for, or where there wasn't a feasible chance of getting legislation through Parliament in time. But neither the monarch nor the Privy Council should be blamed for that. The Privy Council is the collective voice of ministers. The Queen can only exercise the royal prerogative on the advice of ministers. Of course, a lot goes on behind the scenes. Mistakes can be avoided, and sometimes, as in the case of the Diego Garcia islanders, ministers come close to making an apology. Diego Garcia is an atoll in the Chagos Archipelago, which is part of the British Indian Ocean Territory. In order to allow the United States to expand and completely upgrade their naval base there, the UK 're-settled' 2,000 islanders between 1968 and 1973 to the Seychelles and Mauritius. The Chagossians later appealed on the grounds that their eviction was illegal, and won the right in the courts of law to be returned to their homeland. Then, as the Liberal Democrat Lord McNally put it in the House of Lords in 2009, 'the shadier part of our constitution provided by the Privy Council allowed that decision to be overturned by this House'. Jack Straw, who was in the Labour Cabinet at the time of the appeal, admitted that the government should have engaged more fully with the plight of the islanders and that sometimes the Privy Council could be used 'in exchanging legitimacy for speed'.

However, what some critics fail to realise is that all democratic governments working under whatever constitution are sometimes going to have to make decisions and take actions outside their elected remit. That's life. The Privy Council has evolved over the centuries to be highly effective in those situations.

The Council also attracted criticism for the part it played in setting up the Royal Charter for the press. This was ill-informed criticism. Following the phone-hacking scandals, the Leveson Report on the press had attracted much comment and many varied views were put forward for legislation. Eventually the Conservative/Liberal coalition government came up with a proposal for a Royal Charter. This was backed by the Rt Hon. Ed Miliband, the Leader of the Labour Party, Leader of Her Majesty's Loyal Opposition and member of the Privy Council. All leaders of the main opposition parties are sworn to the Privy Council so that if they wish they can receive secret briefings under the Privy Council oath. The proposals for the Charter were put forward by the Prime Minister, the Rt Hon. David Cameron, and his Deputy Prime Minister, the Rt Hon. Nick Clegg, Leader of the Liberal Democrats and Lord President of the Privy Council. With those three Privy Counsellors asking the Privy Council to petition the Queen for a Royal Charter for the press, the terms of which they had agreed with cross-party support, there was never any doubt about the result. The Charter came into being. Some newspaper proprietors tried to get a High Court injunction to stop the Privy Council considering this measure. They failed. The Rt Hon. John Prescott, formerly Labour Deputy Prime Minister, resigned from the Privy Council because he did not want this particular Royal Charter set up in his name. It made no difference. His action deserves a footnote because it is the only time a member of the Privy Council has asked to resign for any other reason than their own behaviour.

The Privy Council will continue to evolve. If we reach a position in the UK where there is increased devolution, or greater regional government, or more political parties gaining seats at Westminster, the Council may have a slightly different role to play. They may also be involved if the

House of Lords reform becomes a reality. But for the moment, the situation of the oldest surviving body of government is well summed up in the ending to a speech by the then Lord President of the Privy Council and Leader of the House of Lords, the Labour peer the Rt Hon. Baroness Royall of Blaisdon. In the House of Lords on 12 May 2009, she said:

> In conclusion, the Privy Council is rather one of those odd bits of the UK constitution, which none the less works extremely well. I am proud to be its President. If we were starting from here we might not invent it but in practice it fulfils an important role in our constitutional and governmental arrangements. Long may it continue.

APPENDIX A

Overseas Territories That Have Been or Are under the Jurisdiction of the Judicial Committee of the Privy Council

Alderney and Sark

Anguilla

Antigua and Barbuda

Ascension and Tristan du Cunha

Australia

The Bahamas

Bermuda

British Antarctic Territory

British Virgin Islands

Brunei

Canada

Caribbean Community

Cayman Islands

Cook Islands and Niue

Cyprus – only for Akrotiri and
Dhekelia sovereign bases

Dominica

Falkland Islands

Ghana

Gibraltar

Grenada

Grenadines and Tuvalu

Guernsey

Guyana

Hong Kong

India

Irish Free State

Isle of Man

Jamaica

Kiribati

Malaysia

Montserrat

Mauritius

New Zealand

Pakistan

Pitcairn Islands

Rhodesia

St Helena

Saint Kitts and Nevis

Saint Lucia

Saint Vincent

Singapore

South Africa

South Georgia

South Sandwich Islands

Trinidad and Tobago

Turks and Caicos Islands

APPENDIX B

Universities Where the Lord President of
the Privy Council Acts as Visitor

University of Birmingham

University of Bristol

University of Hull

Imperial College London

University of Keele

University of Leeds

University of Leicester

University of Liverpool

University of London (but not King's College London or University College London)

University of Nottingham

University of Reading

University of Sheffield

University of Southampton

University of Sussex

University of Wales

APPENDIX C

Order of Precedence

LOOKING BACK FROM THE second decade of the twenty-first century, it is amazing to realise how important the question of social status and precedence was only a short time ago. In living memory, young girls from the upper classes 'came out' – a phrase meaning something quite different now. They were presented at court, curtsied to the Queen, and officially became debutantes, being warned by their mothers about young men who were NSIT (not safe in taxis). You couldn't get into the Royal Enclosure at Ascot if you were divorced, and the letters pages of women's magazines were crowded with enquiries from social climbers and *arrivistes* preparing for their first London dinner parties, wanting to know if the younger son of a duke went in before the eldest son of a marquess. The classic letter was from a women who had both the Aga Khan and a duke coming and received the reply: 'The Aga Khan is held to be a direct descendent of God. An English duke, of course, takes precedence.' What helped – and still does help those who bother about such things – is that there is an officially published order of precedence. There was a brief revival of interest in this from the upper classes during the Cold War, to see in what order they entered the nuclear bunker. The order has evolved over the centuries. In theory, any changes are made by the Prime Minister. In practice, 'ancient usage', raised eyebrows and sharp elbows are probably more decisive. In 2013, there was a long delay on the grand staircase of the Royal Opera House while the Right Reverend the Lord Bishop of London, Richard Chartiss, discussed with a recently created life peer, which of them had precedence in climbing the stairs first to be greeted by the Lord Mayor of London. Interestingly, the baron in question was

Julian Fellowes, the creator of *Downton Abbey*. Viewers of that television programme will know that a hundred years ago, matters of precedence and status were as much a concern below stairs as above them.

In 1915, P. G. Wodehouse wrote *Something Fresh*. He relates a conversation between a young lady and a man thinking of entering Blandings Castle pretending to be a valet:

> 'Have you ever seen a lady's maid, Mr Mason?'
>
> 'Why, no, now that I come to think of it, I don't believe I have.'
>
> 'Well, let me tell you, meekness is her last quality. Why should she be meek? Doesn't she go in after the Groom of Chambers?'
>
> 'Go in? Go in where?'
>
> 'Into dinner.'
>
> She smiled at the sight of his bewildered face.
>
> 'I'm afraid that you don't know much about the etiquette of the new world you have entered so rashly. Didn't you know that the rules of precedence among the servants of a big house are more rigid and complicated than in Society? Try going into dinner out of your proper place and see what happens. A public rebuke from the butler is the least that you could expect.'

That was a much less casual age. Now we have a take-it-or-leave-it attitude to honours, especially in the media. Presenters and interviewees on *Start the Week* or *Question Time* disdain with a shrug their membership of the House of Lords but are only too happy to embrace their titles when they go into the bars at the Palace of Westminster or use their position to vote on future legislation. And there is sloppy research by the media. I've lost count of the times I have seen, for example, Lord Hattersley described as Lord Roy Hattersley, as though he was the younger son of a marquess. That is very much the leave-it attitude. There is also the take-it approach. When the Privy Council discussed in the 1950s where life peers would fit into the order of precedence, no one thought that their children would later assume the title of 'The Honourable'. The law of unintended consequences operates everywhere.

Privy Counsellors come some way down the list of precedence, but a high proportion of them have other, more senior titles which can move them up several places. Although many would regard the whole matter as obsolete, the list is actually used quite a lot, especially by big companies and corporations, charities, local government, universities, and all those giving receptions, launching ships, opening supermarkets or arranging funerals where they want to get things just right. And if you doubt that, just Google the *Daily Telegraph* obituaries page for 14 March 2014 and see how the names of the hundreds of mourners who attended the memorial service for Sir David Frost at Westminster Abbey the previous day are arranged. From the highest in official precedence to the lowest, it is straight out of *Debrett*, with, for instance, the High Commissioner for Bangladesh being given his correct place above the Countess of Snowden but below the Crown Prince of the Hellenes. Some positions in the order of precedence, such as the Lord High Constable, are vacant for most of the time, for fear of giving the wrong person too much power. This is a short list. The best place to find complete details is in a copy of *Debrett's Handbook*:

The Sovereign

Prince Philip, the Duke of Edinburgh

The Prince of Wales

The Sovereign's younger sons

The Sovereign's younger grandsons

The Sovereign's younger grandchildren

Archbishop of Canterbury

Lord High Chancellor

Archbishop of York

The Prime Minister

Lord President of the Privy Council

Speaker of the House of Commons

Lord Privy Seal

Ambassadors and High Commissioners

Lord Great Chamberlain

Lord High Constable

Earl Marshal

Lord High Admiral

Lord Steward of the Household

Lord Chamberlain of the Household

Chief Butler of England

Master of the Horse

Dukes, according to the patent of their creation

Ministers and envoys

Eldest sons of dukes of blood royal

Marquesses, according to the patent of their creation

Dukes' eldest sons

Earls, according to the patent of their creation

Younger sons of dukes of blood royal

And so it goes on, through viscounts, barons, bishops, baronets, knights and dames, judges, the vice-chamberlains, the various orders such as Garter, Bath, CBEs, OBEs and MBEs. Privy Counsellors come below the Knights of the Garter but above the Master of the Rolls.

There is a separate list for Scotland.

APPENDIX D

The Kings and Queens of England

William I 1066–1087

William II 1087–1100

Henry I 1100–1135

Stephen and Matilda 1135–1154

Henry II 1154–1189

Richard I 1189–1199

John 1199–1216

Henry III 1216–1272

Edward I 1272–1307

Edward II 1307–1327

Edward III 1327–1377

Richard II 1377–1399

Henry IV 1399–1413

Henry V 1413–1422

Henry VI 1422–1461, 1470–1471

Edward IV 1461–1470, 1471–1483

Edward V 1483

Richard III 1483–1485

Henry VII 1485–1509

Henry VIII 1509–1547

Edward VI 1547–1553

Mary I 1553–1558

Elizabeth I 1558–1603

James I 1603–1625

Charles I 1625–1649

Interregnum 1649–1660

Charles II 1660–1685

James II 1685–1688

William III and Mary II 1688–1694

William III 1694–1702

Anne 1702–1714

George I 1714–1727

George II 1727–1760

George III 1760–1820

George IV 1820–1830

William IV 1830–1837

Victoria 1837–1901

Edward VII 1901–1910

George V 1910–1936

Edward VIII 1936

George VI 1936–1952

Elizabeth II 1952–

APPENDIX E

UK Prime Ministers

W = Whig; T = Tory; C = Conservative; L = Liberal; Lab = Labour; N. Lab = National Labour

Sir Robert Walpole 1721–1742 W

Earl of Wilmington 1742–1743 W

Henry Pelham 1743–1754 W

Duke of Newcastle 1754–1756 W

Duke of Devonshire 1756–1757 W

Duke of Newcastle 1757–1762 W

Earl of Bute 1762–1763 T

George Grenville 1763–1765 W

Marquess of Rockingham 1765–1766 W

Earl of Chatham 1766–1768 W

Duke of Grafton 1768–1770 W

Lord North 1770–1782 T

Marquess of Rockingham 1782 W

Earl of Shelburne 1782–1783 W

Duke of Portland 1783 W

William Pitt 1783–1801 T

Henry Addington 1801–1804 T

William Pitt 1804–1806 T

Lord Grenville 1806–1807 W

Duke of Portland 1807–1809 W

Spencer Perceval 1809–1812 T

Earl of Liverpool 1812–1827 T

George Canning 1827 T

Viscount Goderich 1827–1828 T

Duke of Wellington 1828–1830 T

Earl Grey 1830–1834 W

Lord Melbourne 1834 W

Duke of Wellington 1834 T

Sir Robert Peel 1834–1835 T

Lord Melbourne 1835–1841 W

Sir Robert Peel 1841–1846 T

Lord John Russell 1846–1852 L

Earl of Derby 1852 C

Earl of Aberdeen 1852–1855 T

Viscount Palmerston 1855–1858 L

Earl of Derby 1858–1859 C

Viscount Palmerston 1859–1865 L

Lord John Russell 1865–1866 L

Earl of Derby 1866–1868 C

Benjamin Disraeli 1868 C

William Gladstone 1868–1874 L

Benjamin Disraeli 1874–1880 C

William Gladstone 1880–1885 L

Marquess of Salisbury 1885–1886 C

William Gladstone 1886 L

Marquess of Salisbury 1886–1892 C

William Gladstone 1892–1894 L

Earl of Rosebery 1894–1895 L

Marquess of Salisbury 1895–1902 C

Arthur Balfour 1902–1905 C

Sir Henry Campbell-Bannerman 1905–
    1908 L

Henry Asquith 1908–1916 L

David Lloyd George 1916–1922 L

Andrew Bonar Law 1922–1923 C

Stanley Baldwin 1923–1924 C

Ramsay MacDonald 1924 Lab

Stanley Baldwin 1924–1929 C

Ramsay MacDonald 1929–1931 Lab

Ramsay MacDonald 1931–1935 N. Lab

Stanley Baldwin 1935–1937 C

Neville Chamberlain 1937–1940 C

Winston Churchill 1940–1945 C

Clement Attlee 1945–1951 Lab

Winston Churchill 1951–1955 C

Anthony Eden 1955–1957 C

Harold Macmillan 1957–1963 C

Sir Alec Douglas-Home 1963–1964 C

Harold Wilson 1964–1970 Lab

Edward Heath 1970–1974 C

Harold Wilson 1974–1976 Lab

James Callaghan 1976–1979 Lab

Margaret Thatcher 1979–1990 C

John Major 1990–1997 C

Tony Blair 1997–2007 Lab

Gordon Brown 2007–2010 Lab

David Cameron 2010 C

Members of the Privy Council as of 1 January 2015

A LL MEMBERS OF THE Privy Council are entitled to use the prefix
the Right Honourable (shortened to Rt Hon.) before their name.
As membership is an office and not an honour, the initials PC should not
be appended to any title. In this list, no honours are appended to names.
Where more than one peer shares a name/title, a distinction is made by
using an abbreviation, thus: Lord Mackay of Clashfern becomes Lord
Mackay (C) and Lord Mackay of Drumadoon becomes Lord Mackay
(D). Full details of members can be obtained by searching the internet or
– more reliably – consulting the annual edition of *Who's Who*, published
by A & C Black. Details of sitting or previous Members of Parliament
can be obtained from the appropriate editions of *The Times Guide to
the House of Commons*, which is published after each general election.

The Lord President of	Ezekiel Alebua	Owen Arthur
the Privy Council,	Danny Alexander	Lord Ashcroft
Nick Clegg	Douglas Alexander	Lord Ashdown
The Lord Privy Seal,	Baroness Amos	Baroness Ashton
Andrew Lansley	Lord Anderson	Sir Robert Atkins
Lord Abernethy	Baroness Anelay	Sir Robin Auld
Lord Adonis	Dame Elish Angiolini	Gregory Baker
Sir Richard Aikens	Doug Anthony	Lord Baker
Bob Ainsworth	James Arbuthnot	Sir Scott Baker
Earl of Airlie	Dame Mary Arden	Sir Tony Baldry
Sir William Aldous	Baroness Armstrong	Ed Balls

Lord Collins	Jeffrey Donaldson	Sir Christopher Floyd
Yvette Cooper	Stephen Dorrell	Lord Forsyth
Lord Cope	Lady Dorian	Lord Foster
Baroness Corston	Denzil Douglas	Don Foster
Lady Cosgrove	Lord Drayson	Lord Foulkes
Lord Coulsfield	Lord Drummond Young	Lord Fowler
Earl of Crawford	Alan Duncan	Liam Fox
Wyatt Creech	Iain Duncan Smith	Mark Francois
Lord Crickhowell	Lord Dyson	Malcolm Fraser
Lord Cullen	Lord Eassie	Sir Lawrence Freedman
Lord Cunningham	Paul East	John Freeman
David Curry	Lord Eden	Lord Freeman
Baroness D'Souza	HRH Duke of Edinburgh	Sir Adrian Fulford
Alistair Darling	Sir David Edward	Sir William Gage
Lord Darzi	Timothy Eggar	Lord Garel-Jones
Edward Davey	Sir Thomas Eichelbaum	Sir Thomas Gault
Denzil Davies	Sir Patrick Elias	Sir Christopher Geidt
Lord Davies	Dame Sian Elias	Bruce George
Ron Davies	Lord Ellis-Thomas	Sir Peter Gibson
David Davis	Lord Emslie	Sir Martin Gilbert
Sir Nigel Davis	Sir Manuel Esquivel	Lord Gill
Terry Davis	Sir Terence Etherton	Cheryl Gillan
Sir Ronald Davison	Sir Anthony Evans	Sir Paul Girvan
Baroness Dean	Sir Edward Eveleigh	Sir Ian Glidewell
Lord Deben	Lord Falconer	Dame Elizabeth Gloster
Lord Denham	Michael Fallon	Lord Goff
Lord Dholakia	Lord Fellowes	Sir John Goldring
Lord Dixon	Alex Fergusson	Lord Goldsmith
Frank Dobson	Frank Field	Lord Goodlad
Nigel Dodds	Caroline Flint	Michael Gove

Earl of Gowrie

Lord Graham

Sir Douglas Graham

Chris Grayling

Damian Green

Justine Greening

Dominic Grieve

Lord Griffiths

Lord Grocott

Sir Peter Gross

Lord Habgood

William Hague

Peter Hain

Baroness Hale

Dame Heather Hallett

Lord Hamilton

Lord Hamilton (E)

Philip Hammond

Greg Hands

Jeremy Hanley

David Hanson

Lord Hardie

Sir Michael Hardie-Boys

Harriet Harman

Sir Alan Haselhurst

Lord Hattersley

John Hayes

Baroness Hayman

John Healy

Lord Healy

David Heathcoat-Amory

Lord Henley

Sir John Henry

Nick Herbert

Lord Heseltine

Sir William Heseltine

Lord Hesketh

Patricia Hewitt

Lord Higgins

Sir Malachy Higgins

Lord Hill

Keith Hill

Lord Hodge

Margaret Hodge

Lord Hoffman

Douglas Hogg

Baroness Hollis

Geoff Hoon

Sir Anthony Hooper

Lord Hope (C)

Lord Hope (T)

Sir Peter Hordern

Lord Howard

Lord Howarth

Lord Howe

Earl Howe

Lord Howell

Kim Howells

Lindsay Hoyle

Lord Hughes

Baroness Hughes

Simon Hughes

Jeremy Hunt

Jonathan Hunt

Lord Hunt (K)

Lord Hunt (W)

Lord Hurd

Sir Michael Hutchison

Lord Hutton

Lord Hutton (F)

Lord Inge

Hubert Ingraham

Adam Ingram

Lord Irvine

Michael Jack

Sir Rupert Jackson

Sir Robin Jacob

Sir Francis Jacobs

Lord Janvin

Sajid Javid Baroness

Jay Lord Jenkin

Alan Johnson

Lord Jones

Carwyn James

David Jones

Lord Jopling

Dame Tessa Jowell

Lord Judge

Sir Anerood Jugnauth

Sir Gerald Kaufman

Sir Maurice Kay

Sir David Keene

Sir Kenneth Keith

Ruth Kelly

Sir Peter Kenilorea

Charles Kennedy

Jane Kennedy

Sir Paul Kennedy

Lord Kerr

Sadiq Khan

Lord King

Lord Kingarth

Lord Kinnock

Lord Kirkwood

Sir David Kitchen

Sir Greg Knight

Lord Knight

David Lammy

Lord Lamont

Lord Lang

Sir Kamuta Latasi

Sir David Latham

Sir Toaripi Lauti

Sir John Laws

David Laws

Lord Lawson

Sir Andrew Leggatt

Oliver Letwin

Sir Brian Leveson

Sir Kim Lewison

Baroness Liddell

David Lidington

Peter Lilley

Lord Lloyd

Sir Peter Lloyd

Sir Timothy Lloyd

Sir David Lloyd Jones

Sir Andrew Longmore

Marquess of Lothian

Lord Luce

Sir Roderick Lynne

Lord McAvoy

Sir Ian McCartney

Sir Liam McCollum

Sir Richard McCombe

Lord McConnell

Sir John MacDermott

Lord Macdonald

Pat McFadden

Lord McFall

Sir Andrew MacFarlane

Lord MacGregor

Ann McGuire

Andrew Mackay

Lord Mackay (C)

Lord MacKay (D)

Sir Don McKinnon

Lord Maclean

Henry McLeish

Lord Maclennan

Patrick McLoughlin

Sir Duncan McMullin

Lord McNally

Esther McVey

Dame Julia Macur

Sir John Major

Lord Malloch-Brown

Lord Mance

Lord Mandelson

Lord Marnoch

Lord Martin

Tricia Marwick

Lord Mason

Michael Mates

Francis Maude

Lord Mawhinney

Sir Anthony May

Theresa May

Lord Mayhew

Michael Meacher

David Mellor

Lord Menzies

Alun Michael

Alan Milburn

David Miliband

Ed Miliband

Maria Miller

Lord Millett

Andrew Mitchell

Sir James Mitchell

Sir Stephen Richards

Sir Ivor Richardson

Peter Riddell

Sir Malcolm Rifkind

Sir Colin Rimer

Sir Bernard Rix

Andrew Robathan

Lord Robertson

Hugh Robertson

Peter Robinson

Sir John Roch

Lord Rodgers

Lord Rooker

Lord Roper

Sir Christopher Rose

Lord Ross

Baroness Royall

Dame Joan Ruddick

Joan Ryan

Sir Ernest Ryder

Lord Ryder

Sir Timothy Sainsbury

Marquess of Salisbury

Alex Salmond

Sir Lloyd Sandiford

Lord Saville

Dame Joan Sawyer

Sir Konrad Schiemann

Baroness Scotland

Lord Scott

Edward Seaga

Sir Stephen Sedley

Lord Selkirk

John Sentamu

Grant Shapps

Dame Victoria Sharp

Sir John Sheil

Lord Sheldon

Baroness Shephard

Dame Jenny Shipley

Clare Short

Lord Shutt

Sir Desmond de Silva

Kennedy Simmonds

Ian Sinclair

Sir Christopher Slade

Andrew Smith

Baroness Smith

Lady Smith

Lord Smith

Jacqui Smith

Dame Janet Smith

Nicholas Soames

Sir Michael Somare

John Spellar

Caroline Spelman

Lord Spicer

Sir John Stanley

Sir Christopher

Staughton

Lord Steel

Sir Ninian Stephen

Lord Stewartby

Lord Steyn

Gavin Strang

Lord Strathclyde

Jack Straw

Freundel Stuart

Sir Murray Stuart-Smith

Sir Andrew Stunell

Sir Jeremy Sullivan

Lord Sumption

Lord Sutherland

Desmond Swayne

Hugo Swire

Baroness Symons

Sir Peter Tapsell

Baroness Taylor

Lord Tebbit

Lord Templeman

Sir Edmund Thomas

Sir John Thomas

Sir Swinton Thomas

Sir Matthew Thorpe

Stephen Timms

Sir Andrew Tipping

Bob Tizard

Sir Stephen Tomlinson

Lord Touhig

Lord Toulson

Sir Colman Treacy   Lord Whitty

Lord Trefgarne   Ann Widdecombe

Lord Trimble   Lord Wigley

Baroness Trumpington   David Willetts

Sir Simon Tuckey   Alan Williams

Lord Tyler   Lord Williams (E)

Viscount Ullswater   Lord Williams (O)

Sir Nicholas Underhill   Baroness Williams

Simon Upton   Lord Williamson

Baroness Vadera   Lord Wills

Keith Vaz   Brian Wilson

Theresa Villiers   Lord Wilson

Sir Geoffrey Vos   Paias Wingti

Lord Waddington   Rosie Winterton

Sir John Waite   Reg Withers

Lord Wakeman   Shaun Woodward

Lord Waldegrave   Lord Woolf

HRH Prince of Wales   Sir George Young

Lord Walker   Lord Young

Sir Nicholas Wall   Edward Zacca

Lord Wallace (S)

Lord Wallace (T)

Sir Mark Walker

Sir Alan Ward

Lord Warner

Baroness Warsi

Justin Welby

Lord West

Lord Wheatley

Sir John Wheeler

BIBLIOGRAPHY

Acts of The Privy Council of England, edited by John Roche Dasent, 1890, printed for HMSO by Eyre & Spottiswode; reprinted by Ulan Press

Baldwin, J. F., *The King's Council in England during the Middle Ages* (Oxford University Press, 1913)

Barnett, Correlli, *The Lost Victory* (Macmillan, 1995)

Berkeley, Humphry, *The Power of The Prime Minister* (George Allen & Unwin Ltd, 1968)

Blythe, Ronald, *The Age of Illusion: England in the Twenties and Thirties* (Hamish Hamilton, 1963)

Bourne, Richard, *Shridath Ramphal: The Commonwealth and The World* (Hansib Publications, 2008)

Brown, Colin, *Whitehall* (Simon & Schuster, 2009)

Campbell, John, *Pistols at Dawn: Pitt & Fox to Blair & Brown* (Jonathan Cape, 2009)

Clarke, Charles, *The 'Too Difficult' Box* (Biteback Publishing, 2014)

Clarke, Stephen, *1,000 Years of Annoying The French* (Bantam Press, 2010)

Critchley, Julian, *A Bag of Boiled Sweets* (Faber & Faber, 1994)

Dicey, A. V., *The Privy Council* (Bibliolife – copy from 1887, 2007)

Ferrers, Earl, *Whatever Next?* (Biteback Publishing, 2011)

Fitzroy, Almeric, *The History of The Privy Council* (John Murray, 1928)

Fitzroy, Almeric, *Memoirs* (Hutchinson & Co., 1930)

Fraser, Antonia, *Mary Queen of Scots* (Weidenfeld & Nicolson, 1969)

Guy, John, *Tudor England* (Oxford University Press, 1988)

Healey, Denis, *The Time of My Life* (W. W. Norton & Co., 1989)

Heffer, Simon, *Like the Roman: The Life of Enoch Powell* (Weidenfeld & Nicolson, 1998)

Holden, Anthony, *William Shakespeare: His Life and Work* (Little, Brown & Co., 1999)

Home, Lord, *The Way The Wind Blows* (Collins, 1976)

Howard, Anthony, *The Crossman Diaries* (Methuen 1979)

Howard, Anthony and West, Richard, *The Making of the Prime Minister* (Jonathan Cape, 1965)

James, Robert Rhodes (editor), *Chips: The Diaries of Sir Henry Cannon* (Weidenfeld & Nicolson, 1967)

James, Robert Rhodes, *Bob Boothby: A Portrait* (John Curtis/Hodder and Stoughton, 1991)

Jenkins, Simon, *A Short History of England* (Profile Books, 2012)

Johnson, Frank; compiled by Fraser, Virginia, *The Best Seat in the House* (JR Books, 2009)

Jolliffe, John, *Raymond Asquith: Life and Letters* (William Collins & Sons, 1980)

King, Anthony and Crewe, Ivor, *The Blunders of Our Government* (Oneworld Publications, 2014)

Lacey, Robert, *Aristocrats* (Hutchinson, 1983)

Lawson, Nigel, *The View From No. 11* (Bantam, 1992)

Lentin, Antony, *Banker, Traitor, Scapegoat, Spy* (Haus Publishing, 2013)

Longmate, Norman, *Island Fortress* (Grafton, 1993)

McAlpine, Alistair, *The Servant* (Faber & Faber, 1992)

MacCoby, Simon, *The English Radical Tradition* (Nicholas Kaye, 1952)

McKinnon, Don, *In the Ring* (Elliott & Thompson, 2013)

Macmillan, Harold, *At the End of the Day* (Macmillan, 1973)

Marshall, H. E., *Our Island Story* (Galore Park and Civitas, 2005)

Morgan, Kenneth O., *The Oxford Illustrated History of Britain*

(Oxford University Press, 1983)

Norwich, John Julius, *A History of England in 100 Places* (John Murray, 2011)

Pannick, David, *I Have to Move My Car* (Hart Publishing, 2008)

Parris, Matthew, and Bryson, Andrew, *Parting Shots: Undiplomatic Diplomats* (Viking, 2010)

Parris, Matthew, *The Great Unfrocked* (Robson Books, 1998)

Paxman, Jeremy, *Friends in High Places: Who Runs Britain?* (Michael Joseph, 1990)

Edward Pearce, *Lines of Most Resistance* (Little, Brown & Co., 1999)

Pelling, Henry, *The Challenge of Socialism* (A&C Black, 1954)

Renton, Claudia, *Those Wild Wyndhams* (William Collins, 2014)

Rose, Kenneth, *King George V* (Macmillan, 1983)

Sellar, W. C. and Yeatman, R. J., *1066 and All That* (Methuen, 1930)

Starkey, David, *Monarchy: England and Her Rulers from the Tudors to the Windsors* (Harper Perennial, 2007)

Titles and Forms of Address (A&C Black, 1949)

Trevelyan, G. M., *England Under Queen Anne Blenheim* (Longmans, Green & Co., 1930)

Tyerman, Christopher, *Who's Who in Early Medieval England* (Shepheard-Walwyn, 1996)

Wells, John, *The House of Lords* (Hodder & Stoughton, 1997)

White, R. J., *The Conservative Tradition* (Nicholas Kaye, 1950)

Young, Hugo, *One of Us* (Macmillan, 1989)

ACKNOWLEDGEMENTS

I OWE THANKS TO SO many people. To my wife Erica for her stead-fast help; to Olivia Beattie at Biteback for her enthusiastic support; and to the Deputy Clerk of the Privy Council, Ceri King – the discussions I had with her and the fascinating details I learnt from her and the former Clerk to the Privy Council, Alex Galloway, were one of the great joys of writing this book and I apologise to them for any mistakes I have made. I must also express my gratitude to Gill Harding of Buckingham Palace and David Banks from the Commonwealth Secretariat for the time and trouble they took in giving me guidance, and Dr David Menhennet, for-mer librarian of the House of Commons, whose research advice was my starting point.

Others whose advice has helped me enormously and whom I want to acknowledge publicly include David Armstrong, Peter Buckman, Sam Carter, Olivia Cottrell, Dan Crewe, Liz Huckle and Andrew Lownie. And finally to three old friends who, way back in the last century, encouraged me to embark on this project: the late and great Tony Howard, Alan Wat-kins and Frank Johnson.

INDEX